"*My Impossible Life* speaks t
of great trauma. Jones's h
she recalls, and ultimately, repairs, the seminal trauma of her young adult self. Set amidst the collective cultural upheaval of the late 1960s, Jones recounts her global quest for spiritual enlightenment and private, and seemingly impossible, psychological healing. In treating herself as narrative and psychological subject, Jones pens a memoir that is compelling as a story of psychedelic youth, and instructive as an account of trauma recovery from the perspective of contemporary psychotherapy, neuroscience and mysticism."

~ Nicholas Balaisis, PhD, University of Waterloo

"Charlene Jones' incredible story of transformation and healing after extreme trauma is truly inspirational. The reader joins her on her life-changing journey—from being kidnapped and sexually assaulted by two escaped felons while a teenager to studying meditation and following her teacher around the world while she looks for peace and healing—until she finally discovers that the wisdom she has been seeking was within her all along. Once she does, she reconnects with a part of her that had been buried for years and learns the truth of who she really is. *My Impossible Life* is a powerful story of overcoming adversity and finding that joy in life still exists."

~ Jennifer Monahan, six time award-winning author of *This Trip Will Change Your Life: A Shaman's Story of Spirit Evolution* and *Where To? How I Shed My Baggage and Learned to Live Free.*

"*My Impossible Life* contains a harrowing story of survival peppered with intriguing travels and fascinating people. Compelling and validating for any who have suffered trauma, this book describes what truly has been an impossible life."

~ Nancy Richards author *Mother, I Don't Forgive You* and *Heal and Forgive 11: The Journey from Abuse and Estrangement to Reconciliation*

"Charlene's tale of survival winds us through the compelling and complicated journey of traumatic memory and her extraordinary will to keep on living. Poetically unvarnished, she possesses the rare gift of being able to cut through the noise and touch the essential. In an age where we have lost the dignity of suffering, Charlene inspires us by revealing the ways in which her "Angel" spoke to her in her darkest moments. This I believe is her greatest contribution, reinforcing the capacity for transcendence yet tethering these lofty goals to the earthy through exposing her deepest longings for communion and friendship; earthly longings that are necessary for survival and most importantly love. It is the love within the cracks of her life that shines through in this rich and beautifully written memoir."

~ Mitch Smolkin, M.A. Counselling Psychology, ICEEFY
Jungian Analyst

"This book is an incredible read. I had trouble putting it down. It carries an unbeatable combination of a well-written manuscript, the words poetic at times, and a compelling and insightful story.

Charlene's story skillfully weaves around her memories of a traumatic event that took place when she was sixteen. Her story, though it speaks of a life uniquely hers, is also universal. It speaks of pain and anger, of searching for self, of healing. Her insights helped me process some of my own baggage. In the Epilogue she wrote that she sometimes used language as a weapon. In this book, her skill with words is a gift, to the readers."

~ Deb Brandon, Professor, Dept. of Mathematical Sciences
Carnegie Mellon University, award winning author for
But My Brain had Other Ideas and *Threads from Around the World*

"It's a stark, raw piece of writing… authentic and vivid… and harrowing at times with immediate fierce impact."

~ B.W. Powe, Associate Professor, English,
York University, Toronto
The Change in the Global Membrane and more

"A harrowing, ultimately uplifting portrayal of a young girl's journey from an abusive childhood to self-acceptance and serenity as an adult. The author skillfully evokes her teenage ability to pretend nonchalance in the face of overwhelming hurdles, her tough exterior and sheer force of will hiding deep emotional scars and the fear of always being an outsider."

~ Kate Gilderdale, Ret'd Editor,
Current Columnist *Stouffville Free Press*

"This is a powerful and important memoir. The writing is simply beautiful…the flow of this book is wonderful and meditative and the language sings. The writer has an absolute gift for description. It's never that gag-inducing, sickly sweet stuff that is often seen in writing about spirituality. The author left me sitting there going "Wow. Just wow," on several occasions. I love how she braided the wiser narrator with naïve narrator and facts with feelings that can't be proven. She has a real gift for ending each chapter on the right note. Every chapter moves the story along, and the final ending is taut and happy and wonderfully done."

~ Lara Lillibridge, award winning author
Girl-ish and *Mama, Mama, Only Mama*, co-editor *Feminine Rising*

"Just finished reading *My Impossible Life*. I followed Charlene's journey around the globe through various spiritual, psychological, and life experiences toward an ability to acknowledge and finally move beyond the traumatic incident that occurred so many years before. The book does a good job of slowly and very gradually revealing what actually happened. Also, I liked the way Charlene's story enlarged to embrace the experiences of many others of both genders who carry similar if less intense burdens of unacknowledged abuse deep within. It's a very informative, compelling, and well-written book."

~ Chuck Guilford, Emeritus Associate Professor of English,
Boise State University

"This is an important and powerful story that flowed effortlessly. It could be made into a movie along the lines of *Eat, Pray, Love*."
~ Kathy Pooler award winning blogger *Memoir Writer's Journey* Author *Ever Faithful to His Lead: My Journey Away from Emotional Abuse*

"…Oh my — read 88 pages at first go — had to get some sleep. Definitely a page-turner — remarkable writing."
~ Lorraine Speer, one of "the group."

"I can't believe all that the author has been through and has emerged to tell the tale and to do so much to help so many. When it's all done and published it will make a wonderful and dramatic movie. I love (the author's) use of scenes and definitely see it's a story that needs to be told…" ~ Lizbeth Meredith M.A., LLC. IPPY, International Book Awards finalist, USA Best Book Awards, award winning author for *Pieces of Me*

"…your book…contains some absolutely beautiful language, vivid descriptions of heartbreaking experiences and most tender insights. (It is a) unique and creative memoir."
~ Laura McHale Holland, author of *Resilient Ruins*

MY IMPOSSIBLE LIFE

*trauma,
travel &
transcendence*

CHARLENE JONES

HEARTONGUE PRESS

Copyright © 2019 Charlene Diane Jones

ALL RIGHTS RESERVED. No part of this publication may be reproduced, stored in a retrieval system, or transmitted in any form or by any process – electronic, mechanical, photocopying, recording, or otherwise – without the prior written permission of the copyright owner and Heartongue Press. The scanning, uploading and distribution of this via the internet or any other means without the permission of the publisher is illegal and punishable by law. Please purchase only authorized electronic editions, and do not participate in or encourage electronic piracy of copyrighted materials. Your support of the author's rights is appreciated.

Cover Photos: bigstockphoto.com and from the author's personal collection
Design & Layout: Stone's Throw Publications - www.stonesthrowps.ca

Published by:
Heartongue Press
7 Rest Nook Lane Stouffville L4A 7X3
Ontario Canada

www.soulsciences.com

ISBN 978-1-987813-326

Printed in Canada

1 2 3 4 5 6 7 8 9 10

Acknowledgements

A DEBT OF GRATITUDE remains to so many people who helped this book along the way, especially since it has been literally 50 years in the making. I wrote the first version of the story when I was 17 years old and still have it, on the original paper where I typed.

First, Sue Reynolds. From the initial six-week writing course I took with Sue I knew her reading of my work mattered deeply. She has the gift of being able to see exactly where the writing does not serve the story and to read every version as though for the first time. For this reason and because of her sensitivity to psychic, emotional wounds, I am grateful she agreed to edit the book for me.

Brendan Gall, my spiritual son, (also writer, Executive Producer for NBC's "Blindspot," and the "Lovebirds" as well as many other projects), read the first finished copy of this in 1993. His encouragement and words of genuine support inspired me to keep going.

To Dr. Ruth Lanius goes a debt of enormous size for her spontaneous generosity and warmth. Her books *Healing the Traumatized Self* and *Surviving the Valley: Trauma and Beyond* offer a path to health.

Liz Meredith offered empowering comments about the structure including the start of the story. Her insight was invaluable. Her book *Pieces of Me* should be read by every parent and every child.

Laura McHale Holland read carefully and applied common

sense to an earlier version and offered general and much needed support along the way. Her books *Resilient Ruin* and *Reversible Skirt* offer a stunning look into childhood, abuse and growing up.

Lara Lillibridge fulfilled a writer's dream by agreeing to read the first 50 pages, then immediately requesting more and finally, the rest. Lara's unflagging and articulate enthusiasm helped me believe. Her books *Girl-ish and Mama, Mama, Only Mama* demonstrate her spread as a talented writer.

Jennifer Monahan read several versions always with great enthusiasm and as if she had never read the story before. She also offered great support and caring throughout the time I wrote. Her book *This Trip Will Change Your Life* still defines the quest narrative for women, and *Where To?* her second book continues in the same vein.

Nancy Richard's immediate enthusiasm told me the book was on the right track. Her books *Mother I Don't Forgive You, A Necessary Alternative for Healing,* and *Mother It's Hard to Forgive You: Ridding Myself of the Family Scapegoat Mantle* are a gift to us all.

Karen Keilt successfully models for me, for everyone, the "after human" of someone who has been traumatically hurt. She also is a wizard at writing and offered encouragement to my own writing process. Read her book *The Parrot's Perch*.

Deb Brandon's sincere articulation to the whole manuscript left me in tears. Her books *But My Brain Had Other Ideas* and *Threads from Around the World* inspire and reveal so much about human strength and the power of writing.

Chuck Guilford's dedication to writing has been lifelong and a huge benefit to all of us, his students. His books *Paradigm: Online Writing Assistant,* and *Altogether Now: Essays on Poetry, Writing and Teaching* demonstrate his continued heart for the art.

Kate Gilderdale who supported my writing with great sincerity and my person with warm friendship over many many years, continues to sustain and inspire me.

b.w. powe gave a short succinct appraisal of the book and heart felt tenderness for the suffering stated in it. His book *The Charge in the Global Membrane* redefines the idea of book.

Mitch Smolkin's words of appreciation fire the bonds of family between us.

Nick Belasius's generous articulate language created a profound sense of the continuation of healthy relationships from one generation to the next.

Lorraine Speer read then responded to my book with enthusiasm. Along with Jean Macklin who helped me remember bits about the Norway trip I had forgotten, these two "were there."

Cea Sunrise Person was kind enough to read, despite her own time constraints, a section of the book and to offer encouragement as well as insight.

Stanley Fefferman (Author-Poet, *Home Was Elsewhere, The Heart of All Music*) read and made concise grammatical suggestions and insightful comments about content for the first section of the book.

Finally, Linda Stitt, Poetry Maven of Toronto, has put her impeccable grammar and punctuation sense to these pages and her unremitting belief in love to my life. Both are much the better for it.

To Harry, my life partner—for your willingness.

Dedication

To the mother and the father of all the fairies.
And to the fairies themselves

Chapter One

I SLAM MY FIST DOWN ON THE DESK. "I just spent three days with two armed robbers, and I want something done about it. Now!"

The man in the police uniform on the other side of the desk straightens his body and begins to question me.

Soon a young tall blond man, a detective, arrives. I am assured he knows what he's doing. We look at a fat album of photos but none of them are Gary or Al, the two men who drove the stolen car I had been held in.

I recite information, Welland, Ontario, a gas station robbery, man shot by two escapees from prison. The police officer belonging to the desk makes phone calls that confirm this story.

The detective and I drive in his car back to the last cabin. I have described the blue Pontiac ditched there, complete to its license plate number.

I show with my hand where the turn off is, we drive the short, dirt path toward the cottage and there in the woods is the car.

The detective radios back to the station, comments on the strength of my memory, hangs up and tells me to stay back.

"They're not here," I repeat, "they're on the highway, the Trans-Canada, going toward Manitoba."

"Stay and don't move," he pulls his gun, points it with both hands in a stand-off with the empty cabin. He breaks in, then returns to the police car, radios the station again.

On the drive back, he tells me this is his first day as a detective. I think, "Of course it is...I am his first."

The first policeman is still there when the blond initiate returns me to the small police station in Marathon, Ontario. The first policeman asks me more questions, writes stuff down.

"Did they molest you?" This rhymes out of him like requesting the weather.

"Yes."

He looks up. "If you jump into that...look, you don't want to press charges against them. It'll mean a nasty court case, trial and you become the one they go after. The way the courts still work is they'll attack the way you dress, every boyfriend you've ever had. Their defense lawyer will question your sexual conduct. Are you a virgin?"

"Technically, yes."

He pauses then. "Technically or not you still don't want to press charges. The courts will tear you apart. Is that what you want? More threats, more trouble, facing those men again, maybe several times."

"I never want to see them again. Ever."

"And they are already in so much trouble you can know they are going away for a very long time."

A flicker of satisfaction rises in my chest. Then gone.

When the flurry of phone calls and men in uniforms walking briskly about ceases, I am sent to have dinner with the area Supervisor, his wife and two small boys. They live in a neatly kept bungalow. She puts an extra plate on the table. Somewhere near the side of my mind I hear them have a heated discussion. This woman does not want me. She does not want me to stay overnight. She doesn't want me to have dinner with her and her two small boys. Is this a real memory? It fits the theme that will rise for at least the next decade: where is home, who will let me stay, where is my home, my body, my home?

Her husband, working late that night, leaves.

This dinner of chicken, canned corn and potatoes is the first I've been near in three days, but I eat only a small bit.

Four round eyes stare at me intermittently, as I pass plates and try to speak reasonably.

"Why do you eat with us tonight?" one of the little round faces queries. I hum and haw not sure how much information to give.

"She is a runaway," their mother states without drama but with an undertone of dislike.

"Did you really run away? How far did you go? Where…" they chime together.

"I did but I have to tell you, you should never, never…"

A car arrives, takes me back to the station, where I am escorted to a cell, given the standard issue grey blanket, instructed to sleep. This time I do.

Late that night I am woken by the guard at my cell door.

"We found the two guys. They were walking up the highway just like you said. The first thing one of them said was she had nothing to do with it. So, you're off the hook."

I hadn't realized I was on one.

Chapter Two

IN YEARS TO COME THE STORY WILL INCLUDE how my father in Toronto started putting on his shoes, eager to pick me up from what he had heard as Scarborough a nearby suburb to our home in Toronto. I was in Schreiber, Ontario, over one thousand kilometers away. I would be sent home by plane from Thunder Bay.

At the foot of the stairs leading up to the open door of the plane, the police officer assigned to make sure that I get on the plane, stops.

"Oh, it's fine," I say to him, "I can take it from here."

"My orders are to get you on that plane and that is what I am going to do."

A flight attendant waits at the top of the metal stairs, so I run double steps to her, smile into her face and say, "Look out, I'm a hardened criminal!"

Over my shoulder I see her laugh, then, as she takes in the full shoulders of the uniform following close behind, her face falls to confusion, concern. The police officer confers with her before turning back down the stairs.

Next, my feet hit the tarmac off the retractable stairs leading away from the airplane. Three men in business suits already walking away from the plane, turn, wave goodbye to me, calling my name as they walk away. I know I do not know them but put my hand up slowly. Inside my head, a narrow memory like a slice of light through a curtain opens. I see myself in that plane again, talking, animated, entertaining those men, making them focus on whoever that was, talking, talking, words, words, words, then gone.

Now here in Toronto's Malton Airport I see my parents streaming forward. My mother crowds toward me, her shoulders leaning into each other, her dark eyes like a bird's. "Honey…" she begins.

I open my eyes from the inside, and she registers their hollow blank depth, empty where my light and heart should be.

She starts back as though slapped. "That's not…that's not my daughter!" She grabs my father's shoulder, the gesture a plea for him to fix this.

My father looks into my eyes and I hold his gaze steady, my depths closed to that inner tomb. We turn toward the car for home.

At home, I sit on the kitchen floor, the avocado green stove to my back, the matching green indoor/outdoor carpet hard beneath my flannel nightgown. I crouch, knees bent, compulsively tucking the edges of the material beneath my toes, then repeatedly stretching my toes beyond the border. School friends come by, fill our compact, orderly kitchen and want to hear what happened.

I tell and retell the story about the two men, the car I got into, stolen, the canvas bags with their shotguns, damp September in North Ontario, breaking into cabins, those two men, Al and Gary. I will laugh they were not very smart, but I convinced them to be my friends.

With every repetition, I shake in spasms I cannot hide, do not control or understand.

"Those men didn't hurt you?"

Whenever I am asked this, a charge beyond my control thrusts upward through my body, rushes against the tightly clamped tissue of my muscles, my mute cells, my trembling bones and flesh witnessing what I have buried within. Those cells leap to release their truth beyond my verbal betrayal.

"No, they didn't hurt me. They wanted me as hostage, nothing more. Nothing went wrong."

I almost never speak of the Angel.

The Angel had appeared sometime while the new blue Pontiac car drove over endless miles, had appeared out the back-passenger window where my eyes stayed following the flow of green shrubs, small trees, highway shoulder as though clues could be found there, clues that might release a most potent mystery. Hour after hour I watched without thought. Then I saw the Angel.

It was an orange, fiery Angel with a sword, surrounded by yellow, orange light, almost a cloud. And the Angel was not moving yet stayed in exact parallel with the car. Somehow the Angel communicated with me, *stay calm as possible, don't run away, ride this through to the end, all will be well.*

When the Angel left, part of my heart left too. It was the part that felt hope.

I believed unquestioningly in this Angel beside the car because Angels had calmed the loneliness and eased the terrors of my childhood.

An invisible thrum might pull at my five-year-old chest, and I would ask permission to walk out to the field behind our house. It was the oak tree at the top of the slope at the very back of that field that commanded me.

I lay looking up at the dappled light falling through the leaves and smaller limbs. I felt calm and peaceful, almost entranced when the sound of the Angels' voices, their wings shoving against the leaves, their faces crowding along one limb, demanded my attention.

Their voices spoke to my thoughts and I asked, *where is Jesus?*

They tittered and chimed, a sound I will recognize many times over my life. The sound decoded to thought, *he will not come here.*

But what if I need him?

You have us. Right now. Focus on now…

They spoke in tinkling tones for a bit, then as easily as pulling back a curtain, they were gone.

"Where have you been?" My mother's voice bounded darkly

about my head. I read all the tones and knew I was not quite safe, not yet in danger. I believed how I responded mattered.

"Up on the hill. Under the oak tree. Mommy, there were angels there and they told me…"

Her beautiful face hidden by the gathering dark mood, she flung words that fell like tacks on my body.

"You did NOT see angels. Don't be so…"

"You mean no one sees angels, ever?" My need to know defeated the need for caution. "Doesn't Gram see things that aren't there? Don't you see…I mean sometimes…" I let my voice dwindle, aware I had strayed far from safety.

"No, I mean yes, I guess your Grandmother and I…some people…" She looked up as she often did when I asked questions, as though the answers lay somewhere above her head. "No…"

"Do you believe in angels? Don't some people see angels?" I insisted past all sense of impending danger.

"Yes, I believe…I mean I believe some people see angels." She turned on me, her dark eyes flashing. I read their rage. She would use words only, this time. "You are NOT…those people are special. You are not. You did not see angels."

As a child I already knew my mother had visions. My mother knew when death would come and to whom. A dark hooded figure approached her, usually in her dreams. She lay in terror, knowing the visitor meant death. The closer the figure came, the closer death was to someone she knew, possibly loved. I knew of this and that my mother was afraid of her visions and their power. She didn't want me to have what so frightened her.

Lineage cannot be wished away. My visionary inheritance stretches from as far away as Scotland. Visionary sight ran true in my Great Grandmother's Scots blood, sang in her sleep all the nights of her life, whispering to her cells the secrets of the future.

It is 1905 in the photo I have. She stands on the dock of Leith, Scotland, a tall, large-boned, dark-haired beauty. I imagine her turning from the camera to study the wooden boxes at her feet, mentally checking their content: silver cutlery, Wedgewood China, white linens, crystal goblets, fancy glass cake plates whose embossed surfaces will make ripples against my child fingers half a century later, a black stemmed fruit bowl, heavy silver birds that shake out salt and pepper, platters roomy enough for both meat and vegetables, all she would need to set up a fine home in the New World.

I imagine she stares across the water's endless grey humpback, her one sightless wandering eye casting about like a homeless waif against the present, finding its way past veils and into the future, seeing what was to come as easily as what was here, now. Had that eye revealed how staying in Edinburgh might mean death for herself or her children, death by her husband's hands? Why else leave with her two children in tow, both under six years old?

The stories of my Grandmother and her mother, how their visions encompassed the rim of time and beyond, dotted the years of my childhood, markers for what I myself would experience and come to understand as normal.

My father told me Gram, Ida, had climbed the stairs to her apartment, where her sleeping son, my mother's older brother, was being cared for by Grandma Great. As my grandmother pushed open the door, she turned sheet white and almost fell.

"What is it, Ida?"

"It's Gord, Mama. I see him, I see my baby in a casket!" My grandmother announced the death of her first born three days before he actually died.

Was it her fear of those visions made my grandmother drink? Or did her drinking soften the thin layer of her conscious mind in the warming liquid, so visions more easily came through? My Grandmother's love of gin or whiskey, vodka if neither were on hand, filled the rumor mills around the East End of Toronto, the Beach, for more than a generation, titillating those who enjoyed a bit of gossip, feeding the needs of those who believed truth lay in their judgments, and blighting my mother's childhood with ruthless shame.

My grandmother's need for alcohol, like that of her mother before her, fueled her other needs, spinning my mother's childhood into a web of being shut into closets, forbidden to play outside with other children, taught to clean and polish endlessly the tiny one room flat they inhabited. As she grew older, and presumably too big to be put into closets, my mother was abandoned for days while Gram pursued her momentary pleasures.

When my mother's turn came to be a mother—something she desired with a fixed and single pointed determination—she would transform her shame into the leaping whip of a leather belt to beat upon the children she loved, so they might know right from wrong.

Sometime in my later childhood, hoping for a guide line, a rope to anchor my own visions, I asked Gram to talk to me about hers.

"I was born with a caul covering my face…" she began. Gram fulfilled the caul's mythology: those born with this added layer of skin on their face or body have visions. Her visions began she believed in earnest after her waist length carrot red hair caught in the tracks of one of the first street cars in Toronto.

Outside the red painted door of their variety store at Queen and Sumac Streets, my grandmother's screams pierced the air where the conductor slammed the brakes on and jumping out was relieved to see only the shining tresses of my grandmother's precious carrot top wound ever more tightly into his wheel, which had attempted and failed to pull my grandmother's head off her shoulders and Mama, running with the scissors, clipped her daughter free.

After that, Gram said, one of her long fingers with its shiny red nail polish tapping the Rothman's against the chunky edge of the glass ashtray, after that the visions started.

"How did you…do you like them?"

"No, no, I don't. I am afraid of them."

She turned smoky brown eyes toward the ceiling as though looking for the Angels to help her stop having the visions. She and my mother, possibly even my Great Grandmother hated and feared these messages. For me they were a source of wonder and comfort.

Chapter Three

MY VISION OF THE ANGEL HAD PREDICTED what came to be. Now I was home from those days and nights of captivity I told what I remembered of what had happened—two men, the damp woods, tramping around. I always said they hadn't hurt me, had been my friends. I did not speak about the Angel.

A week or two later and the excitement around my return dimmed. I began to attend school again, but the most important event was I met David.

He walked into the restaurant where everyone went for lunch, his form in the doorway, light streaming in from behind, his eyes searching the room. My body tingled, cells reaching out for him.

David sat down beside me and turned his face away, then turned back and said with tiny interest, "Oh, you're the one everyone's talking about. You ran away. They say you're crazy." His blue-green eyes pushing against my skin, he commanded, "Look at me."

I wanted nothing else, ever. His eyes found the center of me in mine, then announced confidently, "You're not crazy."

"How do you know?" I believed he would never speak to me again, now I had challenged him.

"Because my mother is schizophrenic. She'd empty all the drawers, stuff all over. Then I'd call social services and we'd find her wandering around the streets."

His beautifully-shaped top lip curled upward slightly, sneering, at all of us sitting there, at me, at the world, at life. He got it.

The school arranged for me to see a counselor who recommended a psychiatrist at the Clark Institute in downtown Toronto.

I took the long street car ride and the elevator up to his office. We spoke briefly, when it occurred to me, I should test him.

"Shhhh," I whispered.

"What is it?" The psychiatrist, a young man with large brown eyes, asked.

"Shhh, shhh," I slunk off the chair, down to the floor, leaned against the wall opposite his desk, my knees bent to my chest.

"Shhh, shhhhh," I put my finger to my lips.

"What do you hear?" his entranced eyes drilled into mine like I held a secret to his future. His pencil flipped loosely about as though uncertain where to land, what to record.

"I want to hear the walls hum. Don't you ever listen to the walls humming? Listen!"

Soon the hour was over, and with it, my visits. I had fooled this trained psychiatrist that easily, yet David, who smoked pot and played guitar always knew when I was really going away.

In his living room, I fall toward the place that constantly compels from inside my skin. That place is dark, empty, silent, soothing in its utter lack of sensation. I fight to keep from surrendering to this reverse Shangri La, this void. I fight and sometimes lose.

"Where are you?"

He sits beside me, his concern a column of energy my skin leans toward. No answer, my eyes on the far wall, I recede toward that welcome abyss...

"Don't do it, come back, I... I don't want to lose you...come back now!"

Slowly I come back, sad to leave the relief of total collapse of sensation. I know if I give myself to this cavern of senselessness it means giving my life over to others who will make decisions, take care of me. Always. For the relief of that void I would easily have given up everything. Everything except David and David wanted me here, for him.

I lived for him despite his frequent absences from me, which he spun into lies I believed. I lived for him because his body was the skin I threw over myself. Without him there was no ground. His body gave boundary to the boundlessness where my body may have been.

I wore his body as a coat because I could not feel mine. The longing for him, for his body whenever we separated, rose from the ghostly space in which I lived. This total emptiness fueled my desperation. I might think a thought, or a fleeting emotion might rise, but nothing much else filtered up from the emptiness within.

Saturday mornings I slipped from my parents' house, walking barefoot on the pavement warmed by the September sun a few blocks to David's. Opening the side door of his grandparents' house as he had instructed me to, I walked down the stairs to the dark, damp basement bed where he lay.

Sometimes as we spooned, my arm tucked into his chest, a scent like damp earth rising from his back snug against me, I matched my breath to his…in when he breathed in, out when he exhaled. Then he might turn his body over, saying softly, urgently, "Do you feel that? Do you feel how we are so connected?" When he spoke like that, I felt confident he loved me.

"Yes. I feel it. I believe this is what love is supposed to feel like."

"But do you feel this? We are so connected, but star-crossed, like Romeo and Juliet. I can feel it." He'd grab me close, rocking us back and forth.

"No, I don't believe that, we can change it…we must stay together!"

He pulled his arms more tightly around me then, as though to keep the world away. His happiness in our closest moments was my addiction, deeper than any of the other dangers, weed, hash, booze, acid, morphine, speed, that surrounded our world. We smoked pot together, but he was my source. As an addict, I distorted my own perceptions to pretend my way into believing him and his lies. That is what makes us crazy: pretending to believe what our bodies, our inner truth denies. We cannot bear such pressure from inside, so we shut down.

If we shut down on one inner experience, one sensation of body truth, we shut down on them all. Soon the inner plane has no feeling, no sensation, but is void, boundless, endless. Then someone or some substance brings sensation, or emotion, even blunted and distorted we are helpless. We take that, absorb it to replace what we cannot sense or feel on our own; we use that person's responses, or the drugs' response, even as it lies and betrays. The need grows for the substance as we keep shutting down on our own body responses. This is addiction.

Angels' wings fluttered about. I ignored them. They fluttered. They whispered, "You have to leave David." I ignored the Angels.

He did love me. He said so. What I didn't know is how the hollow center in that word, love, allows everyone to slip through it with their own interpretation.

For a year, I convinced myself he was not running around. This was sleight of hand but not nearly as deep or deceptive as the one I already maintained, that those two criminals from those three days in September had not hurt me, that I had not fallen through a dark hole, Alice entering a Wonderland gone horribly wrong.

All that year after my return, the family truth remained that nothing was really wrong with me, nothing that a little will power on my side could not fix. When I disappeared into the bathroom after eating and returned to sit at the table, wiping my mouth, my father would say, "Charlene, just try." Then he'd sigh and look at my mother, whose turned down lips blared her disgust at my lack of will.

When I lost a job, or an interview because I was hung-over or didn't bother to show up, the air grew thick around my parents. They looked into my eyes, searching for their daughter inside me, the stranger who lived with them. Their look told me if I wanted to badly enough, I could let their old daughter, the real one who had lived with them before this imposter returned, I could let her live again. If I wanted.

All I wanted was David.

"What do you want?" Lying still beside me, our naked skin as one, his voice brushed my ears, sent shivers inside me.

"I just want you to lie inside me. Don't move, just lie still."

He lay fully erect inside me, perfectly still for as long as he could and neither of us knew this as Tantra. But it was and within a year my body, wrapped around his, echoed the oceanic bliss rising from that cave of mystery deep within.

It should never have happened. With my senses on mute and with what I came to know years later about what I had endured, this first orgasm with its pulsing waves of bliss defied every understanding of human psyche and sex. Yet it happened and in this delivered a tiny slice of sensation out of the dead block of cells called my body. These tiny sensations opened a small sliver of a seam, opened that seam just enough that I began daily to experience some immediate sensation below my neck.

Some would call this a tantric bond, a karmic bond or karmic experience, meaning something had happened in enough past lives to be a natural pattern emerging again in this lifetime. Or did this healing come from our telepathy, a conscious tool we had played with?

David and I had experimented with telepathy. We joined with another friend to see who of us might know what the other was feeling across the few blocks that separated us physically. We kept track, jubilant when correct. We believed we were establishing connection across distance, proving mind over matter.

I also registered when he was flirting or making out with someone else, but I refused to decode my belly's anxiety, that uneasy sensation as though someone with long fingernails drew them slowly and unevenly across the inside of my stomach. Instead I believed what he said, that I was insecure. It was my fault. Now the sensations of my body became the reason to ignore my body's signals.

If I tried to talk to him about those inner fingernails, I knew how he would respond. His eyes would drill into me, focusing me toward him, his warmth and love streaming toward me. I knew he'd use everything he had because he told me, I put a spell on you; you are mine. He sang the CCR lyrics, "I put a spell on you/because you're mine" out to me. I knew I would give in whenever I saw him, I'd believe him and his version of things. I would because I preferred his truth to my own.

The Angels returned, insisting, "You must leave David."

"Or else what?"

"You will be insane."

"So what? I'm not so solid now, anyway. Make me crazy but let me have David."

The Angels continued to insist I leave him. I grew more defiant, more impotently defiant.

Finally, the Angels said, "You must leave. Look."

A few feet from where I stood in my parents' kitchen, a vision opened.

I was inside a cell-like room. I looked out from behind the iron bars of the window. Below me were tightly manicured grounds and David, walking away. He had a woman beside him, a stranger to me, a short woman with dirty blonde hair. She linked her arm through his and looked up at him, her love of him clear. I knew she would mother our children, my children, because the doctors have told David they must lock me up and he should throw away the key.

Relentlessly the Angels continued. They said, "You know what will happen in this life if you marry David. You are not stable." Yet I remained stubborn so the Angels showed me again what would happen if I stayed.

We would have married. He'd have been on the road. Then facing his lonely bed in the early morning hours, he'd empty all the drawers of his mind, as his mother had the physical shelves in his childhood. Tearing through every corner he would find no place that revealed the face or arms, the sex or eyes of the woman he loved. The details that compelled him when we were physically close would resolve in a pale wash, so he'd gather another woman to him. Then another.

He'd insist he didn't care for them, didn't love them even as he'd load up on the young women around him. The silky threads of our conscious connection so capable of reading what was not physically present, would sing to the taut yank of his infidelity.

"Were you with anyone? I felt it; it felt like you left me," I'd confront him when he returned.

"You have to stop being so insecure," he'd deflect. Over and over. I'd ask, he'd lie. I'd ask. His lies my truth.

In my parents' kitchen, the Angels carried on relentlessly. It took only seconds, but I saw the consequences as though living through them. Unable to gain balance and unable to leave David, we would have children. Those children would inherit the pain I was pushing away from me, the pain the Angels' kept insisting I take on, the pain of leaving David and facing whatever else life held.

The Angels keep the vision going and *I see David went on the road again and left me with our three children. Except the me in the vision was an emotional wreck. She prepared to go out for the night, lipstick too harsh, blush too bright, skin tight black pants, a tight black top pushing her breasts up and out, loud rock music flooding through her mind and tiny ramshackle home.*

I watched as she gyrated in the vision through the dingy hallway, into the living room where three small children huddled together against the tide of their mother's unsteady oceans.

This woman looked at them staring at the tv, the empty pizza box opened on the floor in front of them. She acted as if these babies were just fine. One flashed his eyes upon her with a distant look well beyond helplessness and well beyond his years. She wasn't looking at him, but at herself in the dirty mirror on the wall.

Then that future me, that broken woman, raged as she stormed around. She raged at David for not being there, at all men, at her mother for abandoning her, at life for its pain.

The woman in the vision sputtered out loud to those children, "Your Dad is running around with everything that walks. Tell your Dad, kids, when he gets home, it's his fault."

With a dizzying shift in her inner winds, she suddenly brightened like she was anticipating the night ahead, music, drugs, men. She straightened her shoulders, "Ok kids, Mommy's on her way."

She blew her three babies a kiss. None of them even looked up from the t.v. She shrugged her shoulders slightly, then slid out the door, into the blues and rock filled night in that downtown club, unaware her life was under command of a corpse, a ghost from generations of motherless women who had been abused, neglected, abandoned—her real lineage.

If I chose to stay with David, I would live out the pattern of my grandmother, her love of booze and men, and my mother whose shame fired every decision she made. I would have no other choice.

The Angels wanted me to know. *They showed me David returned, put it all back together. From childhood practice with his mother, he'd create the illusion of safety or something near normal. We would be stable, at least for a short while.*

Then he'd go out on the road again. This time one of the children climbed up on a chair to reach a bit of food in the cupboard, to stop the sobs of a younger one, or leaned into a basin of water, a distraction to soothe their loneliness, it was unclear how but one was dead or crippled. This future me, charged with negligence was examined by psychiatrists and incarcerated.

Back in my parents' kitchen it was easy to see all this, but knowing I hung by a thread and that thread was David made it seem impossible to leave him.

The Angels hummed around me in maddening, perpetually uplifting tones, shades of golden light. These were the Angels who had saved me from Al and Gary. I knew the Angels were right: I had to leave David. To do that, I had to first block our connection.

Sitting on the edge of my bed, I thought of David, his mouth, his eyes, and as the emotion of yearning rose, I shut down. All the warmth, the eagerness to please, all the intense yearning rising within my body slammed down under my mind's will, until I felt nothing when his face, his body, even the memory of his smile rose in my mind's eye.

What I did is known by many terms: change the direction of thought, distract away from the pain, in extreme circumstances dissociate. Turn down the volume by turning off the number of brain nerves or neurons prepared to carry the message. Millions of us have achieved this.

Neuroscience tells us how our nerves carry a message and the more they repeat that message the more the neighbor nerves join the chorus, in what has become the mantra of neuroscience, "Neurons that fire together, wire together." Here with David, my instincts had me doing the opposite. Neurons that wire apart, fire apart.

I had learned to do this around my mother. Her impetuous floods of affection nearly knocked me across the room in their fiery warm healing power, but their tides rose unpredictably. Her fickle emotions flooded just as erratically in the hatred and rage she spewed, abrading my tender young psyche with her vitriolic words, my young flesh ripped by her flailing leather belt.

The point of no return came when I was twelve years old. She was leaving, again, but not before her scalding language splashed across the walls, furniture, leaving a hot path of shame everywhere.

"Goddam kids! Nothing but bastards, selfish bastards. Me, me, me from morning to night. I should have drowned you all at birth!"

In this way she stripped the tiny dignity we had in our small house, in our father, even in our own growing bodies and selves.

My father's presence this day prevented her from beating her rage out upon our flesh; helpless in the fury that besieged her cells, she took to the front door. Before she had it open, I stood in front of her, hands cupped to my chest, hot tears of humiliation and pain falling from my eyes. I fell to my knees.

"Please Mommy, please don't go, don't leave."

Her beautiful dark brown eyes shone, their enlarged black pupils distended to burnt out coals, as sharp and black and cold as a winter midnight.

I grew numb at the sight of her back approaching the door. I heard the thought inside: *never again*. My willpower rose around the waves of humiliation and vulnerability rising in my body. This willpower formed into a thought: never again would I be vulnerable enough to ask another human being. For anything. I did not know it then but this moment of her leaving, this experience of learning to shut-down would in time arrive in my conscious mind as a gift, one that would save my life.

Chapter Four

My mother sits on the toilet as her hand pulls back her white panty and she says softly, "Go get me a pad from the second drawer in my bedroom."

I am five years old, swinging on the white painted bathroom door. "What's it for?"

"It's for...for the bad blood. Every month a woman loses bad blood."

"Do boys get this too?"

"No, I just told you. It's what makes us women. Every month."

"If boys don't get it, I don't believe the blood is bad."

"Just go get me the pad from the drawer."

She had longed for a daughter, a soft, pink, pliable daughter she might mold into a woman, someone just like her. My mother had longed for a mirror to shine against the shame she harbored, the shame folded so many times in her body tissues it had disappeared from her conscious mind but directed her needs all the same. She longed for proof she had done something right.

I chaffed at her like a ragged edge of fingernail, every day wearing her down with my endless questions about things for which she had no answer, statements to which she had no response. It often seemed she looked at me, talked to me from the far side of an emotional wall, a wall of shame built on a day I already, at five, did not recall.

I was three and a half. What I recall is my brother's scent of cinnamon, earth and chocolate next me, his body sheltering and warming me. My need for this affection raised inside my skin a feeling I knew as love. I was on top of him, my body rocking with bliss, when my mother threw the door open.

Had she heard noise from the room where my brother and I had been told to take a nap? What made her open the door? Having opened it did the sight of her two children embracing invite every buried cellular memory of being touched against her will, forced to feel a pleasure in her body that her mind did not want, then told by look or by words she was the guilty one? She had invited this unwanted act upon herself, because she was a girl. Did she see in her two children the sins of the flesh, sexual sin, sins assigned since Eve to be the evil power of females? All her efforts to bury her own feminine shame crashed and her rage rose in a funnel cloud that now opened hell.

When she finished whipping me, my mother, breathing hard over her seven-month pregnant belly, stood above me, her eyes narrowed in hate. What I knew was my mother could not, did not do this horrible thing. I saw it was God who had entered her and made her do this. I had angered God and must beg forgiveness.

My tear stained face, my fuzzy numb body approached her legs, sore arms reaching out to her. I felt if I might find her body, her warmth, all would be well again.

"I'm sorry, Mommy!" Baby sobs racked rhythmically out.

Her brown/black eyes stared down at me from the face of a stranger. Her face a slate of hatred, she said nothing, ignored my pleading arms, left.

She took with her my body sensations. From that moment I lived above my body, somewhere in my head. My body lived below me, a cavern of paralysis, a deep cave where no feeling existed. This first layer of emptiness, a cocoon of numbness, swallowed my physical sensations whole.

All of us know what we want through the signals of our senses. From a desire to lower our body temperature, we get up, open a window or take off a sweater. When we feel deep desire, for instance toward a future goal, or a particular person, we try to figure out how to behave toward that desired end. We try to use our thoughts to help our bodies get what they want.

Our bodies send the signal of desire. My body had signaled a natural desire for affection and love and I had reached out for my brother. This single desire cast me from childhood into exile from my family but more than this, separated my brain from my body. Instead of my brain now figuring out how to get what I wanted, my desire-nature remained wrapped in a terror I did not know I had.

I began to use my brain to deny my body.

I learned to shut down whatever desire rose. This meant I no longer knew or trusted what I wanted. From that point, all large signals from my body shut down, layered down below my conscious mind which tried to figure out, without my body, how to live this life.

All who have experienced deep trauma hold this experience, this entombed place of numbing exile from sensory life. Cut off from our bodies we live as wraiths, often acting out, always without satisfaction.

I believed my father would tell me Mommy was wrong, that hurting me was wrong. He came home from work, I heard his voice and Mom's, then his steps as he climbed the stairs.

He said, "Your mother was right to do this. You must learn."

Even today our pornographic culture holds sex as a taboo, inflicting an impossible conflict upon everyone. This was the 1950's, a time when all guilt for sexual misconduct lay in the lap of females. Even tiny girl children. Men and boys were simply enacting their God-given natures.

Later that night I heard the voices of Mom and Dad, sounding normal, their laughter rising from the living room. My body sensed a question: how could they carry on like this, like everything was normal when I was lying on my stomach, back, arms and legs throbbing still? Big tears slid out of my eyes.

My brother came in, lay down on his stomach, turned his head toward me.

"Did you get a beating?" I asked him.

"No. Mom knows it was your fault."

Inside me, everything fell down.

"She knows you did it. Now you have to do what I say. I heard them, I heard them say they don't know if they will keep you. I heard them talk. They said, I think they said you are not really theirs. I am theirs, I belong to them, but they are not sure about you. I think I heard them say…"

"You did not! You never heard this! I belong to them. They know!"

"Yeah? Then why are you up here when we are all down there?"

His logic stunned like a slap. He continued, "I think I heard them say they may give you away."

A cold rush from the great expanse of a world I knew I could not manage swept around every particle of me, leaving me homeless, without boundaries.

Where will I go…I am too little…I don't know how… These thoughts rose as my world crumpled completely.

"I'll go and talk to them, see if I can get them to keep you."

I waited on my stomach ricocheting between despair and a tiny ray of hope, but he did not return.

He did not return, and no one ever referred again to that afternoon. My welted back remained bruised for only a week, but I was orphaned ever after, expelled from the childhood kingdom that had been mine, exiled by Divine forces I believed I had woken with my wickedness. Because no words hooked that memory, no retelling moored it in place, it faded into a ghost, an event that haunted, even as it was entombed.

But Mom did remember. Drifting decades later on the couch, in the morphine that temporarily soothed her terminal agony, she intoned like a prayer, "I almost lost your sister, twice. Once when I was three months pregnant… Another time…I was seven months pregnant."

Her eyes landed on mine with a small shock before she turned her head on the pillow, a signal she wanted to sleep.

My apocalypse, what happened that afternoon, lay like a corpse in a crypt, silent as ice. Within my flesh lay the memory of that beating. The memory sank below my conscious mind because its content was too large.

This is an instinct, as surely as breath. We forget because to remember will cost too much. But the loss of this kind of forgetting exacts a price, too.

The cost is how we make choices in the present. All my choices after that black day funneled into a compulsion to achieve male love. Since he remained innocent, so the truth inside me ran, and I was guilty, worthless, I must follow him, him or another man. This is how compulsion, a drive beyond our conscious control, takes over.

The compulsions that would rule my actions later, rose from my brother's early life repetitions. The animal territory between us, in which he was predator and I prey, had its warnings. His eyes would hold mine a fraction longer than usual, dark with meaning. I'd try to stay close to Mom, but she'd brush me off, "Charlene, stop following me. I'm busy!"

He'd find me then, maybe upstairs, alone. His body in the room felt charged, like an extra layer of clothes on him made him too warm.

"You have to do this. You know she knows. She'll send you away. Take off your pants."

In between, I saved my treats for him, for when he returned from school. His humiliation of me did not stop my love for him, not at this point. The eyes my mother had hidden in her dark brown hair, the ones at the back of her head caught me putting my lunch cookie aside.

"Who's that for?"

I said my brother's name.

"There's no point, Charlene. He doesn't want to play with you. He has his own friends now. Get used to it. Men go out into the world, they leave, and they don't come back. And when they do, it's for one thing, only."

Did she really say that, or have I put language on the cultural truth held by everyone through the 1950's and beyond?

I wanted that grey feeling of being worthless to my brother to go away, but soon realized nothing worked. He told me nobody wanted me and because he was my big brother, I believed him.

Because he was my big brother, I believed him. I was tied to him as surely as if a rope bound us.

We round about a stake, all of us who experience trauma, tethered to it as powerfully as if we had a rope around our necks. The stake is the original experience, whatever is too powerful for our conscious minds to contain. This trauma remains deeply etched past our skin, into our muscles and beyond. Compelled by the tension between the rope, which is our present day, and the stake, the original trauma, we go round and round, repeating versions of the original scene until we clear it with consciousness.

We clear the tension between that stake and the rope through accepting the stake, approaching the original memory and the emotional tsunami it holds. As we approach and consciously relive the memory, letting the unresolved emotion pour into and through our present day body and mind, sometimes repeatedly, we undo the tension of the rope and remove it. Then we step free.

It would take over three decades and unrelenting focus on journals, meditation, and dreams before my memory of this seminal trauma would spill forth from my body, freeing me from the confusion of my brother. This would be the last trauma to spill out and over through my cells. Before this, I would clear those days and nights held hostage by Al and Gary, and the horrible secrets that time contained.

Only when some healthy instinct deep within me knew I would not split apart, only then did the truth of that day from my early childhood rise, with steamy body heat, emotional pain and sweat rivering out, with an experience of throbbing pain on my back and through a galaxy of tears. The price of freedom.

And if we do not have the methods of healing or the knowledge that we must heal, we pass our wounds down to our children. My mother's unacknowledged abuse that cemented her to the adage "spare the rod and spoil the child" would rise finally in her. Once the cancer had committed itself fully to ravaging her cells, this illness and her daily doses of morphine permitted the wall of will power she had lived upon to disintegrate.

Then she'd call out, "Charlene, Charlene quick…" and as I ran to the tiny vial that stopped her pain, she'd cry out, "Don't, Mommy, please…"

"Hush Mom, you're here, now," as I pulled the plunger back on the tiny needle whose cargo delivered her from hell if only I might find enough unbruised skin for its entry.

My mother never stopped believing in the daughter she wanted to have, the one who would fulfill her dreams about being mother to a feminine little princess, never stopped chaffing at me to put away this false, independent self and be what she needed me to be. Never stopped trying and never stopped being disappointed, greeted with my wall of will power.

Therefore, I, who ought to have been a jewel in her crown instead offered constant reflection of her losses. Her father had left before she was two years old; her mother left over and over, sucked into the cavernous inner hole of her own unmet needs where booze, cigarettes and men temporarily took her pain away. That same cavernous hole in Gram gave my mother's early life its ghost of want, inadequacy and a raging desire to be a good mother.

She just hadn't reckoned on having a child like me.

Usually we need no more than the sentence, "my mother was a..." to fill in all the blanks we think we know about another's story. In this narrative, the sentence ought to be "this child was a..." continual frustration, thorn in the side, stubborn creature, a hooligan with enough sass to take on the face of wrath that my mother was sometimes. Understand I do not exaggerate. When I see with my eyes now, I recognize what a wizard I was at putting my mother up against herself.

"Even as a baby," my mother began while my siblings listened with me at the dinner table, waiting their turn to be told about who they were, who they had been and sometimes, what was to come.

"Even as a baby you would clamp your mouth tight. I'd say, now open wide Charlene and you would open your mouth. Then as soon as I brought the spoon close, you'd shut your mouth and look at me."

"Oh," she continued, a knowing look spilling from her eyes, "you knew exactly what you were doing even at that age. I tell you I believe where there's a will there's a way and you Charlene are the most willful person God ever put on this earth."

She said this to me repeatedly, her curse upon me, that I was the most willful person God ever put here, until a year or so later I pointed out she didn't believe in God.

My mother with her rages and verbal abuse, her regular wounding of me was acting on an instinct deeper than culture. Her wounds, pouring their acid on my skin, my heart and mind, her wounds taught me about the world as she truly knew it to be. This teaching would in time save my life and in saving me complete her deepest desire: to be a good mother, even to me, the daughter who disappointed her, who stood as her rival for my father's affections, this daughter who made her feel so inadequate.

On that twilight highway in the September I was 16, Gary and Al and I stood in the drizzling rain.

"Gary has a plan, to ditch the car just off the highway. Then we walk through the woods until we come out at a different point on the highway. That'll keep the police off our tail," Al said.

I wanted to keep the car because that's where the Angel had appeared. I wanted the Angel to come back and for that I believed I needed the car. I also knew the Ontario woods lead in a circle and wherever we entered we would be doomed to exit at the same place.

"We're not going to come out on another part of the highway! That doesn't make sense. The Ontario woods run in circles, we'll end up back where we started," I argued.

Al glanced darkly at Gary who rounded his body, shoulders and head down.

"Shut the fuck up!" Al to me, just before he nodded his head curtly at Gary to begin the tramp through those slimy woods.

I sat down on a tree stump and started to cry. Dread like a living ghost rose, a tangible presence all around me in the damp green shrubs and small trees, everything green-grey in the twilight. The truth of what I had gotten myself into began to seep through every defense and my strength dissolved to a useless bit of tissue flapping in a gale force wind. My crying turned to sobs, my sobs to wails.

"I want…my momma! Mahhhhhm…."

Al's hands and arms above my head, thwack, thwack, a large bird of prey, "Shut the fuck up! Stop your fucking blubbering for your Mama!"

I did not feel the blows.

This was my mother again, her need for me to hold back my tears while she beat or walked out on me. Tears made her hit harder, made her shed scorn on me before she left, so I learned not to feel, not to cry.

No more crying.

Chapter Five

THE KITCHEN SMELLS OF SUGAR AND CINNAMON, HOT JAM and crisped, browned dough and my mother's happiness suffuses this tiny room and spills out, boundlessly. I feel her joy in the rising warmth and pleasure of my body. I feel I may stretch out safely.

She sings along to the small, yellow radio sitting on top of our fridge. It's Dean Martin, or Tony Bennett, it's Bobby Darin or that lover of loves Elvis Presley. Her palms flatten the cookie dough just enough before she places each round onto the cookie sheet where they sit in uniform precision.

Then Agnes, a teenager from three doors away, comes through the back door.

"You home? Can I come in?" Agnes loves to visit my mother. Agnes and her older sister Sharon visit and tell my mother about their dates and their boyfriends, their new hairstyles and clothes. My mother loves these visits.

"Look!" Agnes produces the yellow hula hoop.

"Come on, then!" My mother leads Agnes into our living room, and I follow in the jet stream of their happiness.

American Bandstand plays the music from the TV and Agnes and my mother take turns swirling their hips like the teenagers on that show, twirling and keeping the round tubes of circular plastic from falling.

If these spontaneous eruptions of my mother's happiness remained unpredictable amidst the storms of her rage, the certainty of one holiday year upon year provided safe reliability: Christmas!

My mother's favorite time of year. I come home from kindergarten with a large card of red construction paper, smeared slightly from the heat of my hands, and a chain made of green and red construction paper strips taped together. My mother's eyes grow wet and her body soft as she takes these from my hands.

"Are these for me?" she almost whispers. My chest fills with a feeling that may explode. I nod my head shyly.

"Then I'll put them right up here. Watch now!" and she puts the paper chain on the front of our tree and my card a bit higher up where everyone can see. When Dad comes in, she will hold his hand and lead him to the tree, pointing to the special gifts I have made. He'll coo in that voice he uses that has only syllables and sounds, "uhhhmmmm."

Like that chain made of construction paper decorating the Christmas tree, my mother's happiness circled our lives, a wreath of healing and joy. In the car on Sundays when Dad announced to us, he had to "get your mother out of the house," her smile and her voice as we sang declared we were a happy family, a normal family with the usual troubles and more than usual love.

As calm returned after Mom had given us a beating that is what Dad told us. "We have a normal family," he'd say. "Your mother is right. You kids have got to learn."

And whenever we laughed or wrestled together on the floor, Dad flipping first one then the other of us, he'd drop words into our fun, like whipped cream on pudding, "You kids have the best family in the world."

When the music spread across our tiny living room Dad took Mom's hand, "Come on, dance with me," and they swayed. They had a way of locking their bodies together, their arms intertwined, palms facing, fingers laced and pointed toward the floor, tucked down straight next to their sides. Dad's other arm circled Mom's waist and hers wrapped around his neck so it seemed they wanted only to never again be separate. Then, her face shining and his smiling, they danced to some romantic song.

Or they swirled in jitterbug jive to the Big Bands, Glen Miller, Gene Krupa, Les Brown until each of us wanted to learn how. These moments remain and whenever I have been upset, or fallen into negativity, a point comes where I must get to the music, sing and dance so the good feelings return.

When my mother was warm, she was the source of all the love in the world and when she smiled at me, all my cells reached out for her, like the leaves of a plant turning toward the sun, for nutriment, for happiness. I knew her hugs and her hands had the power to wipe away my tears.

"Mommy, I don't feel well."

"Oh, come here." Her hand on my forehead. "Well, you're not hot. She's not hot, Ed. Her glands feel a little swollen. Should we keep her home tomorrow?"

"How's she doing at school?" My father's pointed gaze at me felt like a beam of light, "You keeping up? You'll have to work hard to catch up if you stay home."

I stayed home for a week every autumn and each spring, and in those weeks, I was safe and loved. Mom made eggnog with fresh eggs and the cream from the collar at the top of the glass milk bottle that was delivered daily. She added sugar and vanilla and I heard the fork lightly hitting against the glass she stirred, and I knew the treat was coming.

"Here, drink this, honey. It's good for you." Her smile was good for me, and my deeply introverted nature thrived through those weeks of quiet calm.

Finally, she and Dad decided my weeks of retreat were emotionally based. Sometimes on Friday, sometimes Sunday, Mom would sit at the edge of the couch where I rested under a comforter.

"Is anything…has anything been bothering you, sweetie?" Her voice, those tender words and the warmth of her presence dredged the tears I had not known I had.

"It's my brother…" the fury stuffed inside me came close to

revealing the truth. Close but never dared to announce the fullest split of my childhood: submit to him or be exiled from the family, thrown out of the house. So I believed.

My mother then took my side, as she took the side of everything vulnerable and in need. "Ed," she'd say, "You have to talk to him…" Whatever talks transpired between my father and brother, nothing changed.

Nothing changed with my brother. But my mother's power to transform the world for good or evil according to her emotional states continued in dizzying fashion. The land of childhood is mythic for each of us and within the boundaries of my childhood, Mom's spell-making reigned as the supreme power. When she was happy there arrived from chaos a splendiferous world, one of order and cleanliness, sweetly scented gentility in which every step was solid, trustworthy. Dust motes danced in precision because she held a dust cloth in her hand, and she polished the sunlight until it too burned more brightly. In her lay a transcendent capacity to take what was ugly, broken and discordant and with an act of will from those dark eyes, birth their whole and natural harmony into the greater harmonic of a safe, reliable world.

She emerges from the backdoor, the laundry basket overflowing with clothes stiff from the outside wind. Her face flushed she looks at me and declares, "Nothing smells as sweet Charlene as laundry fresh from the line."

Next her voice speaks liquid syllables to the small blue, yellow and green budgie whose cage door she opens. She trains the bird to rest on her shoulder as she moves about the kitchen, her voice and the bird's contrasting and melting.

Or her face full of mischief she passes through the living room where we watch TV, in her hand a pee laden diaper from my baby sister. She laughs as she pushes a corner of the diaper toward one of us, teasing, "It's good for your complexion."

She cleaned, cooked, washed clothes and polished windows.

She dusted, ironed and baked. She decided sewing was a motherly thing to do so she taught herself to sew and to knit. She baked luscious cookies and strawberry filled coconut rounds, tiny enough three were needed to fill my mouth but one alone sent my saliva into overdrive. She loved sugar!

In my growing years, I was allowed to visit Sharon and Agnes and I spent some time with Agnes, the younger sister, who was yet much older than I.

Agnes stood in front of the small kitchen mirror, her newly flame orange hair swept up into a neat knotted nest, the fashionable beehive of the mid to late '50's.

"Ow 'oo doin' 'oney?" Her voice mimics itself through her tightly drawn lips, pulled back to receive the oily coat of bright orange lipstick she applied, back and forth, back and forth.

"Fine. Where you going?" Agnes' exploits, at least the part of them she confessed, never failed to engage me.

"Going out with Bill tonight."

She picked up a comb, teeth on one end, skinny handle on the other, gathered an already obedient clump of hair and expertly dragged the comb ferociously down the upright strands, then lying the tormented group against the oval of her hive, squirted another layer of hair spray on top of the whole.

"I thought your boyfriend was Brian?" I had watched Agnes apply black lines of eyeliner into wingtips, watched her brush coat after coat of black mascara on her eye lashes as she prepared for her dates with him, the one she had called 'The One.'

"It's just a feeling I have," she had answered my questions about how she knew he was The One. "A feeling deep in here, you know?" Her fisted hand had landed briefly across her belly.

"And," she said leaning over to kiss me lightly on my cheek, "because I am so happy. That's how I know. And," she stood back, looking down at me, "when it's your turn, that's how you'll know."

Now she was dating another?

"Are you sure?" I asked.

"Yes, that's over. Oh, have you heard this song?" She strode two steps to the top of the fridge and turned the knob on the round brown radio where Bobby Darin sang 'Things.'

"Things...like a walk in the park...Things, like a kiss in the dark..." She sang along as I slowly shook my head. I had not heard it but now absorbed each word.

"What about the night we cried?" she sang, then as Bobby softly recounted more memories, "I love that line. Except, we never did. I mean as a boyfriend Brian did not take me for a walk in the park, or a sail boat ride, or, you know, things, like Bobby Darin says, things you're supposed to do."

"Maybe he was busy."

"Yeah. He was. Busy dating another girl," Agnes said.

"Are you sure?" I blurted out. "How do you know? How do you know he cheated on you?"

"Oh, rumors."

"You shouldn't believe rumors. Where's the proof?"

Agnes paused, considered, took a drag off her cigarette. "She told me." Agnes delivered this with the refined sense of drama her fifteen-year-old contained. My feet flew to the floor from their perch on the chair's rung.

"She did? The one he dated?"

This human feeling stuff was more complicated than I'd imagined.

In the fall of my twelfth year, I'd been visiting Agnes, now married and pregnant for the first of the several times she would conceive. In my questions about her condition, in her talkative way, she had let fall the words containing this universal mystery—how.

I came home, spilled a bit of language, my toes curling, my fingers wound tightly, a bit of language in front of my mother whose face fell as she took in my meaning. This robbed her of another moment of cherished anticipation, telling her first-born daughter the mysterious news of virginity, marriage and then babies.

"You tell her." She directed this, in that voice like sleet, the voice she used to both hide and display her utter disappointment, toward my father.

As he stood in the small living room, he began, "The truth is," he said, planting his feet and spreading his hands. "The truth is, what happens..." He relayed a foggy but basically consistent rendition, including stuff I hadn't heard from Agnes about periods and how menstruation works with conception.

"So, you are saying a girl who does not yet have her period, but is about to get it, might get pregnant if she, if she and a man..."

His grey eyes clouded, and his brow gathered a bit. "I didn't say that...but I guess, I don't know..."

"No, think about it. If a girl is about to get her period and doesn't know it and she does this, it must be possible..."

"Well, I guess so, anything is possible..."

The corner of my eye caught my brother leaning against the jamb of the kitchen door pretending to be involved in eating a sandwich but listening to every word.

"Tell him!" I pointed to my brother.

"What? What?"

My father faltered, so I used a voice I had heard Mom use, a voice that had no ambiguity. "Tell him what you just said to me. Tell him..."

"All right come in here." When Dad finished, he looked from my brother to me.

"What? What is it with you two?"

I stared unblinking at my brother, a slight twist of victory at my lips. Freedom.

Now I stopped reading pre-Socratic Greek philosophers like Anaximander and Diogenes, stopped reading books like *Love, Hate, Fear and Other Lively Emotions* that I thought might help me understand human emotions. Instead, I began to read the magazines I had previously scorned. I read articles describing make-up, hair styles, and most importantly how to talk to boys. I dyed my hair blond, adopted a stylish cut, earned money at my part-time job at the Woodbine Racetrack and bought the clothes I wanted, not what my mother chose. I continued to earn academic honors and play in the school marching band and I began to date.

Teenage years for all of us provide extremes. Every experience comes as a fresh, new adventure. Every success and every failure through these demanding years feels like a life and death truth.

For this emotional turbulence to settle eventually into a balanced perspective, to lean slowly toward maturing, teenagers require someone outside of themselves and their friends. This person must be stable and have the capacity to hold some of the teens' raw emotional energy without getting sucked into their own. That's called being a solid parent, a guiding teacher, a wise counsel.

I had none of this. All of my own emotions if expressed slammed against my mother's needs. All of her emotions dominated our house. There was no room for mine.

Without emotions, I was left with outer appearances. I believed I had only to present the right clothes, the right smiles, the right words to the outside world. Dress it up in the right clothes, teach it to mime the current jargon, prevent all smells, smile it much, make it wake to alarms and when it cannot or refuses to sleep because of all those turbulent nightmares, just over exercise— how you treat a breathing corpse. Never, never feel anything. Call this success.

True to the themes of my life, into this emptiness erupted a single summer that coated my unconscious with a different version of life, one of hope and sometimes joy.

I was fourteen in the golden summer when my parents bought the cottage. A gang from around the lip of the lake quickly formed and convened on weekend mornings at our dock. We occupied the kitchen, tossing toast, bacon, eggs and jokes around, then filed back to the dock for day long water skiing. In the evenings in the back field, under the stars, someone built a large fire, and someone brought a big kettle. We ate roast corn, joked and made out.

That same year, my brother played drums in a band that practiced at our house in the city. A girlfriend and I danced, in go-go boots and tight pants, the very essence of cool, in front of this band in the tiny night club up the street. Did they sell alcohol? I didn't notice.

The lead singer, a young man of powerful sensuality and good looks chose me as his girlfriend. After band practice one night under cover of the darkness of the back porch, he leaned in. I taste this first kiss on my mouth still, the scent of his cologne, his confidence in pulling me close, the feel of his lips beckoning a strange sensation from my body way down below.

Inside the house my brother raged, threw his jacket down, stomped around. My father's confusion fell about the kitchen and escalated into yells at my brother.

I floated inside.

"Why," Dad demanded, "is he being like this?"

Everyone knew my brother and I had a very close relationship. Everyone knew, and everyone refused to know.

Everyone refused to know at that time what we look for now, the signals and especially silence of a child, how silence indicates potential abuse. That was one extreme. At the other end of the spectrum, it was the 1960's. Freedom in all forms seeped into the tightly held life containers of the 1950's path to acceptability. Now it was acceptable to be unacceptable. As these opposites stared each other in the face, literally East came to the West.

The corner convenience store had a small rack of books. One of them was about meditation and yoga. I began meditating by focusing on the single flame of a candle, a practice that years later I would learn was dangerous. I meditated and practiced a bit of yoga.

The whole culture began to soften from the material certainty of the post-war years as people everywhere heard the call of the

1960's: freedom, love, living in peace and yes, magic: the ideals that shaped a decade.

The next year, the summer of love, 1967 brought from California all the hippie thoughts and feelings about love as freedom and life as freedom and freedom from chains and whatever held you down. We drank in the cynical truth of what we were turning away from in songs like "Mother's Little Helper". Simon and Garfunkel's smash hit "I Am a Rock" amplified what I felt, what so many felt that the song became an anthem. And we dwelt in the world of the lyrics of Bob Dylan.

As I grew more distant from my parents, and even from the cottage since I chose to work full time the next summer, my mother's frequent tirades of verbal abuse and her threats of physical violence continued but as though from a far shore. She tried one last time to exert a wave strong enough to stop me. I was on my way out the front door.

"Where do you think you're going?" She flashed the wooden ruler in her hand toward me.

"Out."

"Where out?"

"Just out."

"You'll tell me, or I'll use this on you."

"I wouldn't do that if I were you."

"Yeah? And why not?"

"Because I'll lay you out flat." I was three inches taller than her five foot five and I knew I was much tougher.

"Ed! Ed, come here and listen to what your daughter said. Tell him!" Her sneer contained all the years of superiority she had enjoyed.

"What?" My father looked at her, then at me.

"Tell him!" Mom shrilled.

"I said she better not hit me with that because if she does, I'll lay her out flat." My tone even, my eyes stayed on my mother.

Dad turned to her. "Did you think you were going to be able to beat them forever?" I did go out that day when I defied my mother and increasingly as the weeks went by established independence, coming and going, often without consulting either of my parents.

I found parties distasteful because I had no gift for chatting. The anxious feeling in my stomach before any social event started days in advance, as my physical system reflected what my emotions believed: that I was and always would be outcast, an alien.

Yet one person, Beth Southern, liked me enough to invite me to a wildcat party at her home while her parents were at work. Beth held a pedigree of money and status through her parents and that pedigree opened the doors of the prestigious Balmy Beach Canoe Club. Beth walked like she herself was a canoe, rolling from side to side, her shoulders tilting as though in a futile effort to keep herself steady. She cursed like a brothel owner and refused all attempts of the private school she sometimes attended to employ her very high IQ.

This crowd at Beth's displayed their cool, hippy allegiance to sex, drugs and rock 'n' roll. The girls dressed in tight fitting, revealing summer tops, or blue jeans with bell-bottoms, the essence of cool. They stood in circles casting warm glances towards the young men. The place was packed.

I arrived in yellow knee-high socks, a green tartan wool skirt way too warm for the early September weather, and a long-sleeved sweater, walking like a mummified ghost. Beth jetted ahead of the fashion curves on the energy of her defiance, dressed in blue jeans and a short-sleeved t-shirt, a look that would soon become the hippy uniform.

"Hi Jones. Glad you made it." Everything, especially my name, sounded like sarcasm in her mouth. "Have a beer? Or are you drinking yet?"

"No thanks. Nice outfit."

"You think I have to dress up? For you?" She disappeared into the growing throng taking with her my tiny edge of confidence. Now my nerves stood in their wiry confusion, lit up, so I believed, for all to see.

My face a mask of indifference and boredom, I found a seat on a chair in an alcove where I might watch the others, while hopefully conveying "Stay away." At least 'stay away' is what my head wanted. My racing heart desperately wished someone might speak to me. But then if they did, they'd learn how my tongue twisted to cynicism and sarcasm; they would not hear how my heart yelled for mercy. I thought of myself as a mutant.

Despite my attempts at invisibility a young man's eyes met mine. He zoomed in even as I saw from his clothing, I would reject him. Blue jeans, a strange suit jacket over his t-shirt and tie, he stood out. Yet my heart raced. I wanted to be wanted even if by someone I would never want.

"You see things, things other people don't see," he began.

Inside, I shuffled and looked at my feet, but in this outer world I held his gaze, returning it as from a distance.

"You know things other people don't know. You see…Angels. Yes. You see Angels. But you live alone. It's as though you live in an empty train car, a single train car abandoned in a vast field. People come by the train car and visit, thinking they are visiting you, but you know they are not. You have an emotional power you don't express. And soon each visitor leaves, and leaves you alone, and no one has touched you, and you believe this is what will happen for the rest of your life."

My body had turned to stone as he spoke words intended to name me. Each word shucked another section of skin, revealing the shadowy, ugly, crusted mutant within.

He looked in my eyes. He saw.

"You know how to let others believe you are connecting, even when you are not. But someone is coming…someone more powerful than you."

"A man?"

"Yes, a man, but not like anyone you've ever known. He will come into your emptiness and change it. He will see the alone place inside and that will change things."

What every fifteen-year old girl wants to hear!

I wanted that and feared it at the same time. Without the deep place inside where no one else could find me I was vulnerable. I desperately wanted, and completely shrank from anyone peeling through enough layers to find me. Even the thought of that closeness created pain in my body.

Beth called later. "He said he'd never met anyone who hit him so hard emotionally, Jones. He's not in love with you or anything, he said that clearly, but he said he registered the power of your emotions. Of course, he was tripping on acid, so who knows."

Acid? Oh, that.

Chapter Six

I BELIEVED THE MAN FROM BETH'S PARTY was talking about a romantic partner. The thought at once confused, frightened and elated me. What I had no way of knowing was the person he predicted was a meditation teacher.

That party was when I was fifteen. Within a few months of my return from those three days of captivity when I was sixteen, my brother was insisting I meet someone, someone he had heard about at University and had gone to meet.

"You have to come and listen to this guy. Really, he's talking about all the things we talk about all the time."

"I'm happy where I am, thanks." I was contented in a way. My days and nights filled with smoking weed, or drinking or both, and occasional attempts at job interviews. Since I felt nothing, I was not shamed. And I was interested in the weed, drinking and partying.

This response to my brother's ongoing insistence I meet this man, someone he assured me was a 'real' teacher, continued until I realized my brother was not going to stop. I agreed to meet him, once.

Inside a large west end warehouse, the very high ceilings towered, and the concrete floor spread large enough for the hundred or so people who had streamed in to hear this Bikkhu Ananda Bodhi. I would learn years later his Western name was Leslie George Dawson.

He sat on a hard, high back chair, dressed in beige pants, a maroon colored robe about his thin shoulders. He had even features, thick black-framed glasses surrounded his round, large dark brown eyes and his mouth was full and sensuous. He was Caucasian but when he spoke, I couldn't follow. He sprinkled Pali words among the English and all his words fell down all around me.

He talked and as I focused on him, trying to understand, suddenly a tongue of fire leapt from his mouth! Instantly he looked directly at me and referred to how when we first find beauty it may be so foreign we believe it is the devil. Words like that. Then he went back to his talk, addressing everyone, the whole thing seamless.

"No acid before arriving…not dropped for at least three weeks… a flashback?" My mind tried to place the experience within a context.

He saw me, he saw the inner me and I felt his knowledge and sensed it as a direction I had never had.

I sat in my perfectly formed full lotus posture and tried to make him do it again. I focused intently sending all my mind energy toward him.

His eyes roved the room, just over my head, or landed on the person next to me, or somewhere just to the back of me until I had to believe he was choosing to ignore me! I collapsed out of the lotus posture. Anyway, it was difficult and painful to keep up. Irritated, restless, I longed for the talk to end.

When it did, I found myself lining up with others to shake his hand. I approached and looked up at him, into his eyes. Instantly, that dark planet, the void inside me, the one constantly beckoning reached up as I fell toward it, darkness, a nothing…until I came back just as suddenly to his eyes and to what his voice was saying.

"I knew a woman once," he explained to the man at his side, "who would faint right away in front of you." He looked at me now, as he said, "She would faint right away, in front of you."

He then turned completely away, and I felt loss, as though his presence and his words had outlined me in a new way, providing relief from my total isolation.

We separate actions according to good and evil: if someone does an evil action, we assign to that person the value of being evil. So it was with my brother, who had bent my love for him into a shape of shame and humiliation, to satisfy his need for power. In this he was evil.

Yet the good that would come to me from meeting this Dawson, the power of healing and ability to overcome great odds to gain a sanity none might have predicted, that came from this first meeting. And this first meeting came from my brother. For I knew he would never have stopped insisting, never stop hounding me until I met this teacher, and so I had caved.

That meeting was in the summer of 1969. From my journal:

"I went to a class with Bikkhu. Strangely enough he seemed to know my very thoughts and would direct certain sentences to me, at least, he'd look directly at me, while explaining my thoughts to the class in his own words...He spoke of children as fools and he almost seemed to become the Fool from the Tarot, coming down the Path. And looked directly at me. One time I was wondering if he ever wanted to take a wife or was he ever lonely and he looked directly at me and said that in order to love everyone you cannot be involved. In order to help you must maintain objectivity. I was flabbergasted.

Another time my mind was fading into thoughts other than exactly what he was saying. Slowly I felt myself being brought into focus and he was looking directly at me, talking in his usual tone and by some form of vibrational strength, pulling me into his thoughts again. As soon as I was focused as fully as possible, his eyes wandered to other people again...The total effect of the evening was that I felt a stronger surge of energy than I had in a long time."

Now we believe meeting our teacher will mean good things, positive feelings at least. I had met my teacher, and my journal is full of the desire to pursue a spiritual life, even as I lived in depression, with anorexia and bulimia, even as I ran headlong and consciously to embrace drugs and alcohol, the anonymity of midnight parties. I loved the dark side and it loved me back, providing a relief from

My Impossible Life

the pounding threat of the future, or the dismal truths of the past in a present moment soothed by drugs and friends who, like me, turned their inability to function in society to disdain for what that society offered.

What is noted down next in my journal speaks of the underground tremors, the brewing volcano inside. I was back in my parents' home, from which I was periodically evicted for various crimes like back talking or using the pill as a contraceptive instead of just to regulate my periods, when the Forever Van arrived, heading east.

The Forever Van, a brightly painted VW van full of students of Rinpoche as Dawson was now called, came through Toronto heading to the East Coast. I joined them, then, according to my journal I left the van, hitchhiking with two women to Montreal.

This same journal contains details of the trip, including descriptions of the shops and houses as if someone else, someone not me, wanted to remember I had been there. I have no memory of the experience.

Had traveling in the Van, the rhythm of the wheels turning across the tarmac, sounded deeply enough inside my flesh that cells released the original hitchhiker into this moment, this experience? Had that release resulted in a compulsive need to hitchhike?

We replay our original trauma in compulsive actions in our day life. We do this because to remember too clearly, too swiftly threatens the balance of the daily, functioning mind. It does not matter how well or poorly that daily mind functions. We will not recall memories that lie outside the ability of our mind to believe we are in control. Yet all the while our bodies know differently.

With the truth held at bay because it threatens our daily mind's ability to function, we are compelled toward actions and experiences that we have no choice over, actions and experiences that mimic in some large or small portion the original trauma.

What I remember is waking up, a kind of coming to, on a sidewalk in bright sunshine, looking at a smiling woman, a stranger to me, and asking her, "How did I get here?"

The woman laughs, "Don't you remember?"

That one phrase captures a core of my life. Remember, don't you remember, I am memory, don't remember, I remember both those memories I have consciously, and memories others assure me I have.

Without conscious memory of the sixteen-year-old I had been, the one with burn marks on her skin, bruised breasts, pain from ropes that had tied her ankles and wrists, and the gag that had tied her jaw too tightly, without her I registered consciously only a portion of any experience. I registered consciously only a portion of any experience because I had left her, the scarred and terrified girl behind, but she was the key to my becoming whole. She stayed inside me, did not age, did not heal, until I was strong enough to return to the cells of my body which held her, return and release her from her hell.

As though tied to a stake, we replay bits of unremembered trauma, each time letting go of a tiny layer of the original terror, the original emotion. Sometimes we believe we are making a conscious choice with conscious awareness. We do not have conscious connection to the underlying trauma, but we know we are reaching for a needle, or a drink, a partner or a place to gamble. We provide for ourselves and others all the justifications in the world for these actions except the right one—the original pain.

If we visualize the original trauma as a neon colored spike in our unconscious, each time we re-enact something close to that trauma a bit of the color bleeds out. So, in reaching for whatever soothes, we are enacting a kind of very slow healing. Tragically sometimes that process tips over and instead of healing increases our risk of death.

Despite the obvious gaps in my life, no job, no school, no plans for a future my daily mind believed in a point of view I adopted as mine. Eighteen years old and I knew there was no point. Millions of humans infinitely more capable, much less deformed than I, had given their lives to wholesome, positive activities, thoughts and words, but the smear of humanity, our oppressive insistence upon brutality toward each other and the whole planet, sounded its ugly result everywhere. Nowhere did we get it! Nowhere did any of us stop creating more pain, nowhere.

I found no inherent worth in any part of what people did with their lives. I concluded no worth existed outside our human need to create one. I created mine through drinking, drugging, dancing and sex. My sex partners during this time were really the rapist, slipping off my body out of that room and me, untouched, still roped to that chair, except I remembered none of this original scene.

From my journal through this time:

I am reading Cayce's book on dreams. So many things strike home—home in the joyous, humble sense one knows it as a child—home inside. Yet I am deeply afraid, probably as afraid as I am curious, and probing. Every endeavor so far into mysticism of any sort—yoga, meditation, Zen Buddhism, even my earliest Christian religious beliefs have ended in states of mind I fear are close to insanity and far from God. Part of these dubious results are due no doubt to my own extremist nature, lack of common sense, self-indulgent will (a powerful and lately destructive force) and mental speed. These are a strong combination of characteristics, ones that I'm sure could do great good if channeled and blended properly, just as for the past few years they have led into some harrowing experiences, both external and internal. My own misuse of body and soul have left me drained. I feel dead inside, yet slowly hope is again arriving, with renewed belief in God. This time with His strength and guidance I feel I shall make it, though not before many trials and errors, suffering and painful loss. At this point, my one desire is to return to the state of purity and sure knowledge I remember as a child, that I can again find peace and understanding in myself, to bring it to others. It is my only mission.

I struggled with day-to-day life. I struggled with and started to remember and write down my dreams. Although I did not understand or even attempt to translate them, I drew comfort from the small act of recording them, as though something important had been achieved.

Because those three days of being hostage to those two men imprinted with such powerful emotional intensity, the memory lay more deeply inside my psyche than almost any other. The energy that was meant for living my life in the present was trapped in keeping the cesspool of those memories at bay.

I knew my culture did not contain a map for helping me. I knew the culture understood how wrong I was, how all I had to do was just get up and get a job, or go to school, do something to satisfy everyone's need to believe in a future that did not exist for me. The culture had no way to get me through the woods, to help me find the breadcrumbs that might lead me home. I turned toward the only other possibility that presented itself: Dawson.

He was holding a weekend retreat in the fall after my spring experience with Forever Van. I joined others at the Greyhound Bus station in downtown Toronto and rode the few hours to Kinmount where a mini-van loaded us, and our luggage, for the ten-mile ride over dirt road leading to the Dharma Center of Canada.

Our meetings took place in the newly constructed temple of the Dharma Centre, replete with Buddha statue at the front. The space was sparsely decorated, and high windows let in light all round.

He spoke all morning and again I was unable to decipher much. I also did not see any flames or fire anywhere around him. I was disappointed.

At the end of class, he described what we would be doing in the afternoon.

"We'll be studying movement." He said this as a declarative, like something important would happen, and glanced at me where I sat a row or two behind others.

Good, I thought, *I am good at movement. I'll stand out, a good student.* A warm glow in my chest, I looked forward to the rest of the day.

After lunch, we met again in the Temple and he began, "This

system of movements, developed by Alexander Lowen, from his book The Language of the Body releases oxygen and blood throughout your body, clearing the blocks to your senses, allowing the vital, elementary energies to open…" He described the movement of Chi, how Chi is blocked in the body and the vital importance of learning to unblock this healing life force.

Then we lined up at the side of a tall stool. When it was my turn, I lay my back down against a pillow placed on top of the stool, opened my arms up and over my head and let my jaw drop open, feet slightly pigeon-toed with heels touching the floor as instructed.

Swiftly a red flame burst within, intense heat burning from my root chakra up to my navel. I howled in pain, tears streaming but stayed the full four minutes required, sweating, hurting, fighting my body's impulse to knot up in a fetal position. Standing again, dazed, with the blood draining back into my body, I saw him about to exit through the front door of the temple, a black cape furled about his tall frame.

"Drama," he declared, wheeling around to face the room. "Nothing but drama and hysteria," was his indictment of our, of my, efforts.

The next day, Sunday, I retreated at 10 am into the van that would carry us, at 2 pm, down the dirt road back to Kinmount and the bus to Toronto where I felt safety existed. The van had its back door raised, and I plopped my canvas bag down and sat, my back curving toward the lean of the van's roof.

Dawson happened by, the usual cadre of young men, minions really, who constantly surrounded him, prancing about his tall frame. His black cape swirling, he stopped when he saw me.

"I hope," he said sounding very serious, "you have learned something from this weekend." His tone was respectful in my ears.

I felt pleased he had noticed me and was speaking to me in this way.

"Yes, yes, I believe I have." I smiled at him.

"Good," he continued in the serious tone, "Good. Because," here he shifted his shoulders up to his ears, caved his chest in towards his back in parody of my posture, "we wouldn't want THIS to go on for much longer."

The young men sneered in my direction, laughed in ridicule and floated about him, spores to his holy stamen.

Blood slammed against my cheeks. Rage thrust up through every cell. He had stripped me publicly. He was pernicious, contemptuous, rude and untrustworthy.

I waited silently then, all through the long hours until the van would leave. I waited, promising myself I'd go back to drugs, partying, drinking, to the world I understood where people shared their drugs and their bodies, where we hid from this jagged day life in the sweet cover of night and darkness.

Chapter Seven

Meeting Dawson, following him into that retreat only solidified my sense the world was a mean, cold and corrupt place. David had been my only refuge and without him I was truly lost.

Understand: I ate food, but nothing tasted. It isn't that nothing tasted good, it's that nothing tasted at all. No taste and no smells. I might bury my nose in a bouquet, I might respond verbally with how good the flowers smelled, but inside the dull thud of no smell amplified itself across a vast inner emptiness. Sight? I knew sights, I saw sunsets, I heard others proclaim their beauty, but I felt nothing. Touch remained outside of me about two inches from my body. That is, I knew when someone held my hand, or touched my arm, but I felt nothing inside.

Sound! Some energetic partnership between my body and music still erupted when certain music entered my ears, evoking dance, movement, singing and sometimes tears.

Drugs. Because I could not feel, taste, smell or receive touch, the drugs, especially hash, compounded my sense of being mummified, wrapped in cellophane, layered beyond the world. Hash kept all of it away, leaving me snug in a cocoon of not feeling.

Now it is late spring 1970. I see the lamp in my basement bedroom pooling yellow light in a single cone. My parents at work, Tim's hand on my shoulder brings me gently from sleep as he tenderly lays a lit chillum to my lips, saying, "Char, breathe in. It's hash." He tells me it is 8 am. I drag hard before disappearing into the smoke and smell of what I so love.

Does memory work backward? Do we remember someone we have never met before? Many of us have had this experience, of meeting someone for the first time and feeling, "I know you." What has memory to say then?

I met Tim in grade eight. Stunned to silence by the way the room washed sideways as though a tidal wave had hit, I stammered through our first minutes together. In this lifetime.

I am thirteen in that memory. Five years later my life seesawing on memories unknown to me, Tim provided a bridge between that bright, successful young person who had run away in the middle of the night in early September of my grade 12 year, and the tattered, hollowed out creature who came back.

I had returned with a story about two men, trampling through woods, breaking into cabins. I insisted the men, Al and Gary, "…were my friends. Nothing happened…" I insisted this all the while my body truth rattled muscle and bone up and down as though someone inside had a rolling pin, was rolling my flesh like dough from the inside out.

Tim listened, watching me shake. He listened with that signature acceptance of his, only commenting once over the years, once briefly, about the difference in me, how I had come back changed. Otherwise, he accepted me in that rare way he had of offering loving acceptance to whatever rose in his life. I reveled in not having to explain or try to remember what I could not.

Here in my basement room in the summer of 1970, Tim gives me what I want most.

I suck on the clay pipe, its hot tube wrapped in wet rags, and a feeling of sharp nails hammering underneath my shoulder blades babbles the hurting heat of that fiery inhale until smoke sings to blood its false lullabies and I am gone.

Four months; night dreams of cities reduced to dirty brown

rubble, one flower raising its fragmented, brown curling petals, dreams of brackish streams of water, green with slime, maggots erupting, dreams recorded in my journal. Dreams, the code from redacted cellular memories, all those beatings, rapes, burnings raising their truth in dreams as ephemeral as smoke from the hash, the hash smoke that kept the pain at a distance.

Tim goes off to paint his parents' house. Then, just before my parents get home, he comes back. More hash, more chillums. Four months of my life still hangs within those clouds, entirely gone.

Hyperbole? Consider: even now in my sixth decade when I hear of drug addicts my response is visceral. My nerve ends curl against the inside of my skin, and I see myself, haggard, begging on the hard cement of a downtown somewhere, my filthy hand outstretched, toothless smile, begging for money from the tall well-dressed legs and hands that pass by. I know myself sitting there, all dignity and self-respect long gone in the dissolution of hope, one fix at a time as my body and mind become the drug they crave, and the drug only wants more.

Tim dragged me, despite my need to stay cloistered in the damp basement, to a walk in Toronto's High Park. As I considered my white, white legs moving slowly on top of my bare feet across the grass a thought occurred: I had to stop smoking hash.

The sorrow of this thought filled my head, because I truly wanted to live the rest of my life in the uncomplicated cloud it offered. I longed to place the burden of living, of making choices onto the daily need to score, and then smoke and then go into that darkness some called sleep, to wake and repeat. This was all I wanted.

Was this knowledge that I had to quit from the Angels, the same Angels that had appeared to help me through those three days? Had those dreams I'd been recording brought a thin layer of clarity, thin enough that a tiny stream of vital energy, that sliver of life force David and I had evoked together, might rise now to whisper a healthy direction? I do not know.

What I know is what I knew: against my desires, I had to quit smoking hash and come down.

Tim left in August 1970 for a trip to Europe with his family. I remained in hiding, although with none of my beloved hash. When first one, then two and three letters arrived of flowing, articulate, poetic writing from him, I felt stymied, a mute creature, wordless before his intense command of language.

My conscious plan was to chisel my life toward an early end, yet still I wrote what dreams I remembered. One of the dreams recorded in my journal relates an image of Dawson taking crystal glass and crushing it against my Deva Chakra, my third eye. It was not painful; in fact, I felt a marked if brief joy from this image.

And then in the early New Year 1971 one dream changed my life.

I dreamed I was returning from someplace and Tim greeted me, dressed in a monk's brown, hooded robe. He was attending to people who were very sick and dying. They believed they would heal but he knew they would not. He took care of them until in the dream he lay down on one of the pallets, sick with the same disease.

In the dream, his face bloated with scabs, he grew mad and believed he would recover from this illness, a disease the dream called the Modern Plague.

I still have the original paper where I typed the dream in 1971.

I stormed across the snowy planks of the boardwalk in the Beaches over many hours, muttering to the ice and waves of Lake Ontario the turbulence within me. If the dream was, as I felt certain, about him what was I supposed to do with this information? Why had I at 19 years old been given such a dream? Why did I even believe what I believed to be true from this dream?

We dream every night. Researchers have discovered that if we are woken so our dreams are interrupted, after three nights we begin to hallucinate during the day. Something in the act of dreaming encourages and sustains our ability to navigate this daily world.

Some of the information from dreams comes from our personal history but other layers exist, layers beyond time and space as we know them here in the day world. Many people have recorded the predictive power of dreams and here, this dream predicted with chilling accuracy a cultural event that would sweep across the planet, taking 35 million people to date to an early grave, including my beloved friend.

When I finally decided, I came to peace. I would take this dream to him in Europe and tell him so he might have at least this foreknowledge. Perhaps, just maybe he might change the course of his life and death through the knowing.

I had direction: get a job to get money to meet Tim in Europe somewhere. The Post Office hired me for an evening shift, part time permanent. Every day I left the house about the same time my parents got home and on nights when I took the street car back to my parents' home, instead of partying until dawn with the crew of co-workers called the Pepperland Patrol, I arrived past my parents' bedtime.

They were happy because I was working.

Through more letters and one bleak phone call I arranged to land in London in early July 1971. I made my way to Shepherd's Bush where Tim had lived in a small communal apartment. His friends greeted me warmly and accepted me, although I lost the ability to talk as soon as I landed. No words would come out of my mouth, but I did the best I could to smile at everyone. I did not recognize this as a sign of deep trauma; instead I thought of this as another way in which I was lacking something, an essential something that others seemed to have. I was flawed.

Despite this, my new friends included me when it was decided we'd jump into their tiny car, all six of us and drive to Stonehenge. The moon was full, the night pulsing with promise and the stones breadth and height sheer magic against their towering moonlit shadows. My hands moved across some of the ugly graffiti that had been carved in the stones, as if I might erase the gouges. Then I lay down on one and fell asleep.

"Come on. Freddy and the Dreamers are on to us!" One of my young companions called to me. I looked across the field to see some men in uniform streaming toward us in the grey dawn light. Behind me, my companions scrambled for the car and soon we were laughing all the way back to London.

I was three weeks in London before Tim connected with me with directions for where and when to meet up. Eager, terrified, I climbed aboard a bus for the trek of several days.

The Pudding Shop in Istanbul was a famous dive, a hangout for all hippies. This hole in the wall, always darker than the sunlight outside, felt timeless, as though world events stopped at the door and you entered a place neither earthbound nor time chained.

It was small with enough chrome tables and plastic covered chairs for maybe 30 people. The open kitchen was at the back of the room and kept the moussaka, green beans, and potatoes warming all day. Graffiti on the blue walls and maps of other places focused attention, but the real draw was a large bulletin board.

Pieces of paper, some as old as last month, held secrets of yesterday and tomorrow for all who walked in, personal notes from one wanderer to another, "Doug I was here, sorry missed, Afghanistan tomorrow" or " Sue …where are you?", "Tom, you bastard just letting the world know you're a cruel…", telling entire stories of loves lived, lost and regained, of lives on the move directionless except to escape the directions of a culture gone mad.

Some of the papers had messages like "Treat madness with madness—Tantra," glyphs of hope for those traveling the inner worlds on passports of smack, speed, and more, when the way seemed lost and the darkness infinite.

The Pudding Shop was an underground central where travel plans manifested on tables and just as quickly evaporated in the sudden appearance of a new stream of drugs, where black market traders lined up new clientele for dubious deals, where beer was cheap, drugs available and always someone completely stoned, body crumpled across a table.

Tim would later call all these psycho astronauts "Little Saints and Pilgrims" in an opium inspired letter to me.

I waited alone an interminable number of days and nights, at least three or four, at the Osmanli Hotel in Istanbul, Turkey. I felt I lived forever every day in the Pudding Shop.

Tim finally arrived, skinny and slowed down by months on a Greek Island. A young man 5' 9", sun streaks in his thick, dark brown hair, his skin so deeply tanned his dark blue eyes stood in startling clarity, wove through the people crowding that street in the slums of Istanbul outside the Pudding Shop. He moved slowly, sensually, his ambiguous sexuality clearer than ever before.

He looped his large-boned arm around my shoulders, the familiar scent of his body, an earthy spice, rushing to my head. Did I imagine the smell held a layer of the scent of hashish? He wore patchouli over the deep musk of his own body signature; my nostrils received the message and I felt giddy.

He wanted to travel overland into India. I agreed although a small place inside me began spinning. Not a good sign.

We arranged to exchange checks on the black market, an easy way to make extra money as I had discovered one afternoon through a manic black-eyed Turk before Tim arrived. This second time, it took extra time.

Our meandering soon ripped through to the dark side where the path quickly accumulated wasted bodies of parasitic pimps, desperate dealers, lost souls and auric space travelers aiming to discover the outer limits. All of them came from Europe and North America.

I drank and lay around. Tim smoked and lay around and once a manager laid what he called hash on us. Black and sticky, Tim scraped the stuff onto four U.S. flag papers, making a magnificent joint about six inches long and very fat. He whaled, I sucked and within three tokes we each sank back on the bed wrapped in opium dreams.

The opium released from my cells terror, guilt, visions of Jesus bloody on the cross, an unending stream of pounding questions, "What are you doing? Why are you doing this? This is no good you know." For three days of paralyzing terror, followed by catatonic depression I hid in our cheap, dark room.

From my journal: *I was feeling sicker and sicker (from the opium) more miserable and more miserable and started crying for the pain and sadness of what I see—these people and their unhappy lives, facades of joy, desperation clamoring to a hit, a fix, a high. Fuck.*

Perhaps because his body was clear of excessive unfelt memories his opium fantasies rose in vibrant colors and pleasant shapes, he told me three days later, when he insisted I move, shower, walk with him.

Vagrant derelicts arrived at our room to smoke up. One night the same hotel manager, off-duty arrived at our door with a set of works. Tim's hatred of needles kept him from shooting smack, but others helped themselves, red flags of blood on the walls. I saw the wasted bodies of serious drug addicts, their eyes heavy, some with needles still attached like reverse umbilical cords, limbs tossed on the dirty mattresses, greasy halos of hair, whatever fantasies of a life of freedom ensnared in the liquid or smoke that held them prisoner.

"How can you stand living like this?" I asked Tim.

Tim blinked slowly. "We have to stay here to get my checks, remember?"

"I don't mean that…I mean, how can you stand these people and not have it destroy you?"

"These are part of God's creation, right, I mean, right here… isn't that what it's about?"

He meant the whole Buddhist, Dawson, travel to the East, get enlightened thing that swirled in conversations as frequently as phrases like 'far out' and 'wow man.' All Tim saw was a shining part of God's great creation.

His plan, his need was to head east on one of the vans offering rides through Iran, Afghanistan, Pakistan, and into India. I desperately wanted to go with him, except that I truly, unimaginably did not want to, could not go. The inner spinning had woven a black veil that came down inside my head whenever I thought I'd go farther east so I talked him into returning to Greece. For him this was a regression. For me, it would be heaven after hell.

Jeffrey, an instant friend and just as instantly part of the past when we separated near Athens, drove us in his VW van into Greece. I was in love from the moment we left Turkey, the physical beauty and joyous celebration of life seeming to swell off the hills and shrubs starting in Thessaloniki. Perhaps my love was fueled in the same way one feels clean and whole, even inspired when a bad hangover leaves, when by comparison, whatever the daily life it feels good to be in it.

Did our experience in Turkey, my dive into inner hell states, followed by the sense of relief, of beauty and harmony I found in Greece, reflect the turbulence of my childhood? Did the hell and heaven opposites of those two countries let me live out in material terms, in the physical, the inner states of consciousness I had learned from my family and from Al and Gary? Did the physical manifestation bring a kind of wearing down of the message of brutality and beauty as though once the information is manifest in physical form, it loses some of its power?

But the question is, do we live out our inner most beliefs, the truth our cells hold inside us, do we live this out in the so-called outer world? Do we magnetize ourselves with unerring precision toward experiences that will repeat our deepest held notions and beliefs, unless we become conscious and directly release the emotional and physical pains? Once the energy of pain is worn out, either through physical manifestation or through consciously feeling it, the unconscious lightens up and new attractions, new life experiences may unfold.

Did some of my inner hell absolve itself, wear itself out in the experience I had in Turkey? This is no indictment of Turkey or of the many good people who live there. It is a question about whether some support came to me in the gap left by the manifestation of my belief in life as a kind of hell, so that Greece was able to bring to me a sense of support?

How does it happen that we heal?

Chapter Eight

OUR BOAT FINALLY LEFT VOLOS, the port at the south end of Greece for a tiny island called Skiathos just east of and not far from the mainland.

Midnight, under a full moon, the exquisite village of tiny white buildings with red clay tile roofs grew until it seemed we swam through streams of silver white light bouncing from those buildings, reflecting off the waves, as though we rode moonlight onto the shore.

Tim's eyes flashed with pride as we walked up and away from the shore through the winding whitewashed cobblestone alleys. Instantly enchanted by everything, I eagerly climbed with him, exclaiming all the way on the beauty, the beauty and the cleanliness.

Yoni's discotheque Skuna, at the far end of the island became our home. Yoni kept the small concrete floor clear for that moment when, enough drink, enough music, enough Greek midnight sky overhead, what was left but to dance?

We met others, people who under their need to escape from divorce, bad relationships, bad jobs, were searching. When a copy of Baba Ramdass' book Be Here Now surfaced on this little known idyll in Greece, we felt it was a divine sign. We believed it, we wanted to believe that there was nothing else needed but to keep ourselves in this present moment. That was all; it was impossible, but it was all.

I drank: the beauty and cleanliness, the friendliness of the Greek people and booze. We ate little, slept less, drank, danced and fought.

Through the compelling light that shone on stark small mountains of brush and scrub, the palette of blues, purples, greens, reds thrown up by the Aegean Sea reflecting bottom coral, through visits to a tiny two-room walled enclosure used by shepherds, we fought. Under velvet star stippled skies, walking on dirt roads past carts pulled by donkeys, we fought. We danced and we fought. We fought about money, how he'd spent too much, how I had promised to use my money and now I was taking that promise back, but under it all he wanted to go East and I wanted…something I could not name.

After the poverty and dirt of Istanbul, after the soulless destitution of people we'd met, I had no energy for more. Yet if fighting because we were together but yearning in different directions felt tense, leaving, separating felt intolerable.

Our bodies robed each other in familiarity. We knew the tree lined streets and high school halls each had prowled; our past included playing together in the school marching band, competing against each other in speech contests and later, abandoning all hope of a straight trajectory for our lives together we had mumbled stoned midnight confabulations in the ravine across from my house or while ambling along the boardwalk. All the memories we shared provided a cellular bulwark against the sudden newness of everything here and now. We were each other's touchstone and to break from that now when it felt like we teetered on the very edge of the world seemed lunatic, crazy, a kind of spiritual suicide.

We splurged on a small hotel room instead of the much cheaper communal outdoor rooftop, for our last night together.

The light from the naked bulb appeared to throw a pattern on the wall by my head.

"What do you see?"

"I see a pattern," I tell him.

"I think you are blessed."

"Or cursed. I think I am already crazy."

Sitting on the edge of the bed where I lay, he looked away, stared at the pale blue wall.

"I had a dream, Tim, why I came here at all, to find you, a dream about you."

He turned his blue eyes on me.

"You were taking care of all these people, and you wore a brown, hooded monk's robe. The people were dying and then you got sick with the same thing, you didn't think you would, you didn't believe you were sick, but you got sick with something the dream called the modern plague."

After a long silence he said, "I used to wish I was an invalid. I'd picture myself all in white, lying around with everyone taking care of me. I'm not afraid of dying. I'm afraid, I've always been afraid of going blind, not being able to see the beautiful colors of the world…I don't want to be here if I can't see…"

"You probably won't. You probably, if you go blind, if you went blind, you'd probably just start to hallucinate. Yeah, your mind won't let you go there because it's too scary, so you'll just create pictures and colors…scenes and people from memory."

He wiped his tears.

Next morning my arm hung out the glassless window of the train, Tim running alongside, his hand in mine as far as we could. We recognized the ridiculous sentiment of this moment, the movie scene sense of it, and still played our parts with sincere hearts. He gave that freedom.

Tim died in 1986 from the illness the world would call the Modern Plague, A.I. D.S.

I had traveled to Europe to meet him and bring him the dream. I thought at the time this was a big gift, big enough to change the course of events the dream had predicted. My youthfulness, my failure. I feel remorse for not having had more to give him because he had, without knowing it, provided an essential first step in my healing. The dream about him drove me across the planet, describing in its gripping power a direction I would eventually follow for life guidance for myself and then others—the miracle of nightly dreams.

Back in Toronto I failed at other attempts to work or go to school but returned to the flock of students who gathered in increasing numbers around Dawson. There was, after all, nothing else.

Then Dawson announced he would travel to India. He would go on pilgrimage to India and allow those students of his who asked and received permission, to accompany him. The journey would start with an exploration of Primal Therapy in Morocco, then a trip around Africa by ship to India, overland to visit Tibetan temples, then a time in Australia to gather funds and finally, a three-month meditation retreat in New Zealand.

I found work at a downtown hotel as a room service receptionist. I was living with my boyfriend and in general had a life that others, especially my parents, found acceptable. Divided about my future, I voiced plans to meet up with the group wherever they were early in the new year. That was my best attempt at consciously making a decision—my direction remained divided literally across the planet.

Then a vision brought me round to what my next steps had to be. One night at my job my mind stubbornly, continuously turned to questions about where the Group was and what stage of Primal Therapy was going on.

At home in my living room after work, a vision of Dawson appeared, his tall figure dressed in the kakhi pants and burgundy shirt he usually wore. I knew he was not there in the same way that, for instance, my couch was, but I knew he was there. I knew this in the same way I had known the Angels appeared in the oak tree of my childhood. He looked at me and said, "Come now."

My plan had been to work until after Christmas and then join up with my brother and the group wherever they were then. It was now November.

I said, lighting a cigarette, "I don't go halfway around the world on the basis of no goddam vision. I need material proof."

The next week a phone call came from a man recently returned from Morocco, from Dawson and the group. His insistence was out of all proportion—I knew who he was but had barely exchanged any words with him, ever. He insisted I must come to his apartment for dinner. That Monday my boyfriend and I sat in this man's small place. Our host showed me a newspaper where an advertisement for a one-way ticket to England was circled in red.

"See that? See how cheap it is?"

"Yeah. And it leaves this Friday. So?"

"So, I bought it for you."

"Are you crazy? What are you doing? Why do you even care about what I do?"

"Because before I left, Dawson asked me in for an interview. He told me to tell anyone who was back here thinking of joining the group later to Come Now."

I heard the last two words in capital letters and five days later, instead of the nearly three months I had been planning on, boarded a plane for England and India.

Chapter Nine

INDIA! HOT MOIST AIR PLUMED AROUND as I walked down the few metal steps to the airport tarmac. I inhaled deeply and the cloying smell of urine raced up my nostrils, lodging there.

At the Quonset Hut office, I glanced again at the two names on a piece of paper. Each name held promise of locating my teacher.

The first, a Vihara or place of refuge, sat inside tall, tan clay walls. Striking red flowers luxuriated around the outer wall of the courtyard and the door that led inside, where people lived, ate and slept. By now my body's weight dragged under the effort of my will.

A tall, brown-skinned man opened the gate a few inches and peered down his nose.

"We have no knowledge," his head shook lightly from side to side, "of this teacher or your Group." His tone barely concealed contempt.

"Well, may I stay at least for one night?" I truly expected all doors to open. Aware of the side effects of jet lag and culture shock, I was eager to sleep at least, perhaps shower and eat.

"We have nothing for you." He looked down his long face at me, leaned in and closed the door.

Scientists tell us we make decisions with our brains seconds before our personality catches up. On that street in New Delhi all those years ago I believed I made the decision. On reflection how could I have?

In an impossible growing weight in my body, a torpid stillness of mind I recognized as the first signs of shutting down. If the shutdown completed itself, the ways of the world would dictate my course with no resistance and no direction from me, such that an impoverished street corner in New Delhi would hold as much appeal as a real hotel. I knew the dangers but still the shutdown calmed and soothed in the way of narcotics. I felt its edges climbing to capture my senses.

All of me wanted to just give in, find the nearest bar, start drinking, get some weed or morphine, arrive at the party of anonymous, colorfully dressed vagabonds hanging out so nearby I could almost feel the ease in their veins flushing already with what I craved when Beast howled. Like it howled now.

Beast was the surging drive that wanted control. Beast commanded, sending thrilling little snakes of excitement through my body anticipating what Beast delivered. And Beast always delivered, oblivion, drunken ease, numbing distance from what life demanded, carrying me along in a silken ride on Beast's back to that secret, inner domain where nothing mattered.

The price for Beast was consciousness. Many times I had paid eagerly, leaving my flesh to wander in any direction, no focus or motivation, sweet eclipse from the crippled moon of despair that hung over my internal life. With Beast at the helm my mind emptied its tiny cachet of a sense of self, opted every time for distance from that vice of voices screwing down in my head, release from the straight jacket posture my muscles held.

At this moment in India something, not Beast, chose and I stepped back to the edge of the street, hoping my hand in the air might work to hail one of the three-wheeled, brightly painted taxis scooting in all directions on this major boulevard.

One destination remained—the Canadian High Commission. The bright little vehicle with its thinly padded seat bumped along the road, which grew increasingly into a very wide manicured boulevard of palm trees.

As the small cab streamed forward, that same impossible weight inside warned of shut down. Now its warming edge nudged toward my senses. This time I met it with effort to block. Beast was silent as I saw that shutting down in India had entirely different consequences than being lost in North America.

I stared at the scrap of paper in my hand as though it was a sacred text and the name on it, Commissioner James George, a secret powerful incantation. I made the mental effort to think he must, this Commissioner, be a kind man, a helpful man. Surely, he would know of my teacher's location or in the least know how I might proceed.

"Commissioner James George," the smiling brown face of the man in front of me replied, "lefted here three months ago."

"Three months?" That weight, with its threatening paralysis descended rapidly, alarm fast on its heels. "Where? Where did he go?"

"Tehran!" The same smile, broader now with gleeful eyes, framed the pause into which my world sank. "You must ask Charlotte Singh, she is High Commissioner now, she will know about your teacher, your group."

"Where is she?"

"She is at lunch."

"When will she return?"

"2 o'clock."

Four years earlier, when I had returned from running away, Beth told me, "Leaving like that, Jones, in the middle of the night, telling no one, it's a kind of suicide, but one you can come back from." Here, too, a kind of dying, in the way all travelers must, dying to control, dying to belief in time as something malleable we exert our will upon. Instead, an in-between state, a gap into which the past and one's intentions for the future swirl, a place of emptiness. Tibetan Buddhists call this in-between place a bardo. It must be endured.

"How may I help you?"

Charlotte Singh, short, slightly plump, dark haired with a kind face, looked up from behind her large wooden desk a few hours later.

"I'm looking for my teacher, Namgyal Rinpoche. He's here in India, I think, with about 100 students. He's…"

"I don't know how you people do it! Yes. I know your Teacher. Do you know Sharon Sobilowitz?"

"No."

"Are you sure? Think about it. Sharon Sobilowitz."

"No, I am certain I do not know her."

"Well, she came in only this morning… this very morning… and dropped off the address where your Group is staying in Dehra Dun. She told me she had come here in case anyone came looking for your Group. Just this morning she came in. Did you know they might be in Dehra Dun?"

I shook my head.

"You came to India without knowing where anyone was and just…"

"But I knew it was either here or in Australia and it has turned out all right."

"You are sure you don't know her?"

"I am sure I have never heard of her."

Charlotte Singh was a wave rising from the great ocean of life, playing the role of loving hostess for this vagabond, a child who had not the sense to figure out where she was going, or to whom, before she left on her journey. Charlotte Singh figured out, as a loving mother would, what I needed next—a ticket to Dehra Dun on the overnight train and a first-class ticket at that.

"Spend the extra money. You look extremely tired. You need," she looked at my face, "to sleep."

She instructed her boy to take me through the labyrinth of New Delhi streets. I recall his lithe tan body almost running through the alleys, barely touching down as he leapt across uneven layers of corrugated tin roofs beside dirt paths where the city is built on small hills, one foot here, then there, then both taking him across the patched path. I laboriously followed, but in this memory, I walk on dirt paths and try not to see the details of life and death coiled with poverty.

At American Express he transacted the purchase of a one way, first class train ticket to Dehra Dun, then pointed across the street to the train station.

The train station loomed a large and dark cavernous vault. I clutched my ticket and two very small bags. Dressed in an oversized man's jacket purchased at the Hadassah Bazaar in Toronto just before I left, a pair of corduroy pants, my hair sheared down to almost bald, I walked up and down trying to keep my mind still as the four hours until my train was due inched along.

Between the certainty of the beginning and the finality of arriving, personality fades to a ghost. The mind reaches to wear memories that no longer fit, an echo of something barely remembered, or scurries to a future without shape, while the body stays in the in-between place. It is here the value lies in leaving at all.

My body leaned to enter the small train compartment which beckoned with its cleanliness like an oasis, but a brown hand attached to an arm encased in a khaki uniform fell across the way and a hand yanked my ticket out of my grasp.

Inside the door stood a short, erect woman, elegantly dressed in a silver and blue sari, a well-coifed tiara of silver hair on her head. She burbled liquid sounds of her native Indian tongue to the porters who scattered like birds, then spoke in impeccable Oxford English to two young ones, a boy about 13, a girl slightly younger, her grandchildren.

The two young people glided past as though my body did not exist and the woman looked up, speaking again in the fluid sensuality of her language, her beautifully manicured nails posing in air.

She and the khaki uniform exchanged sounds, then she turned

her palm up, stopping him. Penetrating brown eyes, kind, soft but decisive, met mine with inquisitiveness, a direct stare softened by curiosity.

My body longed for the momentary peace offered by the small space; I knew whatever the outcome my desires meant nothing here. I opened my palms by my side and focused on my heart.

Again, in that cultured British tongue, "She may stay."

Hand man started to object. She flashed her eyes at him, clapped her hands, poured directions through her fingertips and porters again leapt about.

With my two small bags on the floor, I curled my legs up beneath me, keeping a respectable distance on the lower bunk from where she sat next to the window.

Soon the porters disappeared, the train sounded its mournful song, and our bodies absorbed the vibration of steel wheels on steel tracks. We traveled facing the blank wall, me closer to the door and staring past her at the fields and gentle hills dancing through the small closed window.

"Where are you going?" Her tone was almost disinterested and if she had not been so certain I might stay, I would have wished myself away.

"Dehra Dun."

"Oh, well," her eyes flickered momentarily from the window, "that is where I am going. My home is there."

If she'd had a scent it would have been of cardamom and cinnamon, a scent that warmed just by its presence. Whether it was this or her startling personal energy, one of power but also warmth, I relished being with her.

"Well, choose where you want to sleep. I suppose you'll be wanting the lower bed?"

"No, I'll be fine up top, that's just great, thank you."

"Where are you from?"

"Canada. I'm from Toronto."

"Why are you here?"

"I'm looking for my teacher. He's traveling through India with a group of students."

"What kind of teacher?"

"Meditation."

"My dear, you must be very careful about these teachers. So many who claim to be this and that…" Her eyes grew wide and the corners of her mouth turned primly down.

"Oh, but he's Canadian."

"Well, even so you must be careful. How many students does he travel with?"

"About a hundred."

"I see. And you know for sure he is in Dehra Dun?"

I told her the story of my arrival in India, of Charlotte Singh's surprising knowledge about the Group and her helpfulness.

"Oh, my dear, I always thought Westerners were so practical! But here you…" She threw up her hands, laughing, "I must help you then."

She asked if I had brought any food with me, and clucked again, shaking her head when I confessed, then offered me fruit, cheeses and breads. I gratefully accepted pieces of her orange, its flavor only a memory of sweetness for me.

I had no way to question this state of depressed sensory ability, since it was for me normal. A tiny note of disappointment tagged along with every sensory experience, as though something vital were missing. The note was very soft and almost lost entirely in the conviction we all hold that what "I" experience is the way it is. For me, that meant not having direct sensory response to taste, smell, touch, sometimes sound and sometimes even sight. Only a memory, vague, almost gone, of something else, another place, a magical world where senses brought fresh impressions and the world was alive.

She packed her basket and turned back to the window. I followed her into silence. Outside the small window, light flushed pink and orange through the dusty air, then finally all color leached to blue-grey dusk and presently, I lifted myself to the top bunk and closed my eyes. Soon her gentle snores matched the sound of the rhythmic wheels beneath us.

I lay awake for a long time, smoky memories like wraiths rising in wisps, memories explaining why I had come this far. I had spoken the truth about landing in India and all the details from today. What I had not mentioned, what had really propelled me from Toronto was that vision of my teacher. True to my maternal lineage I trusted the visions more than most other sources of information.

I was yet stunned at how the world worked: I had left unexpectedly one week after having that vision, against all calls of common sense and planning. Like a tumbler where the exact numbers convince the lock to give itself over, time had been set in motion with an elegant specificity. I would arrive exactly on the day when someone in India would have dropped into the Canadian High Commission with an address for our group; I would be at American Express where Charlotte Singh guided my next moves...

In the morning, I woke slowly to soft shssshing sounds. Almost closed, my eyes picked out the fresh royal blue sari of my host. Then with a knock at the door a gleaming silver tea service appeared from which she poured and handed me a steaming cup of English tea. Heaven!

"Now get dressed. We will soon arrive."

It was nearly noon when we pulled into the small, dusty train station. Across the yard stood the humble station building, behind which hills fell away lower and lower while tall pines speared the sky all round offering a thin thread of pleasant scent on top of the fresh, cool mountain air.

We peered from the edge of the train where a burly man pushed forward past the crowd of beggars. A few sharp words from him and they fell back, as one. He helped her down and in a moment her bags lay around a black, 1940's gangster-style car.

Even here she directed. To her man she said, "She will come with us."

His eyes twinkled as liquid syllables fell from his mouth. Her head nodded, and coins flipped through the air from his hands, while some of the dirty flock scattered. About half remained, hands outstretched, mouths moving with sounds of yearning.

He thundered this time and they all flew, tiny ragged birds, away. He opened the front passenger seat door for her, helped her in, then came around to where I waited by the back door for a sign about what to do next. To my surprise he opened my door, also.

I slid in, and realized I felt hyper alert, danger signals spilling up. It took conscious effort to not yell this sense of danger to the woman in the front seat. I put it off to nerves, the demands of the journey.

As we pulled out of the station onto the dirt road lined with large pine trees, they spoke softly together in the front. She was not alarmed so I took my cue from her.

Suddenly the driver, his brown eyes piercing at me through their reflection in the rear-view mirror stated, "You are a very lucky young woman. Do you know who Neru is?"

Twenty questions, starting with politics, a subject I avoided. I groaned inwardly.

"Uhm...wasn't he the Prime Minister of India?"

"Yes, yes! Yes, and this is his sister, Madame Pandit. She is Number Two lady in India. She is member of the UN."

When we left the car a few minutes later I was shaking. Culture shock, jet lag, and the shock of caste, how a woman of such importance might bother over someone so insignificant.

Beautiful red patterned carpets lay on the floor under simple but solid wooden chairs and table. A lovely view of small mountains rose outside the window and inside on the mahogany table a plate of toast arrived to go with the new pot of tea. The toast had rose jam, sweet beyond imagining like scooping a spoonful of raw white sugar scented with roses into my mouth. The texture, thick and almost slimy made my throat begin to close over. I stifled the urge to gag.

I tried now to ask an intelligent question or two about India. It was clear my questions only reminded her of burdens.

"India is a place of too many people and not enough for anyone."

She excused herself and came back a few minutes later, smiling, "The group you describe is at the Sakya Tibetan Buddhist Refugee Center, a five-minute walk from here."

Her voice conveyed relief and an undertone of surprise. "Did you know of this center?"

"No, I have never heard of it."

She shrugged once slightly, shaking her silver-haired head, "My dear...I will send my manservant to carry your bags if you would offer him something, a pack of your English cigarettes? And remember, all these teachers are charlatans!"

Her manservant, who was maybe 11 years old, carried my two tiny bags, and as I offered him a pack of English cigarettes he quickly conjured, through broken English and mime, an imaginary sister also in need of a pack. In a land where parents break their newborn babies' bones so the child will be more successful as a beggar, imaginary relatives appear and disappear like smoke.

I turned from the road lined with pine trees toward a wall with a gate containing all the mysteries I had come for.

Chapter Ten

AMONG THE MILLING CROWD OF BLUE-JEANED, bead-wearing people inside the tall tan walls my eyes found my brother. He grinned and strode toward me.

"Now I want you to meet someone. Come on!" He took me to the hotel room he shared with his partner Cecilie Kwiat.

I had heard through my parents that my brother was engaged to a woman 11 years his senior. They had met in Morocco and almost instantly sworn themselves to each other.

Inside this high-ceilinged, wooden-walled hotel room in Raj Pur, resting from the traveler's curse, a stomach bug, the woman who would stir to life part of my damaged heart, sat up, holding her hands out.

"Come closer, I want to see you, look in your eyes." Her soft voice vibrated with authority. I walked forward, took the hands she offered.

Her short brown hair crowned a soft face and full mouth. Blue, blue eyes looked up at me, startling me by taking the time to really see me. In response, I scattered to the far sides of the space just above my head, where I normally escaped whenever someone came too close. But she found me there, found me with her eyes and I could not help it. I funneled down into the space behind my eyes, almost into my body. I was emotionless still, but oddly more present.

It was love, love of the kind between two souls destined to meet again in this life, love of the kind that proclaims, "I know you. I have known you. I am so happy to meet you again."

It was love as love sometimes shows up between two women, deep with emotional resonance, without physical counterpart, the love of a mentor, a mother figure, for she was instantly and would be for many years the person to whom I looked for guidance, for direction and inspiration. It was love in its mystery, its demands and illusions, but love it was.

For three days Cecilie and I did not leave each other's side except when late in the evening, reluctant to part for even a few hours, I tore myself away to toss my sleeping bag across the uncomfortable large ropes woven and tied to the narrow wooden bedframe in my hotel room. The instant my eyes opened I dressed and wandered over to her room where she greeted me, we ordered tea and began our day of talk.

She told me about her early life in Calgary as a cow-girl, riding horses across the open plains, growing up in a family of four siblings, all of it quite ordinary until one day when she was 16, skipping off school, a case of beer in hand, she tried to cross a road and was run over by a 4-ton gravel truck.

"Across my pelvis, crushing everything. I was told I'd never walk again and never have babies. But I already had the names of the eight babies I would have in this life. You don't tell a sixteen-year-old Scorpio she'll never walk again. I stood in front of the mirror and made myself walk, practicing over and over with crutches at first, then gradually on my own. Most people if they notice at all, just think it's another of my weird ways, you know, like, of course she walks a bit strange."

Here was a miracle coming from the myth of her life. Told she would never walk again she defied the authorities. She, who had been assigned to the status of physical cripple when she was 16, had healed herself. What she had achieved fell into my ears. Far below, deep inside me a tiny flame of hope began. If she had, maybe I might. Whatever darkness owned me might fall away. The possibility existed.

She described a map she'd had on her wall, how she had stared at it every day and imagined all the places she would travel to when she finally left that bedroom. In my mind, I see the map and my sixteen-year old friend putting, as she told me, sticky pins in the places on the map: South America, India, Thailand, Australia, Japan, Mongolia, Finland, the carpet of the world beckoning even as her legs relearned how to obey her will.

"Then as soon as I could, I left home, hitchhiked to California, Berkeley, San Francisco Bay area. I was writing poetry…"

As if I had not branded every word she spoke onto my soul already, those last four words tattooed their way to my depths, sealing an unbreakable bond. Of course, she wrote poetry. So did I!

"I began," she continued, "giving poetry readings. I opened for Joni Mitchell a few times, ran with a crowd who hung with the Grateful Dead. Richard Brautigan was a close personal friend." She paused, as though racking up points by name-dropping felt cheap. "But what I did a lot was walk people who were on bad acid trips, walk them around and help bring them down."

"How'd you do that? Did you take them to the hospital?"

"Not back then, man. Hospital at that time meant the man and raids, because drugs were illegal. No, I'd walk them up and down the street, talking and listening, sometimes getting them coffee…" What she did not say was how often she herself was on acid, perhaps on a bad trip.

She did speak about months spent wandering in the mountains around Banff, Whistler and parts north in B.C. "I sang out loud and wandered and talked to the trees."

"How did you eat? What did you…?"

"I don't know. I was mad, crazy, you know. I came home to Calgary, put Mozart on the stereo in my bedroom and listened for three weeks over and over. That was the end of that madness. Then I left again. And you? How did you come to be here?"

I told her, dreams, visions, Madam Pandit and all.

She looked at the clock, "Time for you to go." I got up from where I felt myself being initiated and walked toward the temple for another ceremony.

Inside the plain concrete building, with its single door entrance and small windows placed high in the walls, we gathered for the holy ceremonies of Tibetan Vajrayana Tantra, the Wongs.

Seated on a Dais, his completely bald, round head above everyone else, His Holiness Chogyi Trizen presided over the room of about one hundred westerners and a dozen Tibetan monks. He looked to be in his sixties.

Below His Holiness sat a younger Tibetan man with kind brown eyes, his face framed by large turquoise earrings. Two long braids of black hair laced with turquoise ribbons and coral beads lay over his shoulders. This man, His Holiness Sakya Trizen, head of the Sakya sect of Tibetan Buddhism and therefore head of this simple monastery in Raj Pur, translated the flowing Tibetan of Chogyi Trizen into accented but clear English for the group.

Below both these men about a dozen monks dressed in burgundy robes sat on the floor in front of the elaborately draped thrones supporting the two dignitaries.

Chogyi Trizen, the renowned Master Key Holder in all four sects of Tibetan Buddhism, had been performing Wongs for at least a week before I arrived. These ceremonies, the Wongs, are considered among the faithful to be the essence of Tibetan Vajrayana practice, opening from latent state the individual's chakras, providing the fuel to unlock meditation from a mere ritual, into an active, flowing stream of vital life energy.

Despite its simplicity, the room— so new the damp smell of fresh concrete still infused the air— vibrated with a feeling of warmth and happiness. Every day for almost two weeks as Chogyi Trizen and Sakya Trizen conferred the blessings of these initiations, I was bathed in the transmission energy of both this renowned teacher and his translator.

Sometimes gold, sometimes red ear flaps fell from whichever crown appeared upon the head of His Holiness the Sakyapa. This young man only in his late twenties had offered his fluency in English and generosity of heart to translating day after day for His Holiness Chogyi Trizen. Both these men held the renegade teacher, Karma Tenzin Dorje Namgyal Rinpoche, aka Leslie George Dawson in high regard especially since Dawson's naming ceremony the previous year.

In that historic event, the 16th Karmapa had given the simple monk, Bikkhu Anada Bodhi the new handle Karma Tenzin Dorje Namgyal Rinpoche. Passing the new name to this Caucasian man included the idea that Dawson was, in the Karmapa's eyes, the holder of a lineage, meaning Karmapa recognized Dawson as the latest incarnation of Namgyals, those who bring the teaching to the new world.

Tibetan leaders generally hold the view white people and women, in fact anyone not part of the male Tibetan religious hierarchy, have no chance of attaining enlightenment, the Holy Grail of Tibetan meditation practice. The recognition His Holiness the Karmapa proclaimed about Dawson defied this culturally held truth. Going even further, Karmapa stated, "Where you see Namgyal Rinpoche, you see Karmapa. Same-same."

In an act of unprecedented generosity to Dawson, His Holiness Sakya Trizen offered nearly 100 Westerners including women access in English to the secret ceremonies of the very essence of Tibetan Vajrayana Tantra. Thus, Dawson's fate as a renegade, a white man acknowledged to be the lineage incarnation of a stream of Tibetan teachers, was sealed.

I put my eyes on the bare floor, twisting my body into a full lotus thereby fulfilling the primary mandate of my culture that young women always look attractive. I sat very, very still for what seemed like a very long time, motivated by the knowledge that I looked cool.

My mind had drifted out those small windows built high into the walls; I was dancing in the bars back in Toronto, writing letters to friends, fantasizing about the next man, a man, any man. That fantasy returned to the room where I was sitting, but my only focus was on which of these men might be him. I looked around. None of them were even interesting.

"Oh, yeah, I'm supposed to be meditating, this is a religious experience," I chided myself. Back out those windows in a flash.

The small bits of being present that I do recall remain as a handful of stars: the visual imprint of His Holiness the Sakyapa with his earrings, turquoise and coral braids, and soft voice, a momentary flash of eye to eye contact with a handsome young monk piercing through my dull mind, a tiny physical arrow held in two brown hands pointed straight at me, kind, laughing eyes, the joyous fluid movements of these monks through the throng crowded on the floor, endless sprinkles of rice falling all round, sudden splashes of water from the end of a peacock's brilliant feather dipped in a ceremonial vase and the sun slanting in, marking the hours, through those small windows.

Some ceremonies lasted only a couple of hours; then we had more than one in a single day. Some lasted from sunrise to past sunset, with no official breaks, just concrete floors, Tibetan monks flooding around, the sun slanting in gold streams, rice falling, water sprinkling and the deep voices of those men sounding the mantras and prayers repeatedly. I thought these would never end.

On days when there were no Wongs, or when daylight still shone afterwards, I walked the main dirt road that ran through Raj Pur. The sun burned its light in my eyes even through the smoke rising in dense columns from dung fires; the acrid scent stung inside my nostrils. I tried to practice being aware, walking up and down the small main dirt road, tried to focus my senses, tried to stay present. Inevitably, I found myself singing all the songs from Bob Dylan's Nashville

Skyline, Simon and Garfunkel's Parsley, Sage, Rosemary and Thyme, the songs that ran in my head night and day. I sang out loud.

And those women, crouched down, saris gathered between their legs and hoisted into waistbands, patting cow dung into round shapes to put on the fire, babies slung at their breast or playing in the dirt, what did they see? A young white woman, wrapped in an ochre colored shawl, grey trousers on her legs and hair cut short, singing out loud as she gazed at the trees. Did they murmur to each other in their native language, "There's another one! Crazy. They have everything, and they come here and act this way." Did they shake their heads in pity or scorn?

The truth is I hated it. No bars, no men, whatever drugs might have been available were far too dangerous for me to access, no dancing, no way to douse my chattering, shattered, overheated nervous system, no relief inside the temple or out from the constant inner jangle of songs, commercials, poems, half-phrases, crunch of words, memories, longings and anxieties reeling through a polluted tide of unfelt, unresolved physical and emotional pain. Beast demanded to be fed; without bars, drugs, parties, Beast consumed me.

The yearning for Toronto trawled through my belly fueling a sentimental lurch toward my parents' dank basement where I had lived, the drugs and drink so easily available, the music, late nights and wasted days. It had been my crippled life, and had the choice been mine, I'd have gone back in an instant.

I did not recognize the signs, but I was in rehab.

Some of the Group organized a trip into the foothills of the Himalayas, to a place called Missoori. I remember climbing up onto a sleigh-shaped carriage, drawn by a horse festooned in bells and the ubiquitous orange and turquoise beads and ribbons. I see in memory the hotel to my right, a single-storey wood building with intricate wooden carvings around the eaves of the steeply slanted roof. The hotel perched on the edge of a sudden cliff, with the Himalayas looming across the canyon.

I did wake up the next morning early, to see the sunrise on the snowy face of those rock sisters. I heard a small voice inside tell me this would be a moment I could talk about, the time I saw the sunrise on the Himalaya mountains, but what I craved was to crawl back under the clean, warm sheets and sleep forever.

Whatever happened on the rest of that day eclipses into another memory. This time I walked alone through the dark street, determined to find a bar. Finally I opened the door of a small wooden turquoise building situated on a street corner.

Inside a moon-faced Tibetan woman about my age asked in mime what I wanted. My hand popped to mouth, a shot of something. Her clear brown eyes turned troubled, but she led past a curtain to my right and up one step into an alcove housing a single, wooden booth in which sat two men.

Their braids of greasy, black hair woven with bands of turquoise and coral beads, the jackets of animal fur and knee-high, skin boots with more fur cuffing the tops told me these two men were mountain men, Mongolians.

She hesitated; they permitted. I ordered what they were drinking. Liquid from the shot glass entered my mouth and body as dry fire: Chang! the malted barley indigenous to this area. I coughed, the men's faces cracked wide open with laughter, their black eyes smiled with a hungry intensity I noted but dismissed.

I cared less about them. I only wanted more. After the release of one shot, my body desperately demanded the release that two, or three would bring. I yearned for the softness in my muscles, the feeling of hard-edged thoughts yielding; yearned to be loose, to laugh and most of all dull this present moment out of its sharp shape into something warmer, more receptive.

I asked for another. The young woman stepped behind the men and almost imperceptibly shook her head. Her eyes flashed terror. The room itself seemed to crack open and suddenly I felt the thick, edgy tension in the small space, saw in the eyes of those men now staring at me in an endless acceptance of violence without remorse, murder without conscience.

I stood up. The two men focused on each other as though I had never arrived, as though my presence faded from their sight in the same way the life in my body may have, had I lingered.

Out on the street I took a deep breath, then heard commotion—pots and pans slamming together in the night as a chattering crowd surrounded an aging, skinny, white horse bearing a young veiled bride in her finest dress. Beside the horse, her husband walked, holding the reins of his new life.

While all around the couple everyone celebrated with loud joy, large smiles and whoops of laughter, my eyes focused on the horse's dirt-splattered hooves and legs, how the bride's skinny body sat in the rumpled, cheap cloth and tinseled hem of this, her finest dress, how the groom's jacket didn't close across his thin frame and the uneven cuff of his pants did not hide his ankles. This was the highlight of their lives. After this, every day, every minute, would drip, wringing out their life force as they would scrabble to counter the dreadful truth about India, a land of "too many people and not enough for anyone."

Large pity rose in my chest even as scorn bore down from my head. The two collided in a fire of rage. Here was what marriage meant! A life of imprisonment and penury. Disgust and despair for all of us, everywhere, seeped up and took hold. That was all I could see, life endlessly, senselessly repeating itself in poverty, illness until death.

When we returned to the group, I took this negativity to Cecilie. She listened, even if she did not respond. She listened.

The Group! We were, all of us, the Group and we knew our presence as a power, filling the town's restaurants to overflowing, their coffers to unimagined abundance, their nerves to frayed ends. Our group took on its own identity, floated its own version of wisdom, its own brand of morality. It's impossible to ignore an invasion of almost 100 Westerners to a small village, anywhere on the planet. The locals had seen this troop of pale wraiths filing into the temple of those refugee Tibetans, spilling back out, unloosing a fury of demand and money on the simple resources of their tiny town.

As the end of November came and went and the days of initiation in the temple fell farther behind us, the group divided, an amoeba creating new multiple mini-selves. Some had already left for Canada, returning home with stories and status to see them through the New Year. Those with no money stayed behind in Raj Pur, living on a pittance of cash and hope, living on the promise raised among those with money, "We will not forget you, not leave you stranded in India, we will send for you as soon as..."

And still no Dawson. He was rounding the Cape of Good Hope, he was traveling in Africa on safari, was anywhere but not here.

Plans for those of us continuing on the journey bent toward the next destination, Australia. We would work in Australia, then enter strict meditation retreat for three months in New Zealand. At least, the rest of them would. I wanted nothing to do with any of it.

I sat under a tree and wrote to everyone I knew back home, "Hello, it's me, this has been a trip but I'm ready to come home now. Please send money, whatever you can afford. Send all to our next stop Poste Restante Sydney Australia."

My parents, whose shock at my sudden departure no doubt stirred within them the three days of horror they had experienced when I ran, had refused to speak to me for days prior to my departure. Now I wrote tersely, "I've made a mistake, am ready to come home, will pay back fare, send money Poste Restante Am Ex Sydney, Australia." There it was. I felt certain from the moment the letter left my hands I was on my way home.

My brother kept all our money, which meant his and mine, since Cecilie had used the last of hers to get from Thailand, where she had been in meditation retreat, to Morocco. I never knew how much my brother had, but he convinced me unless he had all of mine Cecilie would be left behind.

We took the overnight train from Raj Pur to New Delhi.

"I don't know why but I'm feeling so much better. Do you think it's the effect of those Wongs?" I felt genuinely excited.

"Hmmm, more likely because you believe you are going home."

"Oh, yeah, that's right," I giggled.

I woke about 3 am, unusually and instantly alert. The train had stopped. I looked outside the glassless window frame, past the iron bars. What I saw pulled me, so I ran to the stairs and shot onto the dirt path beside the train. A small soft voice inside my head said, "Remember this!"

Up and down in both directions small fires glowed warmly, brightly, dotting the dark night. In between, young boys, no older than ten or eleven held on their shoulders poles from which dangled on either side russet-colored baked clay cones, sitting one inside the other, chai cups. With each fire a large aluminum container sat, filled with milky sweet chai. The boys offered their clay cups then ran to the aluminum container, poured the warm liquid and returned it to waiting hands.

Calling to everyone in the lilt of their language they meandered up and down between the fires, chanting their syllables like a mantra of holy invocation.

I bought one, sipped it from the clay tasting cup, savoring each moment, the lit fires bright against the dark night, the boys' chanting voices, the thin warm liquid, its sweetness entering more than my body it seemed, my senses suddenly awake to the timelessness of this experience.

Chapter Eleven

THE NOISE AND BUSTLE OF NEW DELHI created a shock wave that ran through the group after the small, mountain embrace of Raj Pur. New Delhi divided us, who was in which hotel, where was so and so, has the other one who was traveling alone arrived yet, a diaspora of sorts, but chosen.

It was the week before Christmas and Cecilie who had been increasingly sick in Raj Pur, found her health no better here. She took to her bed and was not able to make it out. She tried, we walked together a block or two then she had to return to the hotel, apologizing all the way, "I'm sorry about this. I just have to be in bed and near a toilet. I am so sorry."

"No, no, whatever you need…what about the hospital, a doctor?"

"Do you have any idea what Indian doctors and hospitals are like?" she snarled. I backed down.

Still no Dawson, but other rumors about teachers and teaching proved true. We were to be allowed an interview with His Holiness the 16th Gyalwang Karmapa.

I stood on the rooftop balcony of a friend's hotel room, admiring the bright sunshine bouncing off the vivid reds, blues, greens and yellows of the Tibetan prayer flags flipping around in the light wind.

"Are you going to see him?" she asked.

"Karmapa? No. Why would I?"

"Because he is the head of the Tibetan Karma Kagyu Sect and the one who recognized our teacher, who changed our teacher's name from Bikkhu Ananda Bodhi to Karma Tenzin Dorje Namgyal Rinpoche."

"So, he's a pretty heavy dude?"

My language betrayed the real question: was he strong enough to get me high? We had all noticed this. When in the presence of these masters, we felt, or at least I felt very much the same as getting high on drugs: increased lightness, heightened senses.

"Yeah. All right. I'll tell you," she continued. "We were in an audience with him recently with a group of tourists. A young couple was in that audience, people I've never met, not from the group. The man asked could he take a picture of His Holiness, who agreed, through the translator.

"So, the man, who had a Polaroid camera, snapped the shot. We all kind of milled around. Then this guy was shaking his camera, and saying, 'It must be broken. I don't know what happened…' So, we all kind of looked over. He showed us the picture he'd just taken of His Holiness. What it was, was a mandala, a perfect, clear mandala of Mahakala, (deity of wrath) and the young man kept shaking his camera, talking about how it must be broken. A miracle and he thought his camera was broken!"

Her story of a miracle convinced me it would be worth the effort.

Christmas Eve, 1972, I arrived for an interview in a full-length cotton dress with a colorful pattern of orange flowers, my idea of formal. This entire interview thing leaned against my real desire, which was to hide on a restaurant patio somewhere drinking chai until it was time for the plane to Sydney, Australia, American Express and my ticket home. I didn't know why I had come to this interview, was still arguing with myself against Cecilie's encouragement to take this opportunity.

From the tiny second-floor iron balcony outside the house

My Impossible Life

where the Karmapa was staying, I noticed trees, dirt paths that passed for roads, a few straggly flowers, dull and uninspiring. Later, I learned this building with its simple stucco exterior had been donated to His Holiness the 16th Gyalwang Karmapa to use whenever he was in New Delhi. The donor believed in accumulating merit, a kind of point system where you gain positive energy by doing virtuous acts. If you applied dana, or generosity, toward these teachers who were considered to be very high or enlightened beings, you made double or triple points. This was to offset negative actions or thoughts built from all of one's lifetimes.

A monk in a burgundy robe opened the door. Another door directly across a small hallway opened, revealing two more monks smiling widely. I smiled back, for some reason relieved.

His Holiness the 16th Gyalwang Karmapa sat at the opposite end of the spacious, empty room, staring with fixed intent upon a spot somewhere behind all of us. His eyes were not focused above, but beyond us as though he alone saw a vitally important event past our shoulders. He kept his eyes there, with one exception, throughout the audience.

Reflexively, I moved toward him, his brown eyes never leaving the spot that magnetized his attention, while his monks, like annoying flies, never left my side. About five feet from His Holiness *whomp!* Swift pressure from the hands of a monk on either side of me, a blur of color and swirl of burgundy and my bottom hit *thud!* Suddenly I was sitting on the floor.

Tibetan protocol, rising from their belief some are more equal than others, demanded my head be lower than that of His Holiness the Karmapa. So it was, my head forcibly lower than that of His Holiness where he sat above me, dressed in a gold vest, his bare, swarthy arms indicating a stocky build, maroon robes covering his lower half. No god but a man with a balding head.

He began with blessings, I assumed toward everything. As this boring recitation drone on and on, I gazed at the beautiful paintings of mountains, valleys and meadows hanging on the walls.

I felt nothing.

He finished chanting. He waited. I waited.

Finally, he motioned to his translator who asked, "Do you have any questions for the Karmapa?"

"No," I answered with a slight shrug.

He withdrew without moving. The experience was palpable and disappointing. A sudden urge to have him back, open, like it was a moment ago, had me stuttering, "Who did these marvelous paintings?"

The translator burbled and His Holiness then answered me softly, flashing his eyes for one moment toward me, "Monks in retreat."

"They are so vivid and bright!"

His Holiness made the tiniest gesture with his hand before withdrawing again without moving.

"Is that all?" the translator.

I nodded my head and was quickly escorted back to the outside porch, where I noticed I felt high. An ease in the usual twisting of my inner state, a softening into what might be called relaxation felt almost good. Everything I looked at, the trees, the ground, stucco walls of the house appeared soft as if a brush had smoothed away all the edges. The air felt fine, none of the gritty, tacky feeling of New Delhi's air before I'd entered. Thoughts also all seemed more spacious, surrounded with an emptiness that made it possible for me to note them one at a time. I felt better.

The presence of these high holy beings caused a body shift, a change in feeling tones softening what was rigid and hardened, heightening sense appreciation for this world and in this way opening consciousness to deeper possibilities, more profound harmony. Being in their presence meant temporary relief from the otherwise unremitting dull numbness swathing me like a cocoon.

The high faded. It did not occur to me a precious opportunity had been easily granted, but that, like Parsifal who so easily achieved the Holy Grail, I had failed to ask the question.

Chapter Twelve

THAT EVENING, MY BROTHER REFUSED to turn the electricity on in the small grill in our room. Cecilie wanted it on; he claimed it would waste money. We huddled around an imaginary fiery warmth, the tension lingering in the air until he suddenly sang, "Chestnuts roasting on an open fire…"

"What comes next…"

"Jack Frost nipping at your nose…That's it, I don't know any more…" I said.

"Chestnuts roasting on an open fire…" he began again and all the struggles of travel, uncertainty about the future, sadness of the past, even Cecilie's undiagnosed illness, faded in this game.

"Rudolph the Red Nosed Reindeer…"

Singing! I imagine my father's Irish grandmother, Nell, who immigrated from County Waterford, town of Lismore, Ireland singing even on the dangerous voyage over. Called Ma or Ma Sullivan by all who knew her, a stern-faced, tight-lipped woman in the large photo I have, I see her in my mind's eye teaching her surviving children, Kate, the eldest, Mayme my grandmother, Margaret and John, all the songs of Ma's home land.

These women, Kate, Mayme and Margaret, their spouses and a gaggle of friends who became family because they stayed beyond a dinner, or lunch, gathered for bon fires at Kew Beach. The dark night glittering with stars and the fire, they hunkered in chairs woven with yellow or green or blue plastic strips strung on flimsy metal, while we children ran around outside their circle for a few hours of unrestricted freedom.

They sang, their voices lusty or soft depending on the song, their faces mirroring each other, encouraging as they passed around small silver flasks that reflected the flames from the fire. Each took a swig, many commenting "That was a good one" whether to the warming liquid or the music, no one knew or cared. They sat all cheery-faced in the red glow of the warmth from the fires both outer and inner as they sang.

They sang dirty ditties, these adults, dirty ditties from the thirties, twenties and from the Ireland their mother had left behind; they sang songs too from the World Wars they had lived through. One would begin and someone else nodded her head, taking up the tune until all the voices joined.

Sometimes I curled up next to her on the chaise lounge, watching my mother's face smile as she sang, her voice soft and lilting, hitting right in the middle of each note. Sometimes she pulled me closer for a minute, before encouraging me, "Go along with the other children."

We sang in our small family too. In the car on those Sunday afternoons Dad would start with "My Old Jalopy's a Cadillac" then glance at my mother to see if she was smiling. If she wasn't, he'd say, "Come on Isabel," and if that didn't work, "Isabel, the children!" and she'd open her mouth a little, even if the corners didn't curl all the way up, and sing.

When I'd ask a question, or take a problem to my father, he might just burst into song. "Sunny Side of the Street" was one of his favorites for me. At least that's how I interpreted it. Maybe he was cheering himself up, providing a ballast for his often-stated belief ours was "a normal family, just like any other."

We sang on our way to picnics at the Rouge River with the whole family, cousins, grandmothers, grandfathers, aunts and uncles some of whom were actually related by blood to our clan. We sang in our small living room, every year at Christmas with the lights off except for the Christmas tree lights. Gathering all of us included of course my Grandmother, my mother's mother who lived in our house all the days of my life there and for years after I left.

My father pointed to our couch, "Isobel, you sit there. Where's your mother? Get her in here. We're singing Christmas carols." He wasn't religious. He just liked us to get together and sing.

The songs that fell about that small hotel room in India had few words, and were off-key, more of a satire of music than anything. But still the singing soothed, helped calm a bit of the constant anxiety rattling my days and nights.

On Christmas Day Cecilie woke me up. "Let's go out. I'm feeling better right now."

Out the door and onto the thronging streets where a crippled beggar held out one brown hand, his glance referring to the stump he raised where his other arm used to be, his eyes begging pity, then in lightning speed his rotting teeth appeared, his joyful smile, a brimming helping of, "So what? This is life!" The moment ate at my Western sense of the right moral order, of how to respond to what is known as tragedy.

Much of this experience called India did the same, digging away at the beliefs I'd had about life, even those beliefs that lay unrecognized below the surface of consciousness. This traveling, this plunging into unknown waters following in the spiritual wake of Dawson stirred everything, turning the fields burnt dry with trauma to deeper levels of soil. I had no awareness of this. I only knew the spiritual experiences including meeting these teachers made me high without drugs and that I wanted to follow Cecilie anywhere. I wanted to, had to, be near her.

Cecilie had located an orange juice stand offering freshly squeezed orange juice.

"I just know this will make me better, Char…now, where was it? I know we're going to find it again…" we turned and twisted through the maze of streets. To find fresh squeezed orange juice in New Delhi in those days was a feat of serendipity; to find it twice would be an act of God. We found it!

Cecilie and I drank glass after glass of the fresh, sweet liquid then walked back to the hotel room with even more.

"How was it," my brother inquired of Cec where she lay in bed, again in pain.

"It was all right, you know, a few people dying on the street, beggars, a couple having sex…"

"No, I didn't see that, that wasn't…there were no dying people, Cec…" I protested her report. "Only beggars, right Cec? We only saw beggars! That's all I saw!" A fire about how my senses reported the world to me had been ignited. Incongruity with others was not tolerable, but led to an inner conflict with sharp edges that jabbed their questions: why did she see those things? Why did I not see what she saw? Did I remember what I saw? This last question could be held in my mind for only a moment or two before slipping away, proving the need to have had it in the first place.

Cecilie encouraged me to participate that day in a gathering on the lawn of the Empress Hotel, where the group would meet to exchange small inexpensive gifts. What I noticed whenever I applied awareness to the present moment, as I did in walking toward the Empress Hotel, was the deep heaviness of my body, how it required effort for me to move at all, how very little else penetrated or surfaced from this chunk of flesh I called my body.

The lush green lawn spread out in front of the Empress Hotel like an apron. I looked for a washroom inside. Walking back on the deep plush carpet into which my feet sank, the dark wood interior providing cool temperatures and muting all sounds, I spied into the dining room tables laid with white linen, sparkling glasses, beautiful silverware. I wanted that life, one of luxury and ease. Immediately I judged myself and this desire as not spiritual and therefore not worthy of pursuit.

After the short ceremony, I returned to our hotel; she was gone.

"Where is she?"

"At hospital."

"Why aren't you with her?"

"She didn't want me to stay." He laughed then, a sound meaning he had been given what he wanted. "She doesn't want anyone to see her like this."

The emphasis on anyone, as though the word itself bore an impossible weight, told me he was not going to budge. He held the money and I had no way to get a taxi, to go to her, without it.

Later that day she returned. It was all the relief I needed to see her, physically, to be once again in her presence.

Another portion of the group had arrived in New Delhi and rumors swirled. Dawson was arriving any day, he was not coming to India at all, he was coming to Australia, he was on an ocean freighter somewhere, he…

"Where is he anyway? I came, we all came this way, this far and…"

Cecilie looked at me from her bed with an impish smile. "There's a poem going around. Do you want to hear it?

Yesterday upon the stair
I met a man who wasn't there.
He wasn't there again today.
Gee I wish he'd go away."

(Hugh Mearns.)

Chapter Thirteen

OUR ROUTE TO AUSTRALIA TOOK US THROUGH THAILAND where we spent a few days wandering the covered bazaar, gliding on klong boats down the narrow waters and visiting the Wat where Cecilie had spent three months meditating before arriving in Morocco. On our last day in Thailand, my brother fought with me. He and Cecilie were off to visit the famous reclining Buddha. He had determined I was going too.

"I'm staying here in the hotel, where I can rest," I said.

He responded with that light in his eyes that meant he had thought of a way around a problem, "But it's the Reclining Buddha. You won't have this chance again."

"I don't mind. I need to rest."

"Oh, YOU need to rest…" his mocking tone rang deeply within me, stirring a sense of the worthlessness of my needs. It was an exact replica of the mockery Dawson used so often to persuade us we were lazy, inadequate, lacking.

I screamed, "You don't get to tell me what to do…"

"Oh, yeah?" His sneering face leered down at me from his six-foot, six- inch height.

Later Cecilie will talk to others about the Reclining Buddha. Someone will turn to me and ask if I was there. I will look at Cecilie and she will say I was.

What I recall is standing next to something gold, my hand held out maybe touching. Then everything goes blank again. I will be told I was there. Twenty years old, I visit a statue that's 150 ft long, 49 ft high, this gold leaf Reclining Buddha and to this day have no memory of it.

Our jumbo plane left Thailand eventually flying above the sea of sand, sun rising just over the horizon, spreading its golden spears across this reddening ocean, the famed Australian outback.

When we landed two attendants in starched fresh uniforms walked down the aisles while we stood. They squirted liquid antiseptic throughout the overhead storage, now opened, as well as the seats and floor. That cascade of chemical lemon scent stung through my nostrils. The two women claimed some items, including a brightly colored peacock tail feather which they sprayed to drooping, then took with them.

"Is this obsessive or what? I never took Aussies for being clean freaks."

"We have just come from India." Cecilie's wisdom about travel and the world soothed me. "It's not a bad idea. You never know."

She turned her blue eyes on me, and my righteous rigidity softened.

The Immigration Official detained us for four hours, convinced at least one of our number of thirty or so travelers must be holding. He was right, but never did achieve the satisfaction he so clearly wanted; the one in the Group with the stuff had stashed it in his boot heel.

We scattered that first night, smack in the middle of Christmas and New Year's with every hotel in King's Cross Sydney full. A kind shuttle driver welcomed about eight of the group into his own home for a night on the floor and a drive back in the morning. Someone talked a hotel manager into letting three of us stay in a tiny room built for one. These stories foamed quickly through the porous membrane holding our group: Australians are kind.

Next morning, Cecilie, my brother and I, along with a couple of others sat at a table with a clean linen cloth. I might have stayed there forever, in this western restaurant with the cleanliness squeaking from everywhere, but reminded myself, *I'm on my way home as soon as I get to Am Ex.*

Cecilie accompanied me to the bathroom where I sat in the stall next to her marveling at the white, white porcelain, clean tidy tiles, everything sparkling.

"Bring the toilet roll out with you."

We reconvened over the porcelain sink.

"What did you say?"

"Take the toilet roll, go get it and take it with you in your purse. Look, I have one already."

I stared hard at her plunder then at her. "Isn't that stealing? Isn't that against Buddhist principles?"

"Well, you can look at it that way or you can see that we have nothing and even toilet paper will be helpful and if these people knew they probably wouldn't mind and if they did, if they minded us taking just this little bit of toilet roll, then they need to learn the merit of giving."

Astonished at this sleight of mind, I stumbled toward the stall again and stuffed the almost full roll into my purse.

One of the men had a newspaper in which he had located the cheapest housing in an area called Ultimo. "Sounds promising," he said, his dark brown eyes lit with sardonic humor.

His name was Jack and his presence lit my interest, but I reminded myself, *I'm not staying here. I'm on my way.* This thought created a soft, calming distance from everything.

"When are we going to Am Ex?" I asked my brother eagerly. He was fully aware of how important this was to me, but he delayed. He delayed because he could. He delayed for the same reason he fought to make me do whatever he thought right: power over me. At the time, I did not question it.

The office itself was small, much smaller than I expected for such an important place, where mail of all kinds came and went, communications between people who needed and those who had. I sat on one of the benches, Cecilie beside me, a satisfyingly large pile of letters on my knees.

First, I opened those from my friends, the least likely ones to have any money to send. I opened and read each one, read every word and to a person they all had the same message: no one had any money! One kind person sent me a Canadian fiver, but that was it.

I opened the very small envelope with my father's familiar scrawl across the front. It was admittedly too small an envelope to contain an airline ticket.

He's likely arranged for the ticket, will give me instructions where to go to get it, I thought.

The dog was fine, the new furniture looked good, someone in the family had had a minor operation and come through all right, Gram was doing well, on and on. On the last page of the 3" by 4" pieces of paper my father wrote, "Oh, yes, about your request. Buddha will provide. Get a job."

"No, no, this can't…he can't…they…" tears fell as my voice filled the small space. "I can't stay…stay HERE!" I kicked the bench beneath me, fumed across the floor, my feet stamping. "This can't be. I DON'T WANT TO BE HERE!"

"Yes, but this is where you are," Cecilie's blue eyes lit with humor. "And whether you laugh at this or cry, it is where you are. You are here."

Chapter Fourteen

TRUCKS PUMMELED THE ROAD DAY AND NIGHT flinging an interminable supply of dry dust in all directions. Across the street a vacant lot refused to grow weeds, although plastic bags, a deserted rusty baby carriage, multiple broken bottles, rough, dirty shrubs, old condoms, candy wrappers, used plastic diapers proliferated.

Our house had three proper bedrooms upstairs, a small bathroom, another bedroom (mine) downstairs in the front of the house, then behind that a living room and kitchen, and a second bathroom built onto the back of the house so one crossed through the living room and kitchen on the way to shower or pee.

I often went barefoot as much because I saw myself as a hippie as to keep quiet in the house. One night after we'd been in the house about a week, I trod softly toward the bathroom out back, across the badly worn carpet of the living room. As I walked across the kitchen threshold the sole of my left foot landed on a slimy, slippery surface; I scrambled to not fall and flipped on the light.

Pale, moist looking slugs, four to six inches big, suckered along in all directions, easily twenty or more of them across the floor and climbing up the cupboard doors. A sound like tiny castanets filled my ears from the slugs' companions: cockroaches, the length of my index finger, their antenna waving in the light, their focus undeterred by my presence. I fled to my room, put on my clogs, walked carefully back through the invasion to the bathroom out back, leaned over the toilet and retched hard.

We soon banished the couch, and all the fleas nesting in it to the tiny backyard. That small backyard became the first of many little gardens Cec insisted upon creating wherever she lived around the world. She first removed debris: old glass pieces, cigarette stubs in endless numbers, bits of rubber tire and nondescript items. She then turned that poor soil and planted the damn plants inside the damn soil and gave them water. And they lived, some of them, pink and green providing a shred of the miracle of life.

Jack, who also lived for a few months in this house he had found, sneered, "What's the use in that?"

Tim sent letters in wildly colored envelopes that dropped through the door's low mail slot like shots of sunshine just for me. He wrote about his exploration in bio-energetics, his life on Sullivan St. in downtown Toronto, his sense of being lost. I wrote ferociously in return, our letters flown in airplanes crossing the planet in a trail of passion now dedicated to ideas of healing, connecting with soul guide, learning to live fully.

I dreamed he moved and woke from the dream startled and concerned. If he moved how would I connect with him? His letters kept alive for me the place I longed to be, the East End of Toronto with its beach and bars and bad/good times. I was not so far away in time or space that I was willing to let it all go. Yet.

His next letter arrived within three days, his trade mark mandalas in purples, greens, blues across the envelope where his new address sat: three doors away from the first place on Sullivan St. Tim and I were deeply connected. My dreams continued to bring truth and in that I began to glimpse the possibility of dreams: prescience, foreknowledge, guidance from a source that loves us each with all the wisdom we might ever long for.

In our living room against the far wall, sat a real fireplace. Never mind the 100 plus degree heat from the worst heat wave to hit Sydney in nearly a century, never mind the lack of firewood, Cec and I would have a fire. She found a single piece of wood and we lit it, reading from T.S. Eliot because I told her I had given up reading poetry by anyone.

"They are so good…it just makes me feel I can't so why bother?"

"Then you must read T.S. Eliot, he says the same thing…"

We sat melting in front of the too hot single piece of wood flaming in the fireplace as she made me read out loud,

> *"So here I am, in the middle way, having had twenty years—*
> *Twenty years largely wasted, the years of l'entre deux guerres*
> *Trying to learn to use words and every attempt*
> *Is a wholly new start, and a different kind of failure*
> *Because one has only learnt to get the better of words*
> *For the thing one no longer has to say, or the way in which*
> *One is no longer disposed to say it. And so each venture*
> *Is a new beginning, a raid on the inarticulate,*
> *With shabby equipment always deteriorating*
> *In the general mess of imprecision of feeling.*
> *Undisciplined squads of emotion. And what there is to conquer*
> *By strength and submission, has already been discovered*
> *Once or twice, or several times, by men whom one cannot hope*
> *To emulate…"*

After that we took turns. Cecilie made me read and she read to me from the greats, Yeats, Pound, e.e. cummings, Jacques Prevert, and more.

"I used to give poetry readings, up and down the coast…" she inhaled from the cigarette, "I was called Sam in those days. And Larry, Lawrence Ferlinghetti and I…you know him? He started City Lights press. It's still going…"

"I know his name…you and Lawrence Ferlinghetti?"

"Were mostly good friends…" she drifted then, unwilling to speak more about her days as a poet, giving readings in San Francisco and Vancouver.

In one of our reading times she noticed my deeper than usual withdrawal. "What is it?" she asked, a few poems in.

"Never mind."

Her blue eyes continued to look at me until I spoke again.

"Why are we doing all this?" My arm swept the ugly room, the sad floor and walls layered with years of dirt. "Why can't I just live a normal life? You know what I mean?"

"Yeah, I do." She nodded her head, her blue eyes filling with sorrow. "I'd be hitchhiking down a highway, my thumb out, begging the Gods to let me just please be normal, tears blurring the heat lines rising from the tarmac. Each thought brought more despair, why be this mutant? If only I could just be a secretary…"

We wept together.

"But as surely as I knew," she continued, "the next ride may be someone I might have to talk out of raping me, life like that other one I thought I longed for, with clear rhythms, gentle curves of up, get married, have kids and down, pay mortgage, deal with boredom, that life was not possible for me."

I stared hard at her. She had just eloquently articulated part of my deepest anguish, and deepest truth. I too did not fit into the life proclaimed by all the world to be best.

She went on, "We are all outsiders. Only outsiders are attracted to a teaching like Buddhism. Despair, desperation, suffering, not fitting in, these are motivation for search."

"You talked yourself out of being raped?"

"Yeah. A few times."

"Something happened…I haven't talked about this because…" Here the trunk of my body shook as though someone had my shoulders and was yanking them back and forth. "This is what happens."

Below my chin, I felt myself to be a grotesque creature, wrong in every way. I believed this shaking came from the monstrous aberrations, deformities I tried in vain to hide. My head met these seismic waves with a feeling of betrayal, as though a repulsive creature had escaped and was on display. It was beyond shame.

"When I was 16, like I told you I ran away, and those two robbers picked me up outside of Sudbury. Before this I had been a top student, editor of my school year book, played trumpet in the school band, worked part time, sort of fulfilled everyone's idea of what I was supposed to be. When I got back, I was…different."

Cec lit a cigarette. "Go on."

"They had a canvas bag in the backseat and told me it contained a shotgun. They taught me how to shoot. They said they'd keep me with them…" The shaking intensified just then, as though thrusts of energy needed to earthquake through to the surface of my skin.

"My body always shakes when I talk about this." I reached for a cigarette.

"What happened?"

"Nothing. I just had to stay with them. They held me hostage in case the police caught up with them."

I got up, paced the room. "They had escaped prison…they kept me, then they let me go."

Cec looked at me oddly and said, "Let's get a coffee."

At its peak that small three-bedroom row house sheltered 23 of us, as people ambled in from India, slow in the way all travelers from India are at first. We struggled to house whoever needed shelter, at a small cost, of course. My brother oversaw all that.

In this house, my initial 'bed', a set of rusty springs attached to a single bed frame on which I had spread my sleeping bag, sagged so badly I abandoned it for the floor. Next, I tried to use a door, laid across two cinder blocks. The beveled door left deep imprints after the precious few hours when the stream of trucks that constantly banged their tailgates, screeched their brakes, and ground their gears, slowed to one every ten minutes or so. Then I slept, sort of. So I spent one of my precious days off, walking to a mattress outlet, where I purchased a Queen size mattress and in the heat and cement of Ultimo, walked the mattress, one corner over the other, back to my room.

Somewhere in the four hours this took my mind snapped open and I realized I did not want to be doing this. Recognition dawned: this was why people slaved at jobs they hated! So they wouldn't have to do this!

Then the dullness which gnawed my senses resettled and I continued to walk, pulling one corner up, guiding it up, over and down again, walking back to the back corner, hands smack against the framed coils and doing it again. That was all there was.

In those days Australia had a labor shortage. Job postings littered every restaurant window. Every shop, every café needed workers. I walked across the railroad tracks and into a restaurant/bar called The Explosion Train, lied about my experience in waitressing and got the job.

One night after work crossing toward the bathroom, I flicked the living room light on and saw a pool of bright pink vomit surrounding the unconscious body of one of the men from our group. I put out the light and next day I cornered Cec, "Why was he throwing up? Did he drink too much? I didn't know he drank…"

"He scored. Heroin."

A memory of him and his girlfriend in India, pulling toward each other as though they had the magic everyone wanted, surfaced. They had gazed in each other's eyes, looked at each other in such tenderness! I had believed this one moment held the whole of their story. Now, she had left him, and he was on the needle. Or he had gone to the needle anyway and she left him.

What was the point? Why had he used, when we were here to meditate, get clear and clean? Had Primal Therapy in Morocco not worked? What was the difference between this and any other drug house I'd been in? Questions buzzed around, unwanted flies at a bone, as I went about the work of living.

One night at the end of a particularly busy shift Jessie, the head waitress, said, "You did well tonight. You're getting the idea."

I felt wings on my feet, both during clean up and all the four city blocks across the railroad tracks, to home. Jessie, short with dark blond hair to her shoulders, a crooked front tooth that overlapped just slightly, just enough to lend her language and mouth a welcoming cuteness, pommie Jessie who walked in her hard-soled shoes with a saucy rhythm on the floor, singing the words from the juke box, had no way to know I had been so seldom praised it felt like a draught of liquor.

Hank, who owned the place, came from Georgia USA, had trained in hand-to-hand combat and had served in Viet Nam. In Sydney's toughest, meanest slum he realized his dream of owning/managing his own restaurant where now he served booze from behind the long, shiny bar while he watched over the customers and his waitresses.

One night a customer put his hand on my bare thigh. I poured a full jug of beer over his head. He sputtered to Hank, "Fire her. She just dumped bee' oveh my head."

Hank, who had seen everything, said firmly, "I'm not going to fire her. She's a good waitress. My advice to you is keep your hands off her."

Here on the other side of the planet, my cells were reversing an unconscious helplessness. I had been powerless and humiliated by my brother, helpless before my mother's onslaughts, and captive to Al's rape and torture. But here the cellular conversations below consciousness began to shift. Perhaps because the slugs, fleas, unending roar of trucks, the dirt and poverty, and mostly how much I deeply did not want to be there manifested so powerfully a complete life experience of what I did not want, I began to know what I did want. Personal boundaries, even though this was not even a thought, instinctively rose to top of the list.

I might imagine my cells responded now to new experiences by choosing different words, perhaps more present tense verbs and longer sentences, to describe the increasing changes wrought by my new behavior. What we do now affects the past.

When I related the story of turning the jug of beer over the man's head as a victory, my victory, people at home narrowed their eyes, their lips growing thin with disapproval. No comments, but I felt the air change with something like contempt. We meditated on compassion, we were encouraged to talk only of spiritual things, nothing as mundane as work in a bar, nothing as humane as standing up for oneself. I remember this as one of the first times I recognized I was not really one of the group. Once again I did not truly belong.

At work on another night Hank announced, "I want to upgrade the place. We're going to persuade those surfers who come in there's nothing here for them and we're going to encourage the folks who eat dinner to come back."

Jessie picked up the beat, "Our new policy is no shirt, no shoes, no service."

The jukebox played "Run to Me" by the Bee Gees, Don McLean's "American Pie", and "Brandy" whose woven chain "made of finest silver from the North of Spain/and locket that bears the name/ of the man Brandy loves."

"You like that song, Charlie?" Jessie asked me as she pumped a few coins into the machine.

"Yeah, it's all right."

"Me, too." Jessie, who had smiled the night I dumped the beer over the man's head, had taken to talking to me a little now.

It was a Thursday night, not weekend enough for a full out roust about but close enough for the surfer boys to be gathering come 10, 11 pm for a couple of drinks and to transact a little business, buying and selling dope.

After the dinner rush, we turned the lights down so any late diners had a more romantic feel. When I lifted my eyes from wiping tables in my section, I noticed a group of guys standing by the far wall, their skimpy shirts, large sandals and long hair branding them surfers.

A table towards the back wall was still unwashed, so cloth in hand I walked briskly over, bent down, picked up the lone butter knife still on the table in my right hand and began to swish the tabletop with the cloth in my left.

I felt a palm rub my backside and I wheeled without thought, shoving the butter knife just into his belly. His hands flew up.

"You ever touch me again without permission I'll put this fuckin' thing right through you."

"Whoa, whoa, calm down…I didn't mean…"

"Yeah, right you didn't mean…" I snarled at him. Just then his buddy, the leader showed up at my side.

His blond hair hung just below his collar. The greenest eyes I'd ever seen pierced through my rage; his generous mouth, evenly defined under handsome, sensual features and muscled shoulders, back and neck, marked him as the alpha.

"Now, he didn't mean anything by it. He didn't mean to upset you…he was wrong, for sure, he should…you should know betteh!" He stated this to his friend, who had slunk back into the dark where the rest of the cadre shot glances in my direction.

"And herh'…" the green-eyed one said, "Hold out yer palm…" I did, and he pressed coins, a lot of them, heavy coins, into the flesh of my hand. "Now you look like a smah't one, someone has her eyes on things…"

I listened, mumbling a few sounds in return, uncertain what exactly was going on, a soft cloud filling my mind.

"Well, I noticed some changes her'h," he said more quietly, lifting his thick eyebrows towards Hank who wiped the bar and looked over often. "Like if anything interesting or…" he peered into my eyes, "…strangeh's, show up, why don't you just let me know? Okay? Because we'rh friends now and you don't want to see me, or any of us, get into trouble, right? Okay?"

Far below the surface, in depths to which I had no access, his words started a swell rising. Someone had asked for a favor before, someone, a man, needed something...

In an early autumn scene in North Ontario, Al and Gary, who have kept me hostage are letting me go. The sunlight is bright, the grass still very green. Al is asking, "We're giving you your life, now just don't go to the police okay, give us a day or two to get across the border."

Gary says, "Just give us a day or two, okay?"

Standing with this green-eyed man in the slums of Sydney, his asking something of me, something secret, hidden...what rises to consciousness is just a slight feeling of familiarity. No memory but a stirring through intense confusion, a stirring of what has gone before, and the internal clouds, the fog, rise and block thought.

Dimly, I knew the man was asking something of me, but my brain would not compute.

A few evenings later, Hank said to me, "I've hired some detectives to come in and help clean the place up. You might let your friends know they better stay away."

"They're not my friends! I never see them except for here! They're not!"

Was it difficult for others? I looked and acted most of the time like someone who knew what she was doing, but so often much of me trawled along the floor of an invisible ocean, collecting bits magnetized from what was happening on the surface. With enough bits gathered, clouds from the ocean floor flooded around and my mind did not function well, or at all.

"Well, that's good Charlie because they're going to get busted... now if you say anything to them, you'll get into trouble, you know that, right?"

Under the surface, deep below, a powerful flow of terror gained momentum. Something in what Hank was saying felt sickening to me, something about...

His words prodded a memory that wouldn't be accessible to me for years—of being in a police cell, being in the cell when a guard wakes me up by knocking on the steel bars.

"Your friends," he says, "those guys you were with? We picked them up on the highway just like you said. The first thing one of them said was 'she had nothing to do with it' so you're off the hook."

I had not realized I was on one. Al and Gary were in police custody, because of me and here, without that memory to fill in the gaps, something tugs and pulls within about how important it is Hank know I am not in league with these guys.

A few nights later, Hank announces the detectives have arrested at least a few of them and they will not be back. I have no emotional response, but nod at Hank and say, "Good" before turning to prep for the evening.

One evening I was invited by a customer in the restaurant to a party on the other side of Sydney. I accepted.

I moved through the crowd in the living room, suddenly aware of a column of energy lifting straight out and up from my head. I knew this had to do with something from the Angels, but how I knew was beyond me.

"Yes." I felt this word more than thought it. The column guided me through the kitchen and out the back door. Black night played with the fingers of suburban lights as the heavy summer air of Sydney bore down through the most intense heat wave in over one hundred years.

Against one side of the backyard to my right a figure wove back and forth unsteadily, waving something in his hand as he called out to the second figure, standing ten, maybe twelve feet away from him, "C'merah. Ah'm gonna cah've you' face."

I moved forward toward the paralyzed one, his face distorted with terror. He had wet his pants.

"Go," I said, raising my arm to the direction of the small porch, the kitchen light, the people inside. I turned and looked the short distance at the man still weaving, his body bouncing from the amount of liquid he'd consumed, his voice soggy like his brain cells.

"I'll cah've ye're face." He sneered at me, the large, broken, brown whisky bottle in his left hand, waving wildly about. "Ah'm gonna cah've ye'r face," he repeated.

He had closed the gap between us so his arm with the ugly edged glass easily might connect with my flesh.

"Why? You don't even know me," I said, keeping my tones even, calm.

"Wha? Yer'r jest a sheila, anywah..." recognition leaked through the booze obliteration. Silence for a beat, then, "Ah'm gonna cah've ye'r face," again, but in a quieter tone.

"Hey, when were you born?" I asked, slightly defiant, challenging and flirting at the same time.

"Huh?" The sudden change addled his sense of direction, allowing him to yield.

"When were you born? What month?"

"Whatddya wanna know fer? You so smart, you tell me..." the self-satisfied gleam of the truly drunk lit across his face.

"You're Scorpio, your birthday is in November," I knew the accuracy of this before all the syllables fell between us. His dark hair, dark eyes, shrouded with bushy eyebrows, the intensity of his gaze, the amount of alcohol he'd had, gave it to me.

"Any chick can say tha' outta come 'ome with me," he growled.

"Thank you for the invitation, but not tonight...." I smiled, noticing he had dropped the broken bottle.

I glided up the back porch, into the kitchen, the warm column long since faded.

How did the cab get to that house? Did my date call one for me? Did he argue, as one version in my memory banks suggest? Did he really follow me out into the back seat, trying to grab my mouth, my breasts? Did I yell, fight and beg the driver to just go?

Or is this memory smeared with one from below the surface,

a time when being in a car with two men shifted the trajectory of my entire life? I have no reliable memory, only that I arrived back at our slum house and never saw the man who had invited me, again.

Here in Ultimo the house was clearing of people. Everyone moved on. One of the last remaining men to live there, snarled at me one day, "Your brother cheated us all!"

"What?"

"He and Cecilie have lived here for free while the rest of us have paid!"

More truth about my brother would unravel in the future but for now I continued to follow him, mostly because he and Cecilie were married and for me she was a vital taproot of nutrition in an otherwise desert world.

My memories of Australia include a few precious minutes of feeling good things. For instance, many members of the group knew how to adventure through these travels, to find interesting things to do and then do them. Sometimes I flowed along, caught up in the energetic stream others engineered. One such adventure was a day at the Glow Worm Caves. The dark inside the cave was complete, a darkness such as I'd never experienced and the sudden twinkling of those near stars, the Glow Worms caused the rare moment of a burst of joy in my chest.

From there a friend and I traveled by car to a place on the map called The Walls. It was an abrupt canyon, and when night fell, from deep within the valley beside us rose an intense feeling that we were intruding. We stamped out our camp fire and jumped into the station wagon, huddling down, so strong was the sensation.

And one day in a unique fit of self-determination, I entered the ocean and played with body surfing. The sensation was pleasing, as much just because I had done this by myself as for the ocean's tickling on my skin. When I turned to enter the street again, I saw a tree festooned with what looked like hundreds of parrots. Bright lime green, sky blue, brilliant sun yellow broke the air around them.

They cackled and called to each other further cracking up the air but with sound. As I walked by, I felt a moment of confidence: this was my life.

We left, one by one, the slum of Ultimo and even Cecilie and my brother and I eventually found a new place to live, in a suburb called Manly. We lived in a communal house, but one not run by my brother or in fact, any one person, it seemed.

I traded in my night job and worked selling tickets for the hydrofoil boats that scudded across Sydney harbor each day. It was a job and I went dutifully but when it came time to go to New Zealand for meditation, I was short the needed cash and short the required number of mantras and prostrations.

At the last moment, a generous man from the group gave me the needed money. I learned that very few of us had completed anything near the amount of meditation Dawson required for full meditation. That didn't seem to stop anyone else.

I boarded the ferry, once again terrified and except for Cec assuring me she would be with me the whole time, I'd have skipped out, to the streets of Sydney and the dark world that still beckoned like a lover.

Chapter Fifteen

BEFORE INDIA MANY OF THE GROUP had been in Morocco to experience Primal Therapy, a radical new therapy discovered by Arthur Janov. The theory believes we each carry unresolved emotions from times when our parental conditioning was incomplete. By contacting, feeling, and expressing these bottled emotions consciously, we might gain freedom of emotional expression.

The Morocco trip, with its promise of inner freedom from parental conditioning was the first step. Next India and the Tibetan Temple experience was to infuse us with different sense experiences, challenging our cultural ways of thinking.

In New Zealand we were to enter full retreat, three months with no contact with the outer world. All hours of the day and night would be dedicated to meditation, each person establishing for herself how many hours this would mean. The end goal was Enlightenment, a word no one bothered to define, a word that signaled all the magic and freedom I so desired.

Freedom was what I wanted, freedom from having to spend my life working at some useless job contributing to an insane, meaningless culture, freedom from the oppressive rules of government, Church and family, freedom from the inner judgements that haunted my every waking moment.

The music of our times rose with messages of freedom, "The Chimes of Freedom" by the Byrds, "Share the Land" by The Guess Who, "Goin' Up the Country" by Canned Heat. But even the farthest out rock music, the Doors with "The End" or "Break on Through", or Jefferson Airplane's "White Rabbit", Led Zepplin's "Ramble On" connected to something we felt deeply, a yearning for what lay beyond boundaries.

It was not yet a decade since The Merry Pranksters had painted, in 1964 a VW Van in outrageous colorful patterns to drive across America, demonstrating the possibility of a different way to live, an option to the tightly conditioned reflex of the consumer culture circa 1950's to buy, buy, buy and work for money to buy more.

It was only four years since the Summer of Love had showered the streets of San Francisco with freedom to choose not to go to War, freedom to live, as proved at Woodstock on love and breath and yes, dope. Freedom beckoned a generation on migration, a migration with no guiding star and very little instinct. The migratory pattern of our group led us now to New Zealand and a little town called Rotorua.

As our bus pulled into Rotorua the acrid smell of rotten eggs raced up my nostrils.

"Oh my god who did this? How can we meditate with this smell everywhere?"

Cecilie replied, "Within three days you won't even notice it."

Rotorua, one of the cities in New Zealand's North Island, was built close to geothermal hot springs and the sulfur smell of bad eggs was the trade-off for the pleasure of the warm waters.

We had been instructed to complete 108,000 prostrations as part of Dawson's criteria for entering full retreat. Dawson divided us into three locations according to how many prostrations each of us had finished. Full retreat meant permission to sit, stand, walk or lie while practicing whatever meditation exercise Dawson prescribed that day or that week. People in full retreat lived at an undisclosed location and attended Dawson's classes morning and evening as well as had regular interviews with him.

Medium retreat meant being able to participate in some of these meditation practices, attend some classes, while trying to complete as many prostrations as possible. These meditators lived at Lake Rotoiti a few kilometers from Blue Lake, where laggards like me with only a flimsy few prostrations complete, tried to achieve enough to warrant a move up the meditation scale. The Blue Lakers would be allowed to attend classes only when Dawson said.

Prostrations! A prostration begins with hands clasped in prayer above the head; then hands come to touch forehead, throat and heart center. The meditator visualizes white at the forehead while reciting the seed syllable Om, red at the throat center while repeating the seed syllable Ah and blue at the heart center while repeating the seed syllable Hung (or Hum).

Next, hands still in prayer posture, point down and then out in front, as the meditator goes down and, knees bending, slides forward until lying straight out on the floor, hands stretched toward the shrine. The forehead touches the floor, arms and hands stretched out as the meditator repeats the chosen mantra.

All couples were separated for the duration of meditation, so Cec and I shared a two-room cabin just feet away from Blue Lake, a small body of water. The living and kitchen space, all walls painted in a light blue colour, also held bunk beds. Cec took one as her sleeping site, and every morning constructed a small shrine on the lower bunk where we focused ourselves during prostrations and in sitting meditations.

Because the space was too small for both of us to stretch out at once, we took turns. She prostrated, bending and stretching and as she rose, I went down, stretching my length toward the shrine consisting of a lit candle, a picture of the deity and a picture of Dawson. In front of these three a small prayer book in Pali from which we read morning prayers, lay.

That first morning I rose, sipped coffee with Cec, and in a kind of disbelief this was really happening, began the first prostration. It didn't take long before my world strangled in physical pain and a tightening lasso of negative thoughts like flies, I can't do this anymore, this is stupid, useless, I am stupid and useless, this whole fucking thing is... and on and on. As the weeks grew and our numbers of completed prostrations grew, more than once the flies became vultures and I collapsed, tears streaming everywhere.

One of the struggles created by depression/anxiety comes from the sufferer's conviction nothing better will ever happen, no matter what efforts are made. While I was eaten by these flies of negativity I was convinced of their truth. There was no point to what I was doing. Nothing good would ever, could ever come of this or anything else I tried.

At these times Cecilie was both sympathetic and unremitting, supporting and commending my efforts while turning my mind away from my steadfast belief in the negative. With that tone of will power in her voice, she let me know I had no choice.

"In the long run, you'll discover how much you've gained by this. It's insight, Char. It works like this. Three to six months from when you finish meditating, you'll be lifting a cup of tea to your lips when something you've thought about, or believed in, or wondered about will suddenly open up. From that point on life will be different."

Cec was trying to tell me something vital, but she did not know and so was not able to express how my emotions, triggered by daily life, would rip through me, leaving me panting, sweating and most often in tears. When those emotions subsided my body and mind would clear like clouds leaving blue sky after a thunderstorm. The storm of emotions would sometimes also leave behind a jewel: the memory of their inception. With the memory of the source of terror, rage, and confusion released into consciousness, the hold of these emotions on my body would also be also released.

Over a decade later, memories from those three days and nights with Al and Gary would erupt through my body, releasing the protective layer of numbness in which my senses had been wrapped since each ugly event took place.

Here in Rotorua, I simply accepted what Cecilie said. She had meditated in Thailand for three months in full retreat, begging every morning with the traditional beggar's bowl for her daily food, having shorn her hair and abandoned western clothes for the traditional simple robe. Her faith in meditation rang like a clarion cry. The sound of her voice, her confidence in this as a path to higher consciousness (which to me just meant the hope I might function in daily life) provided a carpet beneath my knees. I tried again.

Always the rumors came to our ears of those who were up to 5,000 prostrations a day, but we were confident, even heroic when our daily total reached 2,000.

One morning as we slammed our bodies down in rhythm, first her body stretching toward the shrine, then mine, I noticed how light and easy the task felt. Lighting a cigarette on our break, I said "Man, this was so easy today. I must be getting used to it."

"Not for me. I'm struggling." Her face flickered for a moment.

"I'm sorry. Maybe it's because I'm a little younger?"

"It shouldn't be. I don't think so…" She was quiet for a moment, then said, "You will do your own work this afternoon."

She prostrated as usual after that, her body bending and stretching across the floor while I put my hands above my head. As she stood back up, I bent and stretched and once again it was a struggle. This was my first lesson in how our mind and body energy sometimes couple up. I had spent the morning "borrowing" from her energy. Her wisdom caught the problem and balance was restored.

A few more memories, clear as stars on a cold Ontario evening stand in my mind from this little cabin on the edge of Blue Lake. The first was the afternoon she surprised me with a visit to town and the hot springs.

Cec led me down the one main street of Rotorua where a few little shops spread trinkets or breads or vegetables in their window displays. Tiny charming necklaces, large bracelets, posters from the late 1960's: suddenly I wanted all of them! I lusted for these as though they held a secret elixir. And bread! Loaves of brown bread, biscuits, rolls filled one window while right next door, yellow bananas, orange oranges, purple grapes, greenest of green lettuce crammed the display case, overflowing with color and shape. It all met my eyes as some miraculous event, put on just for us. I felt very, very high.

"Where are we going, Cec?"

"It's a surprise. You'll see."

We giggled as she pulled open the door to the Blue Baths, the public hot spring baths and as we put on our bathing suits and waded into the large pool.

"What's all that?" I waved my hand at the walls decorated in Roman pastiche.

"How does the water feel?"

"I feel the water, yes," I focused, tried hard to feel the water directly on my skin "but it's as though it slides against a layer of plastic exactly molded to my body."

Despite my blunted tactile sense, Cecilie's anticipation of surprising me, the joy of the waters and their softening heat made me happier than I remembered. That happiness lasted the whole day.

The next memory involves Dawson, who suddenly wanted to visit each of the sites where his followers meditated. He wasn't interested in me of that I was sure. I posted myself at the wall by the sink. The door to the cabin was open to my left. I heard him approach and just as he stood there in the opening, a small dog, one I'd never seen before, ran in front of him. Dawson looked at me, his arms dangling at his sides, "What kind of little doggie is that?"

In a flash my mind covered five hundred responses. What came out of me was, "A mutt."

His sudden laughter rocked through the door and filled the space inside. In spite of myself, I smiled. I had made a joke, made him laugh. Score!

Cecilie began complaining of a pain in her chest. "It's something more than from the muscles, Char." I thought, based on my experience in India, suggesting a doctor was out of the question.

"I'm going into town. I'll get some groceries. You want anything?" Cec frequently made these trips which suited me, since I was growing accustomed to the regularity and rhythm of prostrations, break, cigarette and coffee, more prostrations that filled our days and evenings.

I was surprised when she returned to learn she'd seen a doctor. The pain was a broken collar bone. Dawson reviewed her doctor's note and determined she might attend all the classes and have interviews! She would leave to live in another house, because, she explained, it was closer to where those classes took place. Happy for her, I was also jealous, as much of the others who got to be with her as for her permission to be in class with Dawson. More, in fact.

One day as I prostrated my body down and out across the room, large now with Cecilie's absence, I suddenly saw an eye, with a single vein irregularly shooting across its white part. The vision lasted maybe a minute and for that whole time although I knew I was in the cabin, prostrating, my entire scope of sight was filled with the eye.

When Cecilie next made her daily visit, a promise she'd given me when she left, I asked her about this vision. She directed me to ask Dawson at the next class I was allowed to attend. He said it meant cellular knowledge. I smiled at his response but didn't have a clue what that meant.

One other memory remains seared into my being. I rose one night in the dark of a full moon night, needing to pee. I left the warmth of my sleeping bag, tiptoed across the floor, opened the door quietly and bent to pick up my clogs on the ground when my eyes fell onto all the stars in several universes there, spread out before me like a carpet.

I gasped at the sight of the frost, separated into thousands, millions of shards of beautiful, reflective moonlight. Those ground stars guided my feet around to the outhouse. All the few steps back I saw those magnificent flecks of light on the earth. I glanced upward but the sight that beckoned was on the ground.

The ordinary sight of frost unfolded into a carpet of shimmering points of light. Here in the dark of a winter night, the scene revealed serenity, safety and beauty.

I wonder now at how precisely this memory matched a second, terrifying and unconscious experience. In time the terrifying event of being held at rifle point as I used an outhouse would detonate its truth onto my life through my determination to discover what had happened in those three days with Al and Gary. Here on the other side of the world, that memory slept within, leaving me to experience the safety of the moment.

Word came soon after. Dawson wanted us all in deep meditation retreat, even those who hadn't finished their prostrations. I was to be moved to a house at Lake Rotuiti, without Cecilie.

Chapter Sixteen

"Can't someone move so we can meditate together? You promised me! You said we'd be together!"

Cecilie had just told me I was to live and meditate with someone else. While I remained behind at Blue Lake, she had made me believe she and I would join up again soon. Now this was not to be.

Dawson held morning classes here in this second cabin. The large living room with its huge windows offered a suitable place for all of us, the forty or so meditators now equally engaged in all classes, all Wongs. This sudden equality was because Dawson declared, "Time is of the essence. Only two months left! Get on with it!"

Cec tried to coax me into the idea of liking this new arrangement. As she showed me my new home, new bedroom, she encouraged, "You'll be fine. You'll be meditating and maybe…you'll be able to serve Rinpoche his morning tea!" Cecilie's face revealed her belief in this as a special opportunity, so I smiled as though I did too. Truthfully, the thought of him scared me and his presence rendered me mute. I didn't bother mentioning this. I believed it was another sign of my innate wrongness.

Cecilie left, and I put my bags on the bed in the small room, now mine, opposite the front door. I sat, uncertain what to do next.

Then a thought softly rose to mind, "This is a meditation retreat, maybe I might meditate."

I unpacked my meager supply of shrine objects: a candle, a picture of Dawson in a cowboy hat I had stuck into a white plastic frame for ease of travel, a photo of another Tibetan deity.

An understanding of the physical world was beginning to form within me. It seemed as though an ocean of objects existed somewhere just beyond my senses. Some landed near me, just as waves found shore. So too these objects appeared and then, like waves, some disappeared as though they had a mind of their own. I might not refuse nor hang onto anything. Where other people clearly commanded their lives and the objects they owned, I felt unable to direct my will toward attaining even the most basic things: shelter, clothes, food. Instead, I waded each day through the ocean of items that appeared. Enough food, I was not hungry. Enough shelter, I was kept from the elements; enough landed upon me I was each day granted the next.

I set the shrine up on a piece of cloth from the length I had purchased in Thailand, because Cec had seen how I enjoyed the colors and had insisted I buy a length of the dark blue with gold baroque bordered cotton.

As I fussed, making each decision for myself I became aware each decision brought with it a feeling of satisfaction.

From my room next morning I watched as Dawson entered the cabin. He entered with a slight hesitation, a tiny stall, as though each step mattered. He stared at the ground, then his eyes rose and opened wider, as though surprised to find anyone there. He appeared to be in meditation at all times.

An elaborate process of fussing over the Teacher initiated almost every class, every talk I saw him give during more than thirty-five years. He shuffled to the dais or throne or as in this case a simple chair with a lovely cloth thrown over it. His attendant opened the traditional monk's robe and offered to wrap it fully around him, over his shirt. Sometimes he accepted this, sometimes he signaled for the wrap to be across one shoulder only.

Students stood this whole time, palms of their hands pressed together at their hearts. Then we prostrated three times in the general direction of Dawson, who sat without moving, his face expressionless, waiting.

He might wave his hand to ask for a window to be opened; he might comment on the flowers, fresh cut in the vase that sat on the inevitable small table next his chair; he might indicate that the tea or water, carefully placed so his hand expended the least amount of work to get to it, was sufficient.

Or not. The tea too hot! All students cringed, especially the one who had made and served it.

"Are you trying to burn the teacher's tongue?" his roar rocketed over the heads and shoulders of the students who now crowded together, heads retracted as far as possible into shoulders in an effort to stay out of his line of sight.

I stayed in my room as long as possible and then tried to huddle against the wall next to the door of my bedroom. I believed he did not see me, or seeing me, did not know me.

This ritual worked, until a few days later when at the end of class, he looked straight at me, glared and demanded, "Whose room is that?"

Mine. I thought the word but what came out of my mouth was a very small sound.

"Hmmmm? You? Yes, well…" and he turned his attention away.

My body was shaking everywhere, vibrating strangely as though every cell were a bow and from each an arrow had just been released.

I stood, walked toward the dispersing crowd of students and tried to speak but only incoherent phrases fell from my mouth. I retreated to my personal space, lay on the bed and watched my breathing until the shaking, the alien thrumming, stopped.

For some reason after that I didn't care as much. When it was my turn to serve him, I put tea down beside his chair aware that I did not care if he liked it or not. I didn't think past this, to his voice should he shout, or his displeasure if I did it wrong. I just held my mind on the moment by moment experience and on the inner state I recognized as indifference.

One morning instead of crouching next to the wall nearest my room, I walked to the kitchen cupboards that separated the kitchen area from this living room. I leaned up against the cupboards, directly opposite and facing where he sat. I listened while he spoke. It wasn't that interesting. I looked around and saw the focused, shining faces of the rest of the group. Clearly, they wanted to be here, in this room. This was their choice.

This isn't my choice, the thought in my head was clear. It wasn't my choice and yet here I am, sitting in this room, on the other side of the world from where I want to be, trying out all these meditations because he said so. He? Who is he?

That was the question and it rose in a single whole wave of focus directly flowing from me to him. Without a trace of anger or demand, the calm, deep question flowed from me, with my eyes on him.

He seemed to stand up. The parameters of his body shifted into the shape of a large egg, but a transparent one. From the transparency, snapping lines of gentle electric current glowed blue and white in the uneven oval shape of what had been his body. One or two lines of electric current moved past where his body boundaries had been, through space. It seemed these energy snakes knew me, were unsurprised that I saw them. They were not focused on me, but seemed to be sensing, as though searching for information then receding slightly; then again reaching out as though alive and intelligent. All the while the lines of gentle energy within what had been his body boundaries flowed and pulsed.

I felt forced to look away. When I glanced back, he was in his usual form, ending the class.

Again, that foreign shaking rattled my body. Again, that alien thrum across my nervous system, taut, wired, as though electricity spangled my nerves. The thrust compelled movement and pushed me. I stood, shaking and without speaking scuttled to my room.

Like so many experiences in my life, it took years before I had a sense of what had happened. I believe in that moment we locked nervous systems. My Celtic visionary inheritance made the experience clear in my eyes. My nervous system, ravaged beyond capacity, had flat-lined until his nervous system beckoned to mine, demonstrated, patterned for me what was supposed to be. His nervous system was connected in some way to mine, demonstrating the flushes of energy that provide emotion and sensate experience, providing a foundation of healing.

We know now through neuroscience about the transmission of neuronal patterns from one person to another. This knowledge increasingly supports all psycho-therapeutic work, with the understanding it is the therapist's own health, their own electric neuronal patterns, that provide a client with a basis of well-being. In this same way mothers, fathers, care-givers all provide in their facial expressions, their affection and behavior the outer demonstration of healthy neuronal pathways to growing infants. Transmission it was called by the Tibetans, for a few thousand years before neuroscience validated it.

Dawson had us moving, this one there, that one over here, sometimes because of a request made, sometimes for his own, unfathomable reasons.

My third home was a bungalow, living room, kitchen, three bedrooms and an inside bathroom. Every room was walled in dark fake wood paneling. My roommates, a woman with strawberry blonde hair and another with dark hair down past her waist were already nestled inside when I arrived.

We shared tasks like cooking and cleaning up after each meal in total silence, and other than a few words when one of us shopped for food, remained in total silence.

The floor space of my bedroom held a single bed and a dresser. I created a shrine on top of the small, beat up suitcase that carried shrine items, and underwear, from one place to another.

When I first arrived and closed the door, I pulled out a slinky red, polyester cloth. The beautiful Thai cotton with which I had so happily made my first shrine was too small here. I took this as an outward and visible sign of my inner and constant failure, inability to get even the smallest details of meditation or anything else in life, right.

That was on the one hand. On the other hand, I held to a stubborn recognition that this was all I had, and *Maybe it doesn't matter...*

But the critic remained sharp *...but at least you might have...*

The inner carping continued to shred me even as I consciously tried to buoy my confidence against its ocean, *It works fine. It's not what anybody else has, but it —*

What? It's horrible to touch, not like silk. Others do have silk, you know...

But I don't have silk. What should I do? Break meditation, go to town, try to find in this tiny country...do they even have silk in New Zealand?

The pain of this war, constant, immediate, and concerning every detail of my daily life flooded my consciousness in ugly waves. At first, and for a while, I struggled to keep it all under control, like I thought a good meditator did.

Well, at least I sat today, for ten hours...

So what? That doesn't matter, nothing you can do will help; the whole world is fucked up and you sit here on your ass, contemplating strange figures and mumbling to yourself...what's the point? It's useless!

That's true but Dawson says the Crunch is coming, everything will be wiped out in natural disasters anyway so... Dawson had been teaching about this Crunch. He told us some terrible event, either natural or manmade disaster was imminent and sure to wipe most of us out. Many followers believed so deeply they had moved to the Yukon where he indicated they may be safe.

I wanted to die, so the idea of the Crunch had a different effect on me than those in the diaspora to the Yukon. I wanted to be under square one, the first point of destruction from a tsunami or the initial landing of the first bomb.

How do you know? Just because HE says so? My inner voices often demonstrated this kind of distrust and cynicism of Dawson and everything he represented.

Yes, I guess that's true. But I am here, right now, anyway... so it went.

Ultimately cornered by inner assaults, large tears welled at my eyes, my chest heaved rhythmically as I fought my body's need to express. I felt inferior, a baby, so I stifled those tears. But they returned persistently.

Overcome, I wept and sobbed, then, ashamed, blew my nose and returned to what I believed was the real thing, the true activity of meditation: focusing on the Deity, repeating the mantras. Gradually I learned the tears released something warm and fuzzy, a feeling in my neck and the surface of my face followed by a period of calm.

About the same time I began to recognize some of the verbal dialogues as the repetitive patterns of my parents' marriage. Memories rose like excess fat coagulating on the surface of consciousness. Mom screaming, "I hate it, all of it, EVERY LAST THING IN THIS GOD DAMNED HOUSE!" as she slammed with each word the glass fronted cupboard doors of the kitchen cabinets, slammed them until the small decals of pretty red and yellow flowers she had placed there so happily only a few days before splintered and with the rest of the glass scattered across the small red and white painted kitchen, shattering with them the stability of my childhood.

I learned to translate Dawson's suggestion, "Formulate a question, take that question into meditation," as a way to relate to such memories. Once the tidal wave of emotion had subsided, I returned to the memory, asking, "What happened next? What came before?" until through persistent questioning, the memories with their original emotions rose and released. My body softened a little from the strong muscular tension I usually carried.

I learned my small child self with all her memories still lived within every cell of my body. Within her lived the original emotions of terror, sadness, anguish as well as happiness, joy, as though each of my cells had independently hidden memories in silence, away from my conscious self. And each memory that was painful remained unfinished. The emotion had not passed through, a complete wave, but had frozen at its peak, now perpetuating itself through the tough sinews and tougher stance I took toward myself and everything else.

Here, in meditation retreat, when the "I" residing up top above my neck, had gathered herself away from the dissipations of her distorted, extroverted life long enough to turn inward, to seek and to listen, this child released memory and emotions, leaving a much more relaxed adult. My flesh revealed some of its painful story and "I" learned to sit, a humble recipient of the song of my cells.

I wept. Harder, faster, more and if at times I managed tissues or cloth to stifle the sounds of my sorrow, at other times my dark-haired friend knocked softly on my door to check in and see if I was all right.

The truth was, I was more than all right. The more I approached each meditation session, each hour with an openness of not knowing; the more I accepted the emotional desolation and physical assaults of my life to date; the more I allowed those inner tsunamis of tears and chest heaving sobs to wave across my body, the longer a barely perceptible, gradually growing sense of being calmly present grew.

Cecilie had told me, "All emotion rises in waves, one wave at a time, Char. All you have to do is wait for the end of the wave. Keep your eye on the end." In this, as in so much else, she was right.

The emotional expression was some days. Other days I checked the small calendar I had, counting how many squares on the graph remained: then once seated with mala (rosary) in my hands, my mind busied itself with how many more mantras I might accomplish before the last day.

Bored with this distraction, other memories rose. What was

that movie with that guy? Or music, whole songs, lyrics, harmonies, drums going off inside, Eric Clapton, Joni Mitchell, Janis Joplin, Bob Dylan, the entire canon of rock 'n' roll complete with guitar solos rose within until I wanted to scream.

Then commercials, pop songs, jingles, phrases, slogans, my mother's voice "I believe where there's a will, there's a way and you Charlene are the most willful person God ever put on the face of this earth." And my father's voice, "Don't feel sorry for yourself, Charlene; self-pity is the most destructive human emotion. Focus on the positive. Be good and focus on the positive. It will all turn out all right."

As time progressed and my cells relinquished their burden of the past, a different kind of consciousness rose to awareness, a clarity in my mind resulting from increased release in my body.

During meditation one day I experienced the tension in my neck pulling my jaw open and my face contorting until I saw the outline of a wolf in my skin. I asked Dawson at the next class.

"That's addiction, wolves indicate a complex that resolves in addiction."

That was all he said. I believed at the time I was undeserving of more. What I came to understand was how succinct his words had been.

Jungian therapy, especially as understood by Marion Woodman, relies upon the release of an image from the unconscious, whether in night dreams or daily life. The image brings to the surface a major conflict of the person's life. Once the image has appeared in consciousness, the grip of the complex or conflict weakens considerably. Now the person has the power to begin working directly with the energy caught up in this conflict. In my case the energy was addictions.

Although it would take many more years and some considerable efforts, the image of Wolf in this meditation session released some of the energy tangled in the series of addictions, anorexia, bulimia, booze, hash and bad relationships which compelled my life. Some, but not yet all.

One day my gentle roommates in this third house asked to speak with me. I was warmed by the invitation as I was warmed by any indication anyone wanted me, at all. They gently let me know I was slamming my bedroom door every time I left my room. The effect was upsetting them.

I took their words in, sat with the shame in my small space because here was evidence: I could not control what happened below my chin. I made efforts toward closing the door softly.

Days passed and bored, I grew restless. I played at contacting Cecilie telepathically. I pretended she could hear me. I told her I was sick, so sick I couldn't meditate, but had to stay in bed.

Late that afternoon a soft knock came from the front door and one of my roommates said, "Charlene, you have a visitor."

Cecilie stood in the living room, wet from having walked three miles in the steady drizzle. She held a bouquet of wild flowers she'd gathered along the way.

"I felt you, I heard you saying you were sick…" she looked at my obviously healthy face.

She did not reprimand me, but suggested I not play with these powers again. At least, not when it meant her walking three miles through drizzle to see me. What love is.

This memory and the memory of me building a wall to shut David out of my energy, my thoughts—remain twinned in my body. We know so much more than we allow ourselves to trust. We have methods of connecting that extend beyond time and space as described by Newton.

Back to my bedroom and repeating mantras.

One morning Dawson asked, "Who among you has a gap at the bottom of their breath?" None of us knew if having this gap was the right or wrong thing. His question made many in the room stop breathing.

"Take a moment now and just focus on your breath as you sit there. Is there a gap at the top or the bottom of your breath? Now those of you with a gap at the bottom, get up and stand outside." When those people had left, he said to us, "The gap at the bottom indicates depression. Those of you with a gap at the top are prone to hysteria."

He possessed a creative flair for translating ancient texts to lively and embodied teachings. This was his unique and radical side. On the other hand, he might turn completely orthodox, teaching us traditional behaviors, especially those of Tibetan Vajrayana Tantra. Such was the case with Wongs.

The center piece of Tibetan meditation practice, the noun Wong means "power, energy." It is a ritual for which the teacher prepares by meditating on the deity, for example Chen Rezig. The teacher meditates and performs many mantras, perhaps as many as one million while visualizing the form of Chen Rezig. Why?

Neuroscience tells us that neurons that fire together wire together. By practicing with such vigor, the teacher ensures their own ability to enter into deep meditation, complete with mantra and visualization, at the appointed time, i.e. in front of a room full of students. As the teacher's brain is now firing with these many neurons wired together, the example of this brain pattern may spread to students. This encourages the students' brains to copy.

Wong. Some things cannot be said. Some things are what you cannot say. At Blue Lake my meditation and prostrations consumed up to ten hours a day. Here, at the third cabin, my meditation practice grew to 21 hours daily. The remaining three hours felt less like sleep and more like a deep state of relaxation during which visual experiences flared, like falling stars, then melted away.

As I focused more deeply and consistently inside, it seemed images rose from the deepest part of outer space. The inner cup of my skull, loosed of some of its rust and corruption through the intensity of deep retreat, offered pictures—visions, really—of infinite skies at midnight, pulsing into the deep galaxy, of shiny Tibetan syllables emerging from the night sky and more, my skull relaying information in symbols like the earth caves at Lascaux.

One particular Wong was Red Chen Rezig, known as The Stirrer of the Pit of Samsara. Dawson sat on his throne and when I glimpsed behind him the twelve-foot high Red beings in their elaborate headdresses and with enormous staves, my face opened in a casket of smiles. I knew those beings did not exist in temporal space, but somewhere between time in the space of another dimension.

I approached his throne, eyes on him the whole time as he had instructed us. I knelt, palm facing up to receive this blessing. Dawson poured a small portion of liquid, blessed liquid, from the equally blessed vase into my waiting palm, one of five blessings each student gained through the ceremony. He smiled into my eyes and I knew he was aware of what I saw.

As I walked back to my place in the crowd, he said kindly, letting the smile drop from his face and looking directly at me, "This Red Chen Rezig is for the sorrow of the world."

My smile left, but my body filled with ease and well-being.

Chapter Seventeen

WE HAD BEEN IN THE NORTH ISLAND OF NEW ZEALAND for the retreat. Now, with full time meditation over, some people returned to North America, some to the next adventure with Dawson and some, including myself, my brother, Cec and Jack determined to stay on in New Zealand to make money and catch up with Dawson when possible. We heard jobs were more plentiful in Christchurch in the South Island, so that's where we went.

Jack, who had found the house in Ultimo, Sydney Australia, had shown up at my side right after we left retreat. He had spoken at first indirectly then more and more confidently about getting a job at the Hermitage Hotel at Aoraki, Mount Cook in the South Island. He made it clear he'd help me get a job there, so we would be together.

Our first situation was separation. Jack soon had a job at the Hermitage Hotel at Mount Cook, a short bus journey away from Christchurch, while I was left behind in Christchurch working as a hotel maid in a run-down motel.

I stood in the payphone booth on the street at the time we'd agreed on, tears sliding down my face. "I want to see you. I need you."

"We'll be together soon. I'm going to get you a job here."

"But why can't I come now? I'm doing maid work here anyway. What's the difference? Why wait?"

"I told you. We can do better than maid service for you. I'm going to get you into the office." I wonder now if he had already met and tangled with the hotel maid with whom he had an affair.

Back then, I just shed more tears, then we hung up.

Within a couple of weeks, I was on a bus that left Christchurch, rolled through the MacKenzie Basin in South Canterbury, then climbed up into the mountains finally accessing the gardens of purple and white lupines outside the main entrance to the Hermitage Hotel. Jack was working so I took my small bags into the staff residences. I shared a kitchen and small bathroom with several other women while Jack's bedroom was in the men's quarters. Unmarried employees lived in separate quarters but in the way of all lovers, we found time and space to be together.

That first afternoon, I wandered into the staff bar and soon heard the distinct rhythmic whirring of helicopter blades sounding frequently overhead.

"Why are there so many choppers all afternoon?"

The line of men at the bar their backs to the large window opening onto one side of Mt. Cook all turned to look at me.

"They come to scrape up the bodies off the mountain," a voice from the line-up of men said.

"Bodies?"

"Yeee-ah. Bodies of climbeh's ya know? The ones who try to climb and don't make it." The men turned to each other now, guffawing just enough I didn't know whether to believe these words or not, but I left the employee bar right after, feeling a strange sensation of being in the wrong place, out of tune and out of time.

Later I learned the Caroline Face of Mt. Cook presents one of the most challenging and dangerous climbs in the world.

The second-floor office where I worked running the telex machine was overseen by a warm, good-humored woman from England, and populated with two others, one from Ireland, who was also the wife of the manager of the hotel, and one young woman from the US. The American woman had a relationship with one of the hotel pilots; he took tourists on journeys in a 4-seater Cessna up into the mountains. She arranged for the office ladies to go flying.

Shortly after liftoff I said, "I'm not sure I like this." I said this to the other women, who already knew my gift for drama. When I complained again, about my stomach dipping with each tip of the wings of this suddenly tiny-feeling aircraft careening next to the sides of very real, hard looking rock mountains, they just rolled their eyes.

We flew among the shining white-capped mountains, below the snow line but far above the green and brown ground below, the sun beaming through crystal clear air, flew into what seemed a secret meadow, cupped within the ring of mountains as though the mountains protected a private jewel. The pristine snow caps filled my eyes until I forgot we were floating in space.

The pilot guided us down onto a glacier. The others put on sunglasses to ward off the extreme sunlight bouncing between snow-capped mountains above and glacial snow on the ground. I had no sunglasses, believing they were all about vanity and unnecessary. Or so I told myself. In truth, I had no money for anything, even sunglasses while I pinched and saved for Dawson's next destination.

I wandered a short way from the others, took in the tall rim of jagged peaks, breathed in the sharp, clear air, noted the level ground beneath the icy cover. I felt a small shift internally, as though if the world might offer such beauty, I might be able to partake. Might. I scooped a bit of the crystalized snow up and took the slightly salty taste on my tongue.

"Don't! Remember I said…what if everyone did that?"

We had been warned not to take any of the snow away from the glacier, for what would happen if everyone did? But I lived for myself in my own world and these admonishments were too late.

Cecilie and my brother, now married, lived in Christchurch, where my brother drove truck for a second-hand clothing store, so we got first dibs at new-to-us clothes. I needed clothes desperately and with a deeper desperation needed time with Cec. I journeyed to Christchurch for one long weekend.

Now I lay on the couch in their apartment. Behind the door of their bedroom, they fought. Their voices scarred the air, even though they tried to keep the volume down. They thought I was asleep. I didn't hear words, but the sounds were high, tense.

Then Cecilie flung their door open, light falling out behind her but not angled such that she might notice I was awake.

"Why don't you just go to her? She's the one you really want." Beneath the trained neutral voice of a meditator, streaks of jealousy, loss and humiliation bled Cec's emotions onto the space. I heard my brother's voice in the background, his sounds muted, full of the false humour of one who has been discovered.

"Go on. Go over there and wake her up. It's really her you want. You've always wanted her," Cecilie continued. Now her voice carried the indignant, righteous triumph of a hurt spouse.

My chest filled with confusion, despair and something else, an almost familiar feeling. Hadn't something like this happened before? Not with him, her, but two people talking, one urging the other toward me?

Some memories float like a single leaf on water, unattached, twirling, buoyant, drifting closer then farther away. Other memories contain threads, runners like the roots of plants called rhizomes that shoot under the surface of soil, carrying their potential and blossoming farther along the way.

This present moment carried within it the signature of my past. Here in New Zealand lying on Cecilie's couch I did not recall the original experience, although a couple of decades and much effort later, I would remember.

I would remember how on that first night Al had spurred Gary on, "Go over there and get some nookie, Gar."

"I don't know Al, she's much younger than I thought. It would be like my young sister, I have a sister that young."

I had pretended to be asleep but opened my eyes to see the kerosene lamp lit room, two men at the table at the far end of the room, my ears open to their words. This memory simmered below the surface but niggled at me through these events in Christchurch New Zealand, half a planet and some seven years away.

While I continued to lie quietly on Cec's couch, a small, soft fist in my stomach gripped me. I felt crusted in disappointment, because Cecilie acted as though I didn't exist. She closed the door and I held myself still, breathing, glad I had not moved, thankful they believed I was still asleep.

I began to practice a meditation technique. First establish where my body touched couch or chair or bed or floor. Watch with soft interest anything that happened, then question what came before. The practice helped calm me and I slept a little.

I said nothing to them the next day or in any of the days or years that followed. The scene was ignored, at least in terms of any language among us.

When I returned to the Hermitage, Jack confessed he had cheated on me while I was away. Jack was unaware of the emotional connection I had forged with another man at the hotel. The other man and I had spent some nights talking, necking, nothing more, but it counted. I didn't tell Jack, but this was the reason his confession did not change our relationship.

What Jack's confession did was awaken and intensify questions that had been floating like stars on the event horizon of a black hole. I'd managed to push all the questions away to the fringe of consciousness but now they flooded through, relentlessly.

What exactly was I doing traipsing around the planet after Dawson with whom I had barely spoken? What about my aspirations of writing? I'd had a poem published, my first ever, in an anthology in New Zealand. Word of this success had filled long, joyfully written letters to my parents, Tim, and a few others back there in that increasingly remote place called Canada. That remote place was where I wanted to be, wasn't it?

I was barely writing; no poems, no prose and even my journal entries, so detailed before I left for India, had dwindled to almost nothing. I was following this teacher, something that felt like the right thing for now, but knew I would not spend my life chasing after him.

Only men were allowed to serve Dawson and in serving, presumably gain extra moments of special teaching. Would he ever have any interest in me? For that matter what was my interest in him? What his life trajectory described, constant travel and constantly new adventures, constituted a short season in my life but I knew it was not for me in the long run.

What was for me? Didn't I need to know consciously what I wanted and then act toward that? But I didn't know and what I did know I wanted, which was my writing, erupted in fits and starts, not enough to make headway.

Instead I abandoned myself by the side of my life, drinking in the staff bar, having emotional if not physical affairs behind my intended's back, accepting his cheating as a matter of course.

One night, restless with all these questions and in the light of a full moon, I decided to walk away from staff quarters. Just to take a walk. I had spent endless hours walking the boardwalk in Toronto's Beach, along the wooden planks next to the sandy shore and up and down through winding, heavily-treed streets. I'd push my face against the wind off the lake, smell the wet air and walk until my legs buzzed with the effort that brought a tiny piece of calm.

Now I needed this solace.

I headed out the door and along the path to my left. New Zealand was under a magnificent display of meteor showers, shooting stars every minute or so across the blue-black night flecked with white-gold planets. I strode along, but soon felt a strong presence to my right. It demanded my attention. I slid my eyes sideways.

"Go back!" a Native man demanded.

"What? Why?"

"You do not belong here. If you go one step more, it will be bad…"

I felt a weight in front of me, almost like a body, then a shiver crossed my frame and the presence was no longer in contact. But I didn't doubt, question or disobey. I turned immediately, deeply disappointed, and walked back. Inquiries about the place I had been walking revealed it was a sacred Maori Burial Ground.

Jack's sister and brother-in-law came to visit, and Jack arranged a week off to go traveling with them. Although he wanted me to join them, I protested loudly and strongly. I wanted the week to rest between work hours, to read and to stay quiet. He relented.

Jack's relatives had brought a number of books with them, including Eric Neumann's The Great Mother, a text by Marie Louise von Franz and more psycho-spiritual writings. They asked if they might leave the books behind while they toured in their rented vehicle. I was delighted! I read most of the books, and baked banana bread from the mix I'd brought back from Christchurch with me.

The loaf, warm and fragrant, stayed on the kitchen counter and random residents wandered by, attracted by the smell. More than one said, "Oh, wow can I have a slice," like kids in their mother's kitchen. Another said, "We never have anyone bake anything. This is great! You are now the resident mother!"

What I noticed with surprise was how content, even happy, I felt in the simple act of baking. I had no idea I was activating my shadow, everything I was consciously running away from, including the role of mother and homemaker. My conscious personality, as broken as it was, existed through a romantic attachment to the role of gypsy wanderer, itinerant, mendicant, the attitude Dawson approved of.

When Jack returned something had changed between us. Something about me refusing to tour around with him and his family, something about my need to stay and rest upset the already tenuous balance in which we lived.

With hindsight I see that like many couples we were sexually attracted through a power dynamic. My decision to stay behind increased a sense of my own power. Increased this but not nearly enough to make decisions on my own. My will power pitched against his which I felt to be an oppressive force I had to fight against. And fight we did.

We stood on the shore as his sister and brother-in-law left on a ship and within a few weeks, we too boarded a ship, a Greek cruise ship. Jack belonged to the group, so we had a common root. Dawson was rumored to be setting up another therapy junket, in Mexico. The dozen or so of us remaining in New Zealand including Cec and my brother, wanted to cross the South Pacific in time to rendezvous with the teacher and the group. Surely that was enough! Clearly any troubles Jack and I had had with each other might be erased with enough meditation, with another course, with therapy in Mexico. Surely.

All this would take money, which Jack was making, and I was not. I was covering expenses and putting a little aside but not nearly enough to carry me from this down under place to the next destination. Jack had promised to help me out financially.

We boarded the ship which was headed for Acapulco via Tahiti. What I heard was we were heading to North America. North America meant only one place for me—Toronto and home.

Chapter Eighteen

WE BELIEVED DAWSON WAS PREPARING for a course of therapy in Mexico slated for March of 1974. It was February 1973 in New Zealand when we boarded the ship to take us across the Pacific.

I loved the ship. I was tired in a bone-deep way, more suitable to someone twice or three times my age. The sharp-edged beak of those constant questions pecked away, what am I doing, where am I going, what do I want, until the small inner space I called myself, located above my shoulders, threatened to crack.

My failing attempts at eating daily mocked my sporadic sense of self with echoing sarcasms, "Know what you want? Direct your actions? You can't even decide what to eat and keep that inside."

"We're getting off tomorrow in Tahiti," Jack announced one afternoon from his bed on the other side of the cabin.

Getting off the ship? But it was my refuge! "You maybe, but not me."

"Why not? You have a chance to see Tahiti! You may never have this chance again…"

"I don't care about Tahiti. I am happy on the ship. I like the ship and want to stay here."

"Well, I don't think you'll be able to. I think we'll all be asked to leave for the day." His tone held triumph.

"That's not going to happen. It doesn't make sense. I am a passenger, and if I don't want to leave this ship, no one can make me."

Getting off the ship here in the South Pacific equated in my depth intelligence to leaving the car in North Ontario seven years earlier. I had no access to the tragic outcome of that situation, but all my unfelt emotions rose as one thrust: stay on the ship at all costs.

The threat that the truth might rise from my inner graveyard spurred from me a full out attack on Jack, on the Captain and Company, on all such sea vessels and their unspeakably stupid rules. My rage spewed as defense against anything that might rouse that sleeping corpse, a memory inaccessible to my conscious mind, but thrusting its weight into this experience which seemed so similar.

Next morning Cecilie stood beside me as we walked behind my brother and Jack. I told her about the fight I'd had with Jack over leaving the ship.

When we reached the first cafe, I plunked down at a small, round, metal table, its glass top large enough to hold two soft drinks. I was aware I was losing the ability to speak, and my vision was going.

"What do you want to drink?" Cecilie asked.

I shook my head. She looked at me now, really looked.

"What's happening?" She asked this in tones of buttery comfort.

"...don't know...can't...move, my vision fading... I can't talk..."

"I'm going to order."

Just then a waiter came up and Cecilie requested two soft drinks. They arrived quickly, and she placed her straw between her lips, saying, "You can do this. Place your straw between your lips. I know you can't move, but just do this much..."

I was fading but reached for the straw. I sipped and everyone but Cecilie, dissolved away. All sensation had ceased in every part of me. I did not taste the sweet liquid, nor feel it sliding over my tongue, down my throat. No sensation. The cavernous pit within, the one I had made such furious and distorted efforts to live around, opened its jaws of oblivion. How I yearned for it!

For the rest of the day Cecilie made me walk a little, talk a little, kept by my side and because she did, I stayed out of the pit. Partly paralyzed for a few hours, slowly picking up first one foot, then the other, leaning on her body we walked slowly, so slowly.

Gradually the soft yellow sand, the blue, blue waters came back into focus. If I felt nothing, I could at least see.

This day was eclipsed by the unfinished business from seven years earlier. That was when, seconds after a man's bloodied body collapsed to the ground, I had stood, screaming, not recognizing my own voice. But that shock had not been allowed to complete its cycle.

Instead, Gary had said, "Move or Al will do to you what he did to that man…" My instinct for survival overrode my need to scream, so I had moved.

The unfinished intensity of that experience had carved a crater in the center of my psyche into which my senses threatened to slip. I had spent every minute since the man's murder keeping myself from falling into a space of overload so great, I would lose my life to complete shut-down, catatonia.

The worst part was I did not know this consciously. I only knew every day I struggled against unknown pressures from within. The Buddhist teaching had informed me "life is suffering" and I had resonated with the starkness of this truth since every day felt like pushing uphill against a force going down. I did not know I was working so hard to just maintain. I blamed myself, in the way of so many who experience PTSD for not being better at living and achieving.

Here on Tahiti Cecilie created a tiny pathway to the present moment away from an abyss that may have swallowed me whole. She did it with a simple plastic straw and the generous compassion of her presence. What power there is in just being present with love for another!

Cecilie greeted Jack and my brother as they cheerfully chippered on about the snorkeling, the beautiful coral colors, until finally seeing my unmoving face and blank eyes, they raised their eyebrows at Cecilie, who said, "Never mind. We'll meet you inside." No one mentioned it again.

We left the ship in Acapulco and boarded a bus for Vancouver. I fought for us to go to Toronto. Jack fought just as hard to stay in Vancouver, citing better weather as one of his main points.

Trudging through the slush and biting sleet on a Vancouver street, I couldn't help snarling, "You wanted to come to Vancouver because it doesn't snow here."

"Usually it doesn't. This is unusual."

"Well, unusual thanks but I'm in it. I might as well be in Toronto for all your choice has worked to save us from snow."

We lived in a one bedroom on East Hastings Street. Jack drove cab, I was hired by BC Tel and made it to work through enough hang-overs that I was not suspended or let go. Barely. The plan was to save and get to Mexico Therapy which had been rescheduled for autumn 1974.

Cecilie and my brother moved in across the hall from our apartment for a very brief stint. Then my grandmother, my father's mother, passed away suddenly, and Dad sent my brother the fare to come home for the funeral. I raged, protested, but Dad was adamant.

"He's the first born."

"But I'm the firstborn girl!"

"That doesn't matter. He's coming home. Not you."

Cecilie stayed behind which took away some of the sting, but she didn't remain for long.

"When you leave it will never be the same."

"I'll see you in Toronto. It will be different, but we will still be close." She always wanted to heal my wounds.

So Cec left and Jack and I carried on, fighting more and making love less.

He began one day, "I want to go camping, over to Vancouver Island."

"Fine, you go camping. I'm not stopping you."

"No. I want you to come…you're coming with me."

"Why? Why do I have to come with you? Why can't you just go and enjoy camping, maybe take someone with you who enjoys camping…Camping for me is akin to scraping off my skin with a blunt instrument. I was forced to camp as a kid, I have camped, and I know I don't like it. You go. That's fine with me."

"Because we are supposed to be together. We don't do things together. This is something we can do together, and you can learn to like camping. You're coming too. I can teach you to enjoy camping."

"I don't WANT to go camping."

"Why? Why do you hate camping? We're going to be camping to get to Mexico. Why is that all right but this isn't?"

"Because camping to get across Canada gets us to therapy. It has a purpose. There is a reason to do it, so I can endure it. If I had the money, I'd stay in hotels but as it is…"

"Oh, camping isn't good enough for you? I feel like everything I do isn't good enough for you. Nothing pleases you…"

"Plenty of things please me, I love ballet, the marina but you didn't want to come with me, so I went to those alone. Why can't you do the same for me?"

"What is it about camping you don't like?"

"Too much work for so little return."

"All right, what if I do all the work? That's it, I'll do all the work and you just ride along."

"Why do you insist upon bringing someone with you who is so against this?"

"Because you are my partner and partners are supposed to do things together."

"I believe a couple can have entirely different hobbies, entirely different lives and still be happy together."

"Oh, great so you do what you like, and I do what I like, and we meet in the bedroom every now and then?"

"Look, I hate camping. I don't want to go. What does it take to convince you? You always make decisions when we do things together, is it too much to ask for you to leave me this little bit of space for myself?"

"Oh, I get it. You feel like you have no space. I'm crowding you in this…"

"No, not always…I mean yes, you do crowd me, I don't want to go camping."

All I remember of those three days of camping happened just before we were to leave. I stood in our campsite, looking around. Everything was scattered, pots flung with enough force to have landed in soil or on nearby bushes, milk spilled on the ground weeping in several small white rivers, a coffee cup hanging oddly on a shrub limb. My underwear, jeans and tops spread across the wooden picnic table, and hanging down to the ground emphasized what felt like an ominous question.

A startling silence still rang in my ears as though a large tornado had torn through. I looked up. Other campers stood stock still, offering back to me that whitened look of people who have witnessed an intimate disaster. Their eyes poured utter shock and then, as I looked at them, disgust.

"What happened here?" I managed to ask softly.

"I wonder," Jack's icy smirk.

We drove home in silence. I remember a small voice inside my head, "Serves Jack right for pushing me around."

My past with Al and Gary accompanied us, just like dark demons, on that trip. Something in the last day maybe something Jack said, or even the way light filtered through the trees onto, say, a can of beans, triggered the part of me captive, terrified and mute, to rise, fulminating with rage, scattering everything I could lay my hands on, screaming in anguish. But I had no memory because that part of me, the crazed one returned below my surface like a positron, leaving only the path of the truth of what had happened so many years before.

I had to believe nothing had happened, because to remember what had really happened with Al and Gary still threatened my consciousness with splitting permanently. With the power of survival instinct, the memory stayed shoved down, even as the ghosts of Al and Gary throttled my present life.

Chapter Nineteen

Jack invited another couple from the group to travel with us to Mexico. He told me this was a way to save money. I ragged on him relentlessly about going to Toronto, and finally he decided we would. It meant adding thousands of miles to the trip which he justified through his desire for us to introduce each other to our respective families. He still believed we would marry.

My father told me years later he had been alarmed to see my skinny frame and hear the cough that hacked through me, but because I was an adult, he had said nothing.

After Toronto we started the long, diagonal drive down through the US to Baja California, the site in Mexico where we would experience hands on therapy. The ten-day drive of highway around us did nothing to improve the verbal sparring between me and Jack. Our companion couple suffered through the endlessness of our spiteful verbal exchanges.

We were now at our destination in a general way but lost as to the specifics. Jack decided to keep wheeling the car along the one small, main street in this town.

"Can we just not fight about it?" This plea from the woman passenger.

"Why not just ask someone where the El Dorado Hotel is?" I tried.

"Right. Like there's only one El Dorado Hotel near here. Do you even know what El Dorado means? It means gold. The Gold

Hotel."

Jack tossed his words to me where I sat in the back seat, then flashed a knowing look at the husband who sat in the front passenger seat. Then this man spoke up, suggesting Jack might stop and ask someone.

Jack did. He climbed out of the car, talked with a man, climbed back in and said, "It's just down there." He nodded his head toward the south. "I think we drove past it already."

"How did you ask?" I inquired.

"What?" Jack's face furrowed as though a large bug had landed on his cheek.

"How did you ask about the hotel? Did you ask for the El Dorado?"

Too late he saw my verbal trap. Furious he focused silently on the road ahead.

Finally, we arrived. Dawson of course was not yet present but would arrive later that night. The facilitators, two men and a woman indicated couples were to separate for the duration.

The dusk was deep, purple and blues surrounding us like a soft shawl where we stood on the balcony.

"Look at that!" Jack pointed to the nearly setting sun, its soft rays billowing around a few clouds, the rising moon reflected perfectly with its light orange tinge on the utterly still dark blue waters of the bay. The bay's one long arc of pure white sand, now dark blue in the light of dusk, created two sides of the bay, sides that seemed to embrace the blue waters.

"Oh yeah," I breathed softly as Jack took my hand, "yeah."

Jack held onto me in a long embrace as we overlooked the bay.

"You sure you're going to be okay?" he asked. "I mean, I won't be there to be with you…"

Everything in me went still. What did he want? What was he saying?

Because my neurons had carved large highways committed to

being afraid of men and because I had relatively little experience of tenderness and protection from them, Jack's tenderness in such moments did not register. I simply did not have the wiring needed to move away from my defenses.

"I'll be all right." Tears fell then, tears from fatigue at the endless fighting and from relief I'd finally have some time alone. With a sigh I recognized I already found the distance from him a reprieve.

Next morning, I walked along the balcony that ran outside the rooms facing the bay. The cafeteria of the hotel sat at one end. The hotel was built atop a gentle slope that gradually, after two dips in the land reached the shore of the bay.

Inside the cafeteria I lined up for the buffet of scrambled eggs, white or brown toast, fruit, porridge, lots of coffee and a luscious blender drink of yogurt and papaya which the kitchen staff concocted whenever asked, "una liquado, por favor."

Dawson began the morning class by reading from a dry text book. I felt the energy in the room fall and fade. Dawson looked up directly at me and I saw the words, "Non-clinging" in bright yellow dance in the air between us. I knew others didn't see, except for him.

He started again.

"Sometimes," his big brown eyes full of liquid warmth flashed at me, "the teacher must learn from the student. We'll put this book away and focus on experience, the experience of therapy in your body as opposed to the theoretical understanding of therapy."

He instructed us to meet him by the edge of the water.

Under the blazing white sun softened by the breeze, inhaling with each breath the distinct scent of ocean salt, I stood among the others as he spoke.

"The purpose of all psychotherapy," he began, and my blood leapt, slamming against the perpetually numb state of my muscles and nerves, "is to provide a basis for Rebirth. Carl Jung called birth our first trauma." Here my heart in its dank prison sang. New information! Knowledge! Someone knew the way, the path. Someone knew how to lift the shackles of repetitive patterns of behavior in which most live. Someone knew how to help! His words fell upon me like anointment with holy oil.

"Birth is the first trauma. The conditions of your birth, of which we will speak more later, and to some degree your mother's state of being while pregnant, these are what created the basis of your conditioned responses built right into your nervous system. We can loosen those patterned responses by using body posture, such as described by Alexander Lowen, by using Psychodrama and Mandala technique etc. All are to evoke an experience of the Transcendent.

You know, you really are born from a lotus! Born from the Transcendent! Nothing else exists powerful enough to get you, or what you call "you" through the traumas of birth, never mind what comes after."

Now under his direction we stood in about four feet of water in two lines, our hands holding those of the person opposite. This created an arc above our heads and with the water emulated the birth canal. Each of us had to swim the length, 20 feet or so of this human tunnel.

"Way to go, you can do it, that's it, that's it" rose on all sides as we cheered each baby one of us on.

My turn. I sucked in a large, deep breath, slipped down feeling the warm wet enclose me entirely. An unexpected joy washing every cell propelled me from inside as I slithered the entire length in one go, terribly aware how my long, lean body looked. At the end, I planted my feet below me, started to uncurl my body to the air when hands grabbed mine making the transition easier.

A spontaneous grin of happiness spread across my face.

We ambled back for lunch, which was barely warmed fish, the eye staring blankly up from the plate, and a heap of white rice. But still, the liquados were plentiful and tasty.

Over the month of the course we would experience a rapid decline in the quality of food until barely warmed toast and raw eggs constituted breakfast and a single raw fish with a few pieces of lettuce was the big noon meal. I grew disgusted.

If one of us desired a more luxurious meal, that desire quickly squelched itself under the talk that circulated throughout the room, "These people do not have much, what they have they offer, it is not for us to be demanding…"

"This isn't even warm. I want to take it back to the kitchen. Someone should do something about this…" I complained.

My table mates raised the objection, "It's probably the best they can do."

"Well, their best isn't very good."

Someone raised the point that this was a land of abundant fruits and vegetables. Why were none available to us?

I argued about the quality of food. I believed this urge to question everything that came across my path erupted from the nasty, ill-formed part of me. Why oh, why couldn't I just shut up and be like the others? I listened, grew quiet and tried to comply since I believed others knew better. It would take years before I figured out the food had been manipulated precisely to raise our frustrations and anger.

Dawson conducted class each morning in the cafeteria. With the tables and chairs out of sight, the concrete floor, walls and ceiling and open windows created a feeling of cool spaciousness in the Mexican heat.

One morning he wound into a description of a dream he'd had. "Yes, you see it was down a few steps covered in moss of some green vegetation," his voice calm, he spread his hands wide and looked directly at me. "Down those steps to a kind of cavern…"

Suddenly I saw the entire sequence as though it were right there, in that room, as though I were descending the steps covered in green moss, the stone stairs beneath the green vegetation. I felt the air, uncomfortably close and clammy, then…

"Yes, yes, that's it!" he exclaimed jubilantly his eyes drilling into mine. I knew his excited outburst signaled encouragement for the act of consciousness I had just achieved, recreating in full sensory detail his dream merely from the words. Merely from the words and his power of focus and concentration. Visualization! It must have felt like this when I first learned to stand or took my first steps. Success!

He carried on with the class, his eyes occasionally lighting with warmth on my own.

Days and experiences in this course merge in my memory and flow like water. What remains are a few waves on top, this specific exercise, that precise moment. Here we are gathered on the grassy ground near the ocean's sandy shore. He has described this as a trust building exercise.

On the white sand beach, the sun pouring yellow everywhere, we put our arms up over our heads, and bent backward until our palms clasped those of our partners. Then as we held palm to palm, faces turned up to the sky, we walked together, one slow step at a time, talking to each other.

"How are you doing?"

"Yes, okay. You?"

"I'm good. Now one more step…" my partner splatted suddenly down on me with whooping laughter, her weight squeezing laughter from me too.

Some of her bulk fell across my face, the wire frame of my glasses squishing down on the bridge of my nose. I ended with red marks and some bruising, but our laughter rang across that beach.

The next morning, I dreamed of a bathroom in which the tiles were being repaired. I saw the bathroom and the tiles and the man who arrived with a carpenter's belt on, removing old tiles and readying the new ones. I knew instantly this bathroom scene was my nose, and the tiles were the cells that had to be replaced. The insight filled me with wonder and delight.

I waited for Dawson outside of class.

"Sir?"

He looked at me, listening as though what I said mattered.

"Well, this morning I had a dream of a bathroom where the tiles were being replaced and I know…I mean it's the cells across my nose being healed."

His eyes twinkled and his mouth curved up in a mischievous smile.

"Ah, yes," he chuckled. I knew if I had read the dream wrong, he would have come down on me without reserve. This brief, positive exchange provoked a sense of confidence I had understood that dream. If I had understood this dream perhaps I might again, in future? And so was a small hope born.

He talked about emotional blocks, the evidence of trauma, and how these blocks stay in the muscles and tissues of our body until released. This is the nature of emotional blocks, that they register in our bodies. At the places in our bodies where the emotional blocks sit, our systems slow down— blood, oxygen and lymph— creating good conditions for illness and disease.

Opening up those cells, setting free their flow of blood, oxygen and lymph simultaneously frees their emotional packages for release. The boundaries of trauma may be determined by this: any event too large to be integrated immediately is suppressed into the unconscious, held in the body, where its energy continues to exert powerful influence on the conscious mind including decisions the person makes.

The way to freedom— to being able to be with the present moment minus that influence from the past— lies in releasing those original emotions, feeling them deeply in the body and watching as they naturally dissipate. In this way blood, lymph and oxygen are freed to move naturally, fully.

He roared at us more than once, "This being," indicating himself, "is on about Liberation! Not merely therapy but Liberation!"

He described the stages leading to Liberation. "The four stages may arise in any order, but all must be experienced for real Liberation." The first is that the initial memory must be experienced again in consciousness clearly. The second is the deeply felt powerful emotion of that original memory must be experienced in its fullness.

He said, "It is true that trauma creates a frozen element both physically and emotionally around which the personality lives. To live fully and express real freedom of choice, all the frozen emotions must be allowed to fulfill their original wave: the person must feel the original emotion, terror, rage, even laughter."

The third part is body expression. The emotion of the original memory must be experienced within the body. That may be shaking, vomiting, a pink flush to the skin, heat…any response from the body. But it must be present.

Finally, he told us a kind of domino experience takes place in which you see automatically rising, unbidden but clear, the moments where you made decisions about life based on that original experience. Once these four have been completed there is no more being subject to becoming.

"To wrap up: you must have memory of the original trauma or incident; you must experience the original emotion that now moves through you, unfrozen, free. You must experience a body response: heat, rash, nausea, even bruising may erupt without present cause. Fourth, you will see how decisions you made in your life took place out of that original trauma. You will no longer be compelled to make the same choice whenever that pattern pushes up from the unconscious. You are free." He paused, pursed his lips together, then continued.

"Your senses are Deva. When you experience all four stages of Liberation in whatever order, you understand. The word Deva means light, Angelic. For instance, writing in Sanskrit is called Deva

Nagari or shining snakes because originally the monks in meditation saw the letters shining in gold dancing in the air, in space. Perhaps Deva Nagari was delivered to them by space beings. Nagari means snakes, the shimmering forms and Deva means shining.

"Your senses, when cleared of the claustrophobic conditioning you call 'You' make your senses Deva and those same senses are the doors to the Deva, Angelic realm."

Angels! The doorway to Angelic realms! How the Angels arrive to us. My heart leapt.

"When your senses are clear," he continued, "your brain naturally creates order and meaning. You are neither obsessive-compulsive on one hand, nor hysterical on the other. Now…" his eyes roamed ours, truly seeking, "Does anyone know by heart the poem Jabberwocky?"

My hand shot up; I might be the best student today!

"Ah, you," he replied as though disappointed, "No one else?" No other hand appeared.

"Well, then," he continued with a tiny shrug as though the lack must be accepted, "Stand up!"

Oh, I hadn't thought I'd be standing, the thought crossed my mind.

Embarrassed, I struggled to my feet. My mind retreated behind a blank screen as I gaped at the eyes all staring directly at me. Just then I heard a small, soft voice from the crowd say, "'Twas brillig and the slithey toves…"

I glanced toward the lifeline sound. It came from a soft face under blond hair, and large, round blue eyes, a young woman whose name I knew, but with whom I had never spoken.

In a flush of gratitude, I proceeded confidently, "'Twas brillig and the slithey toves / did gyre and gimble in the wabe / all mimsy were the borogroves…"

"That's it!" Dawson's finger flashed out from his hand, pointing and shaking at me, his head rolled back, his eyes round as though startled, his mouth grinning, "That's it! That's you! You are the

Borogrove, a true Hysteric!"

Laughter rang across the concrete room, bouncing up from the concrete floor and back across the hall between the cement walls, raining down from the ceiling. On all sides, laughter at me.

"You are hysteric! Now sit down!" He was still laughing.

A terrible thunder rolled from my stomach, lurching upward. My sense of self, that numb, grey person railed down on this uprising, trying to will the tsunami of emotion and sensation back to its grave. Facial muscles held taut. Breath stayed shallow.

I tried and partly failed. The first huge wave of humiliation along my arms, across my chest, up my throat promised to fill my face. I refused this sensation with everything in me. Tears clouded my eyes. The conflict raged as I watched the familiar inner terrain, its bleak numbness, return against those waves of true, physically demanding emotions. He, Dawson, had made me feel.

At least for a moment. My practiced will power, fueled now by rage at Dawson soon suppressed those waves of energy, bringing me back to my usual state of indifference.

When I recall this moment, I wonder how I knew to "watch"? What intelligence remained focused and calmly alert, seeing the storm of emotions rise without physically reacting? I have come to believe we are not separate. When we are in close proximity, in the same room say, as another, we share mind. In this moment, Dawson's consciousness, clear, focused, calm, powerful and serene held the entire room. It was not his personality; that was something very different. It was the consciousness he had honed through so much meditation. His consciousness permeated the room and everyone in it. Being held in his energy, his field, I experienced how to watch the emotions he had invoked in me. This is how after many years I have come to understand how he taught me.

Back then, as I sat down, and my mind began to clear, emotion to recede, I remembered something—the face of the one person who had helped me. Someone had helped me. Between ever smaller waves of humiliation, for the rest of the class I recalled that moment. Someone had helped me.

A rhythm quickly established itself in our days: breakfast, a short break, class, another short break, lunch, an hour for rest then some kind of exercise. Our evenings were free time in the beginning but soon Dawson arranged for Wongs.

Dawson explained that each Wong, given with a distinct Tibetan deity at its center, expresses an aspect of human consciousness: female peacefulness, male peacefulness, female wrath, male wrath, peaceful intellect, wrathful intellect. The list extends over forty major deities. Each Wong provides the potential for meditating upon that aspect of human consciousness, until it grows easier to access. Dawson was a fan of Wongs and provided many on every course I attended.

Down the two small slopes from the main building, our hotel enclave included a flat, square concrete pad surrounded by palm trees and green shrubs on all sides. We called it the Enclosure and it was here we experienced Wongs, classes and eventually mandala therapy.

He sat at the front of the Enclosure, on a chair festooned to indicate his elevated position. Our silence indicated the seriousness with which we received his blessings of this Wong. Silent that is until a ripple of laughter began at the back of enclosure. I felt a snap of negativity, *Who is laughing? That can't be the way to appreciate this experience!* Then as the laughter grew, I turned around.

A donkey had ambled into the enclosure and stood contentedly looking at Dawson. Slowly I felt a slight expansion in my chest. I turned to look at Dawson and his grin pulled a sense of relief from me. Then I laughed softly at the sight of the donkey, standing quite still, staring at Dawson.

Another evening Dawson recited the Heart Sutra in Pali for us. We were each given a candle which was lit by one of his attendants as we approached his chair to offer the traditional white scarf, known as a kata. He continued focusing on the words, occasionally raising his finger to indicate that person might stand beside him. I was given the opportunity! I felt blessed!

I stood and waited and as the others one by one left the enclosure I came to stand, then sit in front of him. I had no forethought, simply did what my body felt was right in the moment.

I waited and watched as Dawson indicated to his attendants what they might do with the extra cloths, surplus vases and candles, incense, all the implements of the recitation. He dismissed the last one then turned towards me sitting at his feet.

Finally, he looked at me. "Have you received?" He asked this gently.

"Yes, I have." I leaned in more closely as though we had rehearsed this. He leaned forward wrapping a long white scarf around my neck and pulling my head toward him, so the crown of my head bumped into his heart chakra three times, as he said, "Boom. Boom. Boom." I was in bliss; when I looked up, he smiled radiantly.

"Thank you, sir," I said clearly, tears rolling down my cheeks. Then I backed up, stood and walked to my room. He had broken through again, again had reached the vulnerable part of me, touched and embraced my frightened core.

Jungle Drums! On another day someone had pushed the button of the boom box and rhythmic drums pounded through the Enclosure. Dawson separated the men including the two male facilitators taking them back through the palm trees where the women might not see.

When the men spilled back into sight, they had bare shoulders hunched up, their chests inflated, their legs diving up and down to the beat of those drums as they approached the women. More than half a dozen men singled out one of our women, provoking the cold fingers of instinctive fear. We had no hero, no one to whom we might run. Any one of these men easily outmuscled, outweighed any one of us.

The men advanced, their eyes roaming across us as we shrank back a little. Dawson surely would not let anything terrible happen, would he?

Just then one or two of the men circled a woman and cut her from the group, hoisting her, effortlessly it seemed, upon their shoulders. She was on her back, her belly exposed to the sky, riding on the shoulders of all the men.

Dawson called out, "Now you just relax! Let your head fall back!" as the men paraded around the space, their bodies pumping up and down to the drums, sweat gathering across their faces, their muscles shining as she lay as still as possible, her head upheld in the palm of one of the men, her face glowing!

I stood beside Dawson watching as this first woman disappeared on the shoulders of the men, disappeared beyond the palm tree wall to whatever lay on the other side. The men reappeared, temporarily just ambling about, then as if possessed of a single mind, flowed toward, circled and hoisted the next woman.

This time the sensibility of the woman as a great treasure, something rare and precious flooded through me as these macho men strutted around the enclosure seeming to proudly exhibit their prize before exiting as before.

Every one of the women one by one experienced the sensation of six or more men lifting, carrying, parading her. Soon a kind of alchemy seemed to take hold so the physical attributes of each man whether short or tall, muscled or thin, faded in the burnishing light of the slowly lowering sun, in the monotone consistent insistent drone of the drums, in the heavy warmth of the salt air, all distinct attributes faded leaving only a single thrusting masculine energy, dynamic, fluid, protective and trustworthy.

I realized I was to be last. This felt familiar and natural. I listened to Dawson's commentary on each woman, uttered softly to the female facilitators standing on his other side. "You see, that one can't relax…there's one that must be in control…that one is letting go…" It was not judgement, not indictment, just observation.

Six or more men approached, their eyes lit with certainty, confidence. Their hands gently scooped and lifted my body up, even from my standing position and a hundred sensations rippled through my legs, buttocks, shoulders, back, a hundred sensations parlayed into a single thought, **Good.**

I forgot what I had so newly learned in listening to Dawson so held my head up until I heard Dawson's voice, serene and clear, "Just let your head drop."

Neck muscles relaxed, blood rushed to my face, the men undulated up and down and paraded me for what seemed like a long time in this inverted world. It seemed they were reluctant to end their fun, until finally they carried me off in the opposite direction from the others and carefully, gently, with tenderness, lay me on the grass outside the palm wall. The drums stilled, the men left, but not before one bent down close to my ear and whispered, "Are you all right?"

I nodded as the men left. I lay still, a bit stunned, then a kind of fluid happiness fluttered at the edge of my mind.

Now as I write this my eyes fill with tears. What a powerful sense of true masculinity, undistorted. What a sensation of being held up by the masculine, treasured as rare and worthy because of being female. All this flowed through my cells, the cells that still held on that day so much damage, emotional and physical, from men.

Those cells must have taken in the signal from this experience; the neurons must have joined together whispering how some men are kind, trustworthy, supportive. Those whispers would eventually transform into a chorus of neuronal information balancing, through conscious hard work and through the serendipity of life, what evil, what damage had been done to me.

Against the backdrop of increasingly inedible food at the retreat, another memory remains. As I stood on the arm of sand surrounding the bay one evening, there, just past the hotel in the twilight a small fire burned.

Suddenly a man, one I did not know very well, was at my side.

"What is that?" I asked him.

"Haven't you been?"

I shook my head.

"Have you got a couple of bucks?"

I nodded.

"Come on." We walked under the satin blue-black sky, under the orange sliver of moon, along the beach and beyond to the fire.

My friend spoke Spanish to the man and the boy who was clearly his son, as the boy ladled up two large white paper cones filled with the pinkest, most perfectly round shrimp, a mound, small mountain of these sea morsels, upon which the man drizzled from his frying pan fresh melted butter generous with garlic. The first round, ridged flesh to touch my tongue convinced me I'd never eaten before.

My companion spoke more and softly with the pauses that reflect the politeness of strangers.

On the way back, my mouth and nostrils still dreaming the memory of shrimp, my friend said, "I asked them what they thought of all the noise, the crying and sometimes screams that come from the Enclosure."

"What did they say?"

"He said he understood. He said the white people have come to release their demons. They were possessed before and now they would be better. He said it was good."

Mandala therapy had begun the previous week when one person per day volunteered to enter the Enclosure where his or her own psyche would come to life.

Dawson had explained, "Mandala indicates an enclosed space in which something happens. It also indicates some degree of wholeness, or the spontaneous arising of wholesomeness from within the human mind, as Carl Jung discovered. For instance, if you dream of a mandala, or even four corners, or a circle, the beginnings of a mandala are present. This indicates strength is emerging in the psyche.

"What we'll be doing is exploring mandalas made of human beings. If you sign up, you'll chose four people to represent the main aspects of your psyche. For instance, you'll choose from everyone one person to be your positive masculine, positive feminine, negative masculine and negative feminine. Of course, you may choose to use another format: good mommy and daddy, and bad mommy and daddy.

"The person whose mandala it is first sits in front of each of the four aspects, giving each a bit of information about how they function in the person's life. For example, if the center person feels there was little positive feminine, she might say, "You are a mystery to me." From that clue the person playing the role of positive feminine relates mysteriously through the whole time the mandala goes on.

"The unconscious, that is those people not directly involved in the center of the mandala sit and watch and wait. Sometimes a tip, a word or two of wisdom may come from the unconscious. Whatever is spontaneously erupting from the unconscious is offered to the center as a complement to integrating consciously the four aspects. This struggle also shows the struggle with life. This is a rare opportunity! Don't miss out!"

A few brave souls put their names on the list but still many spaces remained, even as the days passed. I hung back, aware of a nervous tension from my stomach whenever I thought about writing my name in that empty square.

On the last day for mandalas a woman completely new to the group signed on. We gathered in the Enclosure, where Dawson wasted no time.

"You call yourselves students of this teacher!" He always referred to himself in third person, a trait I assumed meant he had transcended his ego. "But you have no faith. Not enough faith to put your names forward! You pretend to have faith in This Being, but someone unknown has real courage, true faith to experiment and try!"

With that and a curt nod, he signaled the beginning. The woman unwound her increasingly tragic tale, a tale embracing all the major distortions of my own early life—severe beatings with a leather belt, sexual abuse, verbal and emotional humiliation, no protection, no safety. When she got to the person picked for negative father, that man stood up and took off his leather belt.

Surely this can't happen! Surely Dawson will not allow…

The therapist snapped the belt in the air a few times as the woman shivered visibly in fear. We sat paralyzed.

Then Dawson stood up. The therapist handed him the belt. A smirk of derision across his mouth, Dawson raised the leather strip in the air and brought it down across her huddled shoulders, bent back, a scream of terror and pain filling the space. Then Dawson his face now twisted in triumph laid the leather whip across her arms and legs again. After a few strokes Dawson handed the belt back to the therapist playing the role of negative father.

The woman tore at negative father, her fists flailing, arms swinging, her face contorted as she screamed syllables at him. The man beat her back with his fists on her face and when she cowered, he again took the belt to her.

Tears slid out of my eyes. I looked at Dawson who saw my tears, looked around at everyone and said primly, "All of you should be crying. Go back to your rooms and cry."

Did I sleep that night? I do not recall talking with anyone for the rest of the evening, only that I retreated to my room, shame, guilt, terror mixing inside me. I remember crying softly. In the end a single thought rose. I would speak with the woman who had been beaten. I would tell her how sorry I felt for not helping her.

Next morning before breakfast we were all called to a meeting in the Enclosure. Dawson began, "You call yourselves students but most of you were unwilling to put yourselves forth. No trust! No commitment! There is nothing you can do now. It's over. What's worse, some of you belittled the efforts of the rest by imbibing alcohol and drugs! At this course!" He raged at us turning everything back on our incompetence, our failure, our sins. He uttered not a word about what he had done or what he had sanctioned in the facilitator's actions, although the memory of it hung like a shroud in that space as though it were all taking place again.

On and on, he heaped blame upon us: we had behaved horribly with drugs and alcohol and partying and none of us had taken the course and the opportunity seriously....

We deserved it but not for the sins he cited. We deserved to feel guilt and shame for not stopping his abuse the day before. I sat ragged with the urge to get up, scream at him, at the others, at myself. Then he dismissed us, and I walked back to the balcony outside the cafeteria.

I stood there, my morning coffee and cigarettes in my mouth as others streamed around with news.

"Dawson's leaving..." one spoke to me.

"What?"

"Today!"

"Today? Now? After reaming all of us out? We didn't do anything. Maybe that was the worst part of it. We did nothing to stop it."

"That's what he says! We didn't really participate, get involved... and he's vowing to never give another therapy course again."

A woman from the group walked toward us, her mouth opening and closing although none of us on the balcony could hear her. She continued talking as she approached close enough the words made sense even if her sounds acted as a wall around her, keeping us out.

"Stop it. Stop talking," I yelled at her.

She carried on, continuing and I watched as my arm reached out with my hand at the end of it and met with something of her flesh. The spout of blood that opened up at the side of her mouth told me where my palm had landed. Inside I registered relief.

Are we a contagion upon each other? I would prefer to remember that Dawson's violence from the day before had left some kind of trail, maybe like positrons, such that we all felt enabled around violent eruptions. Instead my own human failing gathered my arm, pushed it forward towards her. The sight of her blood shocked me and registers still as a kind of warning.

She dabbed at her mouth, her eyes filling with tears, then said, "It's alright," turned and walked away.

Just then I saw the woman from yesterday's mandala, her face flowered purple and blue. Her arms ran with the same colors, red, purple, blue, a bit of yellow as the bruises on her face.

I took a step toward her.

"Thank you. Thank you. You did this for all of us. I'm so, so sorry…" tears surprised me.

"No, no it was a great gift, a blessing. I've been in abusive relationships, tied to them, to repeating what…what you saw, all my life. No more! This has been a gift to me." Her eyes shone with a kind of triumph.

I did not understand her response, but I trusted it.

And now I had had an experience of trusting myself. I had not signed on for a mandala, despite what Dawson had encouraged. And I was certain I had been right not to sign on.

She melted into the cafeteria. I remained waiting on the balcony listening to the voices of other students around me. Some demanded Dawson be stopped. Some declared their emancipation from him and his dangerously bent teachings. Some stated their allegiance.

I didn't think Dawson was the authority. I believed she was.

Chapter Twenty

Jack's voice echoed in the nearly empty cafeteria, "I'm going across Mexico, to visit the ruins in Chi Chen Itza and Palenque. You're coming with me."

Exhaustion weighed on me as though I was wrapped in another, a second body. I knew I needed to go home, to Toronto. I also knew my parents would not help and I had no money without Jack.

"I could hitchhike out of Mexico," I pushed, hoping he'd fold.

Cathy, a fan of the idea of a cross Mexico car trip, chimed in, "You can't! That's too dangerous! You'll be killed!"

Jack said, "Do what you want. I'm going across Mexico and into Belize. I'll pay for you to come with me. But I'm not giving you money to go home or anywhere else."

Tears surged up, blood hammered below the surface of my face, but I wouldn't let go, wouldn't give him the satisfaction of knowing his power had depleted me.

I became one of five people who would drive in two cars the distance from Baja California to Belize.

Once more, I got into a car to travel with a man who made all the decisions. My daily mind, the person I believed I was, sat in that car as though present. Underneath, where I was unaware, simmered a bloody stew of memories, another time when I was in a car against my will. This body memory punched up against the ever-thinning will power to resist its eruption into conscious mind. What was unfelt tore at me just below the surface.

It was like two sides of a coin were wearing increasingly thin, threatening to collapse into each other. On one side my daily life activities, especially meditation retreat and now therapy, conspired to drive up everything I had no memory of including the horror of being held against my will. At the same time on the flip side of the coin, an instinct as powerful as breath worked to keep all the ugly truths from my conscious mind.

Yet without conscious memory in place I was not free to see how I had replicated the circumstances of being helpless, penniless and at the mercy of a man's decisions. I was as captive with Jack in this trip across Mexico as I had been with Al and Gary. The difference was I had forged the chains myself.

Nature, I believe, has designed a particular plan for us. We live into whatever we have not yet reconciled through consciousness. We are bound to the memories we do not access, bound to repeat a past we have not cleared. We manifest with startling precision the exact material circumstances we have not emotionally released and resolved. My unremembered experience compelled me in this present day and time into the space with Jack. My unrecalled rage and terror focused all-out assault against him.

"Hey, we can go..." he'd begin.

"Why? Why bother?" I'd respond, pleased to watch his face crumple to a glower of anger and disappointment. He wanted my approval even as it seemed he worked in every way to prevent me from giving it.

Another person offered, "What a great view," as we stood just outside Mexico City looking down across the vista.

"What? This and all the poverty you can handle."

I sat looking out at the world without registering it, mile after mile of tarmac beneath my body as my mind seethed with negativity. Only once in a moment of clarity, I thought, "Open yourself to what is happening. Be here." I opened my eyes, willed myself to take in what my eyes saw: a mountain of filthy garbage, wasted food festooned with flies, old clothes like flags of defeat, arms of chairs waving out at the sky as they slid under the sheer weight of all that waste and dirt, and two children picking hopefully among the ruins. Tears slid out and down my face. I returned my focus to the inner grey landscape of my own consistent despair.

We reached the eastern portion of Mexico. Jack's interest in the ruins peaked as he gushed excitedly on about going to see them, newly hatched from their centuries of green jungle growth, just a few buildings cleared at this time, the third week of December 1974.

Jack got us to the site of the ruins. I watched my companions walk with evident ease up the many steps of the pyramid at Chi Chen Itza, while I felt only the heaviness of my body. How did they do it? The energy and speed of my companions described another way in which I was wrong.

I looked up at the grey stone steps, so many steps. The sun beat mercilessly down, and I felt a fatigue like defeat. Did I try to climb? I heard the others encouraging me to make the ascent, their voices pulling against this enormous weight of my body, too heavy, far too heavy to make it. I gave up.

When we visited the Observation Tower at Palenque, my feet flew. I felt mysteriously energized, suddenly light in body, easily climbing the stone stairs. I climbed, then abruptly turned a ninety-degree angle, then again up and again turned. At each turn the view out of the glassless window filled my heart and mind, first a view of the surrounding green, the jungle and gradually, as the steps rose, the panorama of far fields.

I saw clearly, and in memory still do, the grey stones, carefully placed. I hear the same question: Who? Who placed these heavy weights so succinctly in a rising square? Part way up, having turned all four sides of that square once, twice, three times, I realized, *Today is December 21st. It is nearly noon. When it is noon, the sun will be shining directly through these little openings.*

If we live many lifetimes, it is possible our cells retain memories of those times. Like the code a monarch butterfly carries, a code that unfurls its patterned colors when the sun brings warmth, our DNA may hold information for our own unfolding based in memories of times past. When we stand on land where this history took place, does an echo unfurl, called forth by the land in the same way the sun calls forth the colors of the butterfly?

The Palace Tower was used for Observation, for Astronomy. Standing at the top surveying the bulges of buildings immersed in green jungle growth below, I almost laughed at recognition of my passion for star gazing.

We crossed back from Belize into Mexico, but not before paying off the border guards. Jack's rage at this almost got us thrown in jail as he fumed about not giving them what they demanded.

"Jack, if you don't pay, we'll all go to jail," I repeated what our travel companions had said. "It's only five dollars each…" I kept on in a reassuring voice, my own calm a seasoned response to danger. Gradually he settled down. He paid for us and we boarded the bus for Cancun, a town he had heard about and wanted to see.

It was the week between Christmas and New Year so every room in every hotel was booked. We sat in the deepening shadows at one end of the single main street, literally on a curb, out of options.

I looked away to the left, down toward the shore at the far end of the street, the golden sun streaming still upon a group of bronzed people, at ease, laughing together. I saw one tall, utterly beautiful young man, his salt blonde hair set above a classically sculpted body.

"Go and ask him. He knows where we can sleep," I said to Cathy.

"What? I can't just go up to him and ask, hey, do you have a place for us to sleep!"

"Yes, you can, and you will. He has a place for us to sleep at least for tonight and you will go and ask him..." I carried on until, flummoxed and sighing, she walked toward him.

She ran back and gasped, "He says he has a boat in the harbor, it's a yacht called the Sugar and it sleeps six and we can sleep there, at least overnight, he won't be using it tonight..."

That is how we met Ajax, the gorgeous green-eyed captain and owner of the Sugar who would sail us across the Gulf of Mexico to Key West. In my mind that meant home.

My first quick turn around the cabin, its tight galley and narrow walls had convinced me when he said the Sugar slept six, Ajax had meant six very small, very thin, very short people. I felt the air leave my chest and walked back on deck.

Jack had called dibs on the Captain's bed to allow for his over six-foot frame.

"Fine," I said, "you sleep there."

"Where are you going to sleep?"

"On shore, in the tent."

We'd been aboard for a few nights when Ajax hauled and stashed the first of many boxes of fuel oil. Then someone mentioned it was New Year's Eve.

"That right?" he looked around at our faces. "Well, all right then. You ready for an adventure?"

Ajax sailed us up the coast between the mainland and Cozumel Island. He seemed vague about the destination, but the beauty of the sunny day, the glorious color of the Caribbean water and the green living walls on either side of our tiny vessel buoyed our spirits.

Ajax easily slid from under one canvas sail to the next, so smoothly it seemed as though he was the gentle wind itself. Occasionally he yelled at Jack or Mick to pull on a rope more tightly, encouraging them to watch how that made the Sugar move.

I bathed in the sun, breathing the salt air, content to watch the shores on either side shift their green vegetation to rocky mouths of bays, then back again to walls of vines and green living things expressing profusely as they clung to high cliffs.

We even drank a little and that too made me happy.

"Are you all enjoying this sailing experience?" Ajax suddenly asked. "Better this than trying to get used to sailing by going out on the ocean side."

"But we're going on the ocean side to get to Key West, aren't we?" I asked.

Ajax just smiled and turned those eyes, luminous and colored like the sea, towards the shore. "I'm looking for something," he said in his enigmatic way, "I'm looking for it."

"What? What is it? Tell us, we'll help look…" we chorused like children.

"I'm looking…" he sang out softly, ignoring our pleas. His eyes grew to the shore, holding it like a rope our eyes then also gripped.

"That's it, at least I think…yes, that's it!" he stated suddenly confident. "Overboard!"

"What?" I asked as Jack dove in.

"How else," Ajax said to me kindly, "do you think we'll get ashore?"

I looked around. No tiny boat, no rubber dingy, no small rowboat snugly fit to the sides of our craft.

I rolled my skin-tight jeans up to the knees, tightened the knot in my green flowered bolero top and dove into the deep salt crystal water, weighing under and rising again, cutting waves across the calm surface as the sun scooped the horizon behind us.

At the cliff's edge Mick had already discovered a small ladder, almost completely covered with green vines, which led to a staircase on the cliff wall. Mick was an American whom Ajax had found in town and like a boy bringing a lost puppy home, had added him to our crew. Like the rest of us Mick too had no experience sailing.

As I gained the ladder and began to climb, I watched each of our crew disappear through a small door at the top of the cliff.

Then it was my turn.

A small number of mostly elderly people emerged into view. They spread across a large room, clearly a nightclub by the mirror ball lights, the defined dance floor and sitting areas.

To my left a band continued to play as one by one the patrons of the room turned to look at us. The four of us grabbed each other's hands and the hands of everyone still young enough to stand by themselves. We snaked around the room, concocting a dance, then lined ourselves up across the breadth of the space and began high leg kicks, at least, those of us who could.

One of my breasts popped out of the knotted top; I pushed it back in, looking swiftly around but besides one grey haired man whose eyes grew very merry watching this, no one else seemed to have noticed.

My glance around picked up the fleshy matrons, jewels rippling in the light from the disco ball, their wrinkled faces beginning to smile as their eyes looked wildly around as though searching for someone to grant permission. A few balding men sat; a few others joined in, ready to dance. We slammed our feet in time to the music, clapped our hands.

"You are Pirates!" came to my ears, so I nodded, grinning and said, "Ahoy!"

We carried on pulling everyone forward, whoo, hands up and back again, bending at the waist; everyone followed whatever move we did. From the corner of my eyes I watched as the band members glanced at each other.

The music stopped; we sat.

"Ah, great, you're here! We were really just saying how dull it all was and then you arrived…" an old woman with sparkling eyes, her flesh wrinkled like an old apple decorated with too many jewels on her neck, arms, fingers, said.

"Yes, thank you. Thank you! You too!" I replied as she had directed her comment at me.

She laughed, her hand at her throat, jewels sparkling, "Oh, no, of course, we're the audience…"

My eyebrows came together, I shot a glance at Jack who was listening in.

"Aren't you the entertainment?" she asked.

"Ah, no, not really."

"Well, what was all that about?"

I looked for help from Jack who clearly was not going to say anything and then at Cathy who looked at the floor, then I shrugged, "Just having fun, I guess…"

A drink later I felt way more drunk than I should have on only one, plus a few from the afternoon. I picked a fight with Jack who did not drink and wanted me to stop.

We climbed back out the little door just shy of midnight, down the cliff and into the water. I swam through the dark wet, seeing the black star splashed night all around, hearing "Midnight at the Oasis" in my head and feeling exactly like I was living in a commercial for good rum. That had been the highlight. Otherwise, for three weeks we had waited while Ajax kept disappearing every night, assuring us he had plenty of other places to sleep. Right after we firmed up plans for our gulf trip, he started disappearing in the daytime too until he was gone altogether for several days.

When he returned Jack and Mick tried talking to him, but all Ajax ever said in that calm, cheerful manner of his was the supplies weren't in yet, the supplies we had paid for.

"Nope. Not ready today. Not tomorrow either," he'd say happily when asked.

"Why not?" Jack tried.

"Just isn't time yet. Now…" When he saw Jack about to object, Ajax leveled his eyes at him and continued, "…if you want to find another way to Key West, that's fine by me. No hard feelings."

Jack and the others had already sunk too much money into these 'supplies' which we believed would be mostly food, maybe some alcohol for our lovely journey, to change plans now. We waited, through many anxious conversations about whether or not Ajax might be trusted, even as we put all our trust in him.

What I see now is how closely this experience with Ajax mirrored the larger one with Dawson. In both I put my life in the hands of a man who seemed unable to speak clearly and simply about what was going on. In both I rallied to the side of a group of others who also felt anxious about the leader. None of us were capable of putting a boundary in place. It seemed Ajax had us where he wanted us.

Finally, we left Cancun. We barely finished watching the straggling group of waving people shrink behind us as we sailed toward the grey curtain of clouds that now puckered the sky in front, when Ajax announced, "You will all take your turn at watch."

My time was midnight, so I descended into the hold to sleep. I was already seasick yet fell out of consciousness immediately. Mick came to get me for my turn at the wheel and as I climbed up out of the hold through the small hatch my eyes exploded with stars, stars, stars everywhere blue, white, large and dazzling, blinking against a perfect dark.

"Oh, my god," I uttered as he handed me the wheel.

"Yeah, pretty spectacular," he grinned.

"I must go down to the seas again/ to the lonely seas and tide," I began. "For the call of the sea is a wild call/ and cannot be denied/ And all I ask is a windy day/And the white clouds flying/And the flung spray and the blown spume/ And the seagulls…"

I'm not sure the seagulls ever cried, but the stars swung in a spiral whirling away in all directions as my head opened, and I passed out.

Voices floated clearly above me, then faces, two or three bobbing with furrowed eyebrows, stern mouth lines.

"Just can't walk…" I muttered, trying to make it better, to remain strong and independent, this latest falling just a tiny trick, over soon, nothing to worry about. Jack had to help me downstairs and onto the bed, where he covered me with a blanket then melted into the darkness sucking everything to its insides.

Everybody gathered deep in the hold, all around my bed. Or, Cathy was sick, vomiting into a pail, inches from my face, several feet away. She only showed up at the bottom of the tunnel through which things, some physical, reliable things shone for a moment, the pail, or her eyes before her face grew into the rim of that bucket, the stairs all at odds with themselves, before the tunnel turned over and everything split apart and faded to dark.

A voice said, "High fever." Either that or the dream spilled across the floor of the hold, its colors, red, dark brown, a putrid green, unable to keep the shapes from falling out everywhere and someone may get into trouble, all that mess.

Jack, leaning over me said something about water and drinking.

I shook my head sadly and muttered through the thick band of unrelenting pain where my throat used to be, "Can't swallow. Hurts." Passed out again.

Everyone was gone when I woke, so I slid my body out of the bed; I was giddy, suddenly feeling better.

My head popped out of the hatch, my mind ready for everybody to look at me, see my face and ask about how I felt, my tongue ready to say I felt a little better, although seasick. As my eyes caught up with the grey light, I saw the profile of each face grey, stricken and hooked on the horizon to my left. The humid air was a strange green color in bands, so I thought I might be still hallucinating. The ocean began to bulge upon itself rhythmically.

"Hi." No one responded. My eyes followed theirs to the three large, grey funnel shaped clouds dominating the eastern horizon. As if a director had clapped his hands, Ajax leapt from stillness to a frenzied action around the boat.

"What's that?" Mick pointed to a piece of wood floating a few feet off starboard.

"That's the rudder," Ajax voice betrayed no panic, but a shudder it seemed ran through the rest of us. "Now everyone who can, will bail! We have a hole in the bottom of the hull and will have to sail the rest of the way to Key West. Start bailing!"

Mick walked past me and smiled in a ghostly way, saying, "I sure am glad none of this is really happening or I'd be very scared." It made me laugh a little as I sank again beneath the deck.

Down in the gloom I heard the motor go off. Then the tiny craft gave a terrific tremble and keeled at a steep angle on her side. I knew this as death. The thought of water relentless in all directions, its cold, eerie claim entering first the room then my nose, choking as my throat filled…no! I realized I would pass out with fever before that happened. Grateful for the fever, I pulled out my Tibetan rosary, and began to say mantras but those exotic beings seemed distant and useless now.

Madam Sosostris from T.S. Eliot's Wasteland sauntered through with her line, "Fear death by Water." With sudden clarity and utter calm, I said out loud, "I never thought I would die by water." Or the thought ran through my mind, now so full of strange holes like mesh that what was happening ran through one hole, became something I not only thought about, but said or did or…

I prayed to the Christian God of my childhood, and to my friend Jesus. When I thought of his Mother, Mary, a surprising thrust of emotional pain wounded my chest. I saw my own mother's sorrow at losing me. To everyone else I said good-bye, David, Jack of course, my fellows on this boat. I gave them all intense prayers, but it was my mother's pain that saddened me. Then I accepted Death and passed out.

I would be told later our passage took three days, during which the others had no hope of rescue, but bailed the water continually out from the bottom of the boat and clung to whatever thought they had to make it ahead of the tornadoes bearing down on our tiny craft.

Jack's voice, "Come on. You have to see a doctor," his hand pulling my shoulder gently back and forth.

"I won't. Don't want doctor…want home…did we die? We didn't die, did I die?"

"No."

"Wheressss…everyone?" Words slid around my thickened throat.

"Everyone else is off the boat." He said it meaning everyone had leapt off that vessel at the first possible chance. "We're in Key West but can't officially dock until you've been seen by a doctor."

"Don't want a doctor. Tonsillitis, strep throat, get me home."

"You have to see a doctor or the rest of us have to stay here, on the boat." The intensity in his voice told me there was no other way out.

I tried and failed to sit up. Jack helped me stand and held me steady against the still rocking rhythms of my body swaying from side to side, a real drunken sailor.

Mick waiting on deck reached his arms down through the hatch to pull mine up, helping Jack get my weight out of the hold, on deck and then on land.

Jack's arm about my waist, my hands grabbing onto him since the lurching back and forth throwing me from side to side left my feet falling unsteadily at each step.

"Why'sit..'appening?" Words now slid as unreliably as my legs.

"It's the boat. We all went through it, but we've had a few more hours on land." It was early evening. The streets looked very clean. Soon we walked into the medical clinic.

The doctor, an aging, corpulent man whose face leered slightly from beneath his mustache and overly full lips, ignored me when I announced, "I have tonsillitis or strep throat. I need antibiotics and morphine."

He put a shot of penicillin in my bottom, gave me a container of antibiotics and a bottle of over the counter painkillers.

"I am in pain," I begged him, "real pain. I need something strong for it." He refused.

It took me many years to understand he had seen in me just another drug addict coming in from Mexico.

The hotel room Jack found was clean if simple, sparsely furnished, and cold to my body temp of 105. The bed with its clean white sheets looked like heaven.

Lying beside me, Jack insisted, "You'll be fine in a couple of days. When that happens, we'll bus overland to Canada."

"I've had this before…takes months…call my mother, please, please Jack, call my mother and tell her I'm sick, get me a plane ticket…"

How many days or nights chased each other through my dreams? Jack tried to get me any bit of food I mentioned; I tried to eat. He brought me any liquid he thought I might take in. The shot of penicillin had helped, but I did not gain strength nor did the fever leave completely.

Suddenly my eyes opened. The relentless ache in my back, the sharp swords in my throat had gone. I sat up easily and there at the foot of the bed sat my friends: three Native men. I knew them! They were there for me! One, with his back to me had a blanket draped across his shoulders. One to my left had a feather in his headband and a very, very white shirt on, over calf-colored animal skin pants. The man to the right filled more space than the other two, was less clear to me.

I crawled then floated, feeling totally well, better than I ever remembered, to the bed's edge as the man with his back to me turned with such a warm welcome I wanted nothing more than to stay with him.

They were seated on the dirt ground, around a small fire, rattles and ceremonial items spread about.

"Do you know what we are doing?" the man with the blanket asked. At the sound of his voice, this astral body of mine resonated with joy.

"I want to go with you, now," I shot the thought back to him, to the man whose welcome still bathed me. He laughed, repeated my words to the other men who also laughed so I believed for one precious uplifted moment I was to be allowed. They transferred thought energy together so quickly it was only a blur to me.

Then sorrow abruptly filled the warm space I'd been bathed in, as the man to my left addressed the others in a voice without sentiment, a voice of complete command, "No. She has to remain. She is not finished, has more to do..."

With an animal yowl I eclipsed back into my body. Pee, warm and smelly spread out around me.

Jack came back soon, or he was only outside the door, or had been in the room all along.

"Jack, I just saw three native men, sitting there..." I pointed to the bottom of the bed. "They were here for me, they knew me, I love them, I, I..." unstoppable tears rolled, "I wanted to go with them, but they said I couldn't, I..."

Jack was gently rolling my body over, stripping the bottom sheet of the bed, checking the top sheet to see if it was dry.

"Jack, call my mother, I need to go home, maybe I'm losing it, do you believe me?"

"I believe you. I don't think you're losing it," he said.

"Is there blood?"

Jack stopped suddenly. "What? You have your period?"

"No, no I was...back there, at the tent, I was peeing blood...is there any blood?"

Jack's face drained to white. "You were peeing blood and did not tell me?"

"What, take me to some Mexican doctor who wouldn't even know...Jack, I need to go home...please, please..."

"All right. You'll get your way. I'll call your mother right away."

Relief capsized my willpower and I collapsed against the bed. "Thank you," I whispered.

Ajax came to visit.

"You are really sick."

I nodded my head a little.

"Do you have everything you need? Is there anything I can bring you?"

"No, fine, thank you. Jack phoning home. I'm going home. I'll be fine now."

Ajax lay down beside my fevered body, stared into my bloodshot eyes, saying over and over, "Oh, you are so sick. I am so sorry," as though he'd had something to do with it.

He told me a brand-new catamaran with three very experienced sailors, a few hours behind us, had made it, but only barely. The crew had limped into Key West looking shaken and grey.

He stayed a while longer, then swung his legs off the bed, sat up and said, "If there is anything you need, let me know..."

I didn't ask why he had attempted the voyage during tornado season, with a crew of four unseasoned sailors, knowing the boat was barely sea worthy.

Since then I've wondered was this the material manifestation of my own consciousness, beleaguered with holes, barely skimming across dangerous tornado infested waters.

At that time, nothing else mattered: I was going home.

Chapter Twenty-One

I HAD LEFT AS A VISIONARY VAGRANT, a young woman who wore her inability to function culturally as a sign of superiority, someone whose exaggerated sense of confidence prevented others from touching her inner wounds. I now saw myself as fragile, a homesick waif who had made it across the Gulf despite tornadoes, disease and an unseaworthy vessel. Deep in the hold of that tiny boat I had believed I would die. I had closed my eyes and accepted my death. Then in the hotel in Key West I had crossed over to where time has no meaning. I had experienced the wholeness, the joy and contentment of being on the other side. But the laws of life and death must be fulfilled and I was sent back. Now my task was to live my life, this life I had been given with all its tatters and holes, my one and only life.

Vaguely the question of why I had put myself in such danger crossed my mind, but it was fleeting.

As I lay on the couch contemplating what the last few years had brought, I silently vowed to never be under another person's will again. I saw my struggle with Jack as one of power dynamics and I felt relief when we decided to part ways.

I was offered a job, to work as a part-time receptionist in a local medical clinic; I gratefully accepted. I walked to the door of the small, narrow building where I sat at the front desk, answered phones, retrieved patients' manila files and greeted those who arrived. From the woman who trained me I learned to laugh about little things in life.

My parents asked if I'd stay at our house in the city when they moved full time to the cottage. After the constant shifting and upheaval of the last years, I found the sweet simplicity of a job, and a nice place to live, the reliable repetitions of this small life a soothing balm.

I learned how to bake bread, make yogurt from scratch and embroider. I read Carl Jung's Treatise on the Hero and some of the work of his first disciple, Marie Louise Von Franz. All my readings did not provide the insight that came with later years: during this period of happy domesticity I uncovered and lived out my shadow, everything gypsy me had held in contempt.

I meditated daily, including prostrations, walked frequently down the steep green ravine across from my house to the loud, busy Queen St., heart of the Beach. There I had chiropractic sessions by another Dawson student, who with his wife began to host a weekly evening group meditation. I accepted his invitation to join. Soon another group started, doing the same Western Mysteries based meditation, on another evening and I joined this group as well.

Cecilie came to visit from the other side of the city, lugging a large number of poetry books all the way on the subway and bus connection necessary. Sitting in that small kitchen our voices ringing with the surprise and delight of reading out loud to each other remains a memory of great love.

David accepted my offer to come and have dinner. I cooked for him before he left for his gig, guitar as always at his side. He came back another night for a massage and with my hands on his body we returned to that one deep place together, our bodies curled like twin seashells washed in the waters of an ancient insistent tide.

When he had to leave, our kisses at the door had him turning back many times. When I closed the door at last, I stood in the center of the living room, the trucks and cars vibrating the floor slightly, and thought, *what am I doing? I don't want any of this Dawson stuff, this meditating. All I want, all I've ever wanted is David. I'm leaving the rest of this stuff and going back to him.* Pleasure flushed through me.

Instantly a large, grey, clammy cone shape, narrow at the top, descended around me, holding me as tightly as David's embrace had moments before.

"You have not done the work yet," came a voice followed by an ocean of my tears. I knew from the sensation in my body I had no choice. I had to leave David, again.

This vision commanded my actions but did not stop my stubborn heart. In the early 1990's, after much healing and even more practice in meditation, I came back to David, finding him in the downtown bar that had become his second home. We began again but he was often on the road, in distant places and even when he wasn't, he refused to communicate, no texts, emails, phone calls, except in person on the nights I showed up, eager to wait and listen, eager for his touch.

Then like a light flashing on inside me, I asked myself what I was doing. I had carried the energy of him in my daily life for over thirty years by that time. I realized I did not have to continue. Mentally I built a dark blue sphere around myself, rimmed it with an impenetrable substance for a shell and meditated inside it. When a thought of him rose in me I'd distract myself with tasks around my home, or with singing, dancing or walking, purposely putting him out of my mind. Within days I felt better, lighter than I'd felt since he first walked into that restaurant so many years ago. I wondered if this was my energy, just mine, when I did not carry or connect with him.

This continued for a few weeks. Then his name popped up in my email. My fingers hesitated, then dropped to open the message. No salutation, just a single sentence: "If I ask nicely will you let me back in?"

In one sentence he captured exactly what I had done and how

he had felt about it although we had not spoken, and he was at that time half a planet away. He taught me in this one sentence about telepathic communication. Shortly after his return to North America I left him finally, because he could not be true. Left him but have kept the jewel of information he offered: telepathy exists. It is real.

Two of the facilitators from the Mexico therapy began a Wednesday evening mandala group. It was held in the back rooms of the office of Dr. Tom Varnay. Dr. Varnay's fascination with womb and birth led him to write a book titled *The Secret Life of the Unborn Child*. He had nothing to do with our sessions but graciously opened his space for our explorations.

"I want to know there will be no violence like in Mexico," I began with the woman facilitator. She agreed. I made myself the silent promise that if any violence did begin, I'd respond very differently.

We quickly became the Mandala Group, those initiates committed to weekly engagements in the fearsome and challenging work of mandala therapy. The closeness of our quickly knit group identity made it impossible for me to refuse when several members invited me to join them on a trip to Norway in the summer with Dawson.

Dawson! He was still the Hurdy-Gurdy man, Magician and the Fool, the Mystic Master and Visionary. I had gained in his presence access to an experience of life so immediate, so fresh and vital the world itself seemed to come alive. And for that, I willingly entered the possibility of his mockery. His ridicule would burn away what was most corrupt in me. Or so I perceived at the time.

Through insight made famous forever by Alan Ginsberg's poem "Howl", Kerouac's novel *On the Road,* Bob Dylan's song "Mr Tambourine Man", I glimpsed Dawson as living a freedom I envied—impervious to the dictates of money, in command of his life, his vision, his sense of purpose here.

The men of the group so wanted to be him they took to growing moustaches like his, wearing a beanie-toque as he did, sporting dark rimmed, very thick lensed glasses, and whenever possible strolling with their hands behind their backs. It seemed they believed imitation a valid road to an improved state of consciousness.

Whatever failings began to seep through the threads of his presence, whatever questions from the dubious and violent therapy in Mexico, another summer in Toronto paled in comparison. Ready to try exploring the planet again, this time going north close to the Arctic Circle beat staying in the hot mugginess of another Toronto summer.

But first, I had to have my own mandala. I had waited as long as possible and when I might not put it off any more approached the center of that darkened room.

I spoke to the woman counselor, "You are my Positive Mother. You know what is in my heart, but I can't find you. I don't know where you are most of the time." She bent her head and stared at the floor.

I turned to the sandy haired PhD, the one whose belt and fists had done such terrifying things in Mexico. "You are my Positive Father. Again, I don't know much about you. You read the newspaper, you read books." He began to mimic opening and settling in to read a paper.

"You," I said to a woman I had chosen from the ring of people surrounding the center, "are my Negative Mother. It doesn't matter what I do, what I say, you constantly criticize. You are unhappy, negative and nagging at everything I even attempt."

"So why are you telling me this in that tone of voice?" she started, her role leaping from her spontaneously. I shrank.

I turned to the other man. "You are my Negative Father. You ignore when she," I pointed to Negative Mother, "beats me. You ignore her negativity, her criticism. You spend your whole time vying for her favor, her attention." Right away he began to walk toward Negative Mother, who stood haranguing me. He linked arms with her and together they began to walk around the center. It had barely started, and I was already overwhelmed.

"Wait, listen to me..." my voice fell in vain.

"No, wait," I tried to take the hand of Negative Mother who turned on me in rage and began flailing at me with her arms. Her efforts were mostly symbolic, without the thrust of real flesh contact. Besides she was not as strong or tall as I was, so this quickly dissipated.

"No, I want your help. Yours and his..." I pointed to Negative Father.

"Oh yeah, SHE wants help," a voice from the Unconscious began.

"Yeah, just like her, all about her...me, me, me..." taunted another.

"As if she had ever done anything deserving..." the anonymous voices carried the mirror image of my internal states, the dialogues I prostrated, meditated and cleaned house to avoid. With their insults came the tsunami of shame I fought to keep back.

The Unconscious gathered energy and strength, finally spilling over, everyone walking everywhere all around the square, everyone talking at once, demonstrating the chaos of my inner world.

Someone whispered, and I caught it, "What about Positive Mother?"

Desperate my eyes wildly scanned the room. Positive Mother! There she sat, silent, in a dark corner. I strode over, knelt in front of her and wept, "Please tell me what to do. It's all making no sense, look at it and I can't...I can't..." hot tears poured down my cheeks, sweat pooled across my body.

She looked up then, gently taking a strand of my now wild hair, putting it behind my ear, and said softly, "Why don't you ask your Positive Father?"

"He's not there. He won't listen, I don't...I don't know how..." I wailed, harsh sobs racking a lifetime of confusion out of my body.

"Just go to him," she insisted so gently, "and ask him nicely if he will help you."

I stood up, the sobs stopped for now, and walked slowly over to Positive Father. In response, the Unconscious, all of them, sat back in their places, and stopped talking.

As I approached, he stood up, and when I was in front of him, he just looked at me, neither of us smiling.

"Ohhh, loooook, she wants DADDY!" a voice from the Unconscious erupted.

"Yeah, does she ever," the slime in the sounds slid around the room.

I was certain, however. I did not want Daddy sexually. That wasn't it. But then, what was it?

I just kept looking, waiting for a signal, a word, anything from this Positive Male. After a few moments, he reached out his palm and put it softly on my hair, then, as my chin quavered, and tears slid down, he scooped me up in his arms, and carrying me, laid me down gently on one of the mats. Then he stroked my hair, as though I really was the beloved child, the loved and wanted one.

When we sat again in a circle, I remained soft. My long hair fell in waves and my dark rimmed glasses stayed off my face. A man from across the circle blurted out, "Why, without your glasses you are almost pretty! Why do you wear them? Why not get different ones?"

"They are camouflage."

On the streetcar going home, I began to review the evening. As soon as I started my body began to shake, and I knew what had been opened had to be closed again. I put it away, pushing all thoughts of it out of my conscious mind.

Meditation, star groups, embroidering to classical music, cleaning my home, working part time—my life was settled and increasingly calm, but not for long. By the end of June, I boarded a plane for Norway and whatever adventures lay in wait.

MY SINGLE ROOM IN NORWAY lay snug inside the one-story

Chapter Twenty-Two

building used by Norwegians as a place to train their teachers. I had my own heater, a small desk and a single bed with clean sheets. Down the hall was an indoor bathroom with real porcelain.

I sat in the straight backed, blue padded chair, a circular embroidery hoop clasping the off-white cotton where reds, blues, deep green threads emerged from the silver needle I pushed in and out. My gaze wandered out the window, looking across the dark purples, deep reds, vibrant oranges and yellows of the Norwegian countryside in the clean, clear after-rain air of late summer. Dark grey clouds layered the sky, then suddenly the sun punctuated those clouds throwing streaks of light across the land.

My feet felt almost warm in the knee socks I had put on against the continual damp. The electric heater snapped on with a click; I relaxed again in delight at modern conveniences and gave thanks I was no longer in the Farmer's Field. It had been just that, a seeping wet mound of dirt and grass, a meadow of thistles, and our destination up and down, back and forth along the arduous Norwegian coast. I had believed that once we attained this much storied Farmer's Field, we'd engage in daily classes and exercises, but Dawson's classes had stopped quickly and as suddenly as they had begun.

We'd arrived in Europe six weeks earlier, touching down in Amsterdam, a city my friend and traveling companion, Jake, wanted to explore. Jake had been part of the mandala group and instrumental in persuading me to come. Together we wandered Amsterdam that first day, took a canal ride, lingered over the art in the Van Gogh museum and walked the small interesting streets.

Meanwhile several others from the Group had bussed directly from the airport to Paris, to pick up and drive back to us the new Citroens that would carry us along Norway's famous fjords. Vaguely the recognition grew in me that someone had done this. Someone had arranged all this, the details of cars and planes, hotels where we gathered, destinations and rendezvous points. It was a fleeting thought. My brain still registered very little outside my immediate experience. That experience included items like the cars we needed rising on schedule and disappearing again, mysteriously and without effort on my part.

From Amsterdam we had driven north to Copenhagen, where I sat with Cecilie in the beautiful clean square of its downtown, sipping coffee. I fell into a mild reverie about the women, some my age, who strolled around on their lunch break. I imagined they had houses, partners, steady lives full of cozy rhythms, reliable repetition.

Cecilie watched me out of the corner of her blue eyes. "Yeah, you know, I used to cry when I was hitchhiking on the highway. Why couldn't I just be like them?" She nodded toward the women. "How many of them do you think have ever written a poem?"

As recently as a few weeks before, her response would have settled me but now raised a more difficult query. Why did I believe being a poet meant living without what I longed for? Why did longing for those things, the rhythms, cleanliness, porcelain of an orderly life make me feel such shame? Was that life of regularity anti-poetry or anti-spiritual? Dawson regaled us frequently about the truth of impermanence, how all material items, all status in the world rise and fall away again. Therefore, the best attitude is one of non-clinging. I had translated this to mean the most evolved life was that of an impoverished gypsy traveling around after him, even as I began to see he lived and traveled everywhere in comfort and often luxury.

In our first class in a campground in southern Norway, Dawson had asked, "Who has looked at a map of the coast of Norway?"

Jake had, so he raised his hand. Dawson nodded. Jake began to speak, "The road winds up north in a...a torturous fashion..."

"Oh, now we've heard from you, that it's TORTUROUS!" The room exploded with laughter, Jake's face glowed red and inside I saw red.

We all knew the risk. Answer Dawson's question, speak a thought, offer an idea, and his icy, withering contempt might be the result. His flashing words and cutting mind created a wide swath around him, a moat few dared cross. Everyone acted as though they believed Dawson's ferocious mind was the embodiment of an extraordinary compassion manifesting in wrath. So intent were they on developing this same compassion, they rigorously practiced these same tactics on each other.

The open space in which we had gathered for this first talk seemed to fill with their ridicule. Jake's humiliation shaded his cheeks pink and drew faint spots of water to his eyes. I glanced at Dawson, one hand leaning heavily on his knee, a smirk dancing across his mouth and wondered why we sided with him against each other.

In Toronto when I had queried Dawson about the theme of this trip, he'd responded with one word, "Movement." My head had lit with ideas of learning about how to move the body to maximize healing. I imagined I would learn how to flex my muscles, stretch, breathe in such a way that increased healing would follow naturally.

Now in Norway every morning we collapsed our tents, stove our clothes, boots, extra pillows, sleeping bags, toiletries, books, journals and pens, flashlights, pots, dishes, dish cloths, and cooking burners inside the disappearing emptiness of the tiny cars. Then we drove, hoping to catch a coffee on the way.

Having made the effort to get there, sometimes morning class was as meagre as "Meet us later today at such and such a place."

Then every night we met, pitched camp, dislodged all necessary items from the car's boot, gulped a fast dinner and appeared for class.

Dawson's sporadic classes focused on non-clinging, on keeping our minds in the present moment, on Emptiness and its Sanskrit translation, *Sunyata*. To help us understand what the Sanskrit meant, he spoke of impermanence, about which he intoned "Nothing lasts, even your worst fears, worst traumas or nightmares. You should be celebrating! This, this is your liberation!" Then his tone turned, "You people! Clinging to your ideas, your ways of being, the very ways that chain you! You are stuck in useless, habituated cycles of thought, stuck in the past, when it is a dance with ghosts, with mere shadows, with Nothing!"

One evening class took place on a grey brown piece of earth, ringed by bushes, barely large enough for the few of us determined to brave the millions of tiny insects in the late dusk of the midnight sun. Dawson's face was all but concealed behind the mosquito netting falling from his Tilly hat, his sonorous voice inciting mantras encouraging us to experience the various insects, no see-ums, and gnats as without meaning, without intent, empty.

What I experienced in my head were visions of destruction. I'd bring death to all of them— insects, fields, roving, the gypsy life, teachers and students! I'd create emptiness, all right, by destroying all of it! Hatred, rage and a passionate negativity flooded through my head, the only place I ever felt anything. Then, suddenly, my mind went still.

The buzzing outside my head from those little insects no longer bothered. As I held focus, I realized none of the insects were landing on my exposed face. I saw this as a minor miracle and attributed it to Dawson. Surely, he created such extraordinary events as this!

Increasingly as we inched ever northward, switching back and forth along the edgy Norwegian coast, it was wet. And damp. Wet, damp and very cool. I had already gained a point of no return, living in damp clothes, sleeping in a bag that never had the chance to take advantage of what meagre sun there was, before we hit the Farmer's Field.

By the time Jake and I arrived, our compadres of stout heart had already erected a large white tent and inside had laid a carpet at the far end that Dawson's feet might land on something other than the ground where the rest of us sat.

We had challenged ourselves to get here, challenged ourselves in the driving and daily ups and downs of tents, of switchback roads, of gas and coffees, of miles and miles of driving, we had proven our devotion and dedication, had put ourselves on the line. Now surely, he would teach us some of the secrets of living and living well!

But what I heard fall from his mouth was like sharp pins on open wounds. "You students, you think you are..." he mimed us, batting our eyes at him, fawning creatures. "You know, I have a new word: Stew Dent. That's for you all. Stew because you are in a stew and Dent because you are all Dented." The male attendants ever present to his right and left, chuckled, their shoulders shoving up and down as they showed solidarity with his humor. And most of those in the tent also laughed.

I had stopped laughing somewhere along those Norwegian fjords. I heard what I heard but could not believe I was hearing it. He was sneering at us, insulting and deriding us. This shaming fest with him as the master of ceremonies in lieu of any real teaching fell all around. Yet everyone else seemed to accept what I increasingly saw as his contempt. They seemed to accept it, even called it "teaching."

At the end of one class, he performed what he often performed at the end of a Wong, the dispelling of gathered energy. He did this by snapping fingers of both hands while saying the Tibetan syllables, "Benzra Mu" which, he told us, was the way to dissolve energies so they do not linger.

"I hear," he said with a straight face, "You have no place for, you know, uhm...and..." he leaned toward one of his attendants, "You have assured me porta-potties are due to arrive today, or..." the attendant vigorously nodded.

"Yes, well in the meanwhile you must take advantage of the bushes, the trees farther back and just... Benzra Mu!" He exploded the syllables and the people in the tent collapsed with laughter. Except me. What I understood was we still didn't have even the most ordinary needs met.

The next day and the next, until every day I heard him berate and belittle us. And I heard a truth I'd never heard before, when Dawson said, "If the Lama could Liberate you, do you not think he would wave a magic wand and do it? Yes, he would. But no one can liberate you, only YOU! Get on with it!" I registered his honesty, even as it snagged an unwelcome question: if this was true what was I doing following him around?

Between his ridicule and his open declaration he could not affect the change I wanted, I slowly started to see things differently. A group were gathering to try to construct a yurt, because Dawson had said he wanted one. Here, in Norway, minus proper tools, instruction manuals, their hearts beat strong to try to create for him, their teacher. When the "opportunity" as it was called came to me, I refused to volunteer. He had insulted, denigrated, laid contempt upon us and now these people wanted to create something for him?

It came as no surprise when I heard how he had walked up to and unloaded upon them, going on about their stupidity and short sightedness, their inabilities and lack of skills. His actions and words were no surprise, but I felt stronger within myself. I had decided against the grain of many, and it had worked for me.

Chapter Twenty-Three

I ROLLED OVER, HUNCHING MY SHOULDERS under the A-frame of the pup tent. *Should have,* I scolded myself for the one hundredth time, *should have bought a larger tent, a one-man tent even, just the next size up.* But that would have meant all of me stood in the store, all of me including my ability to think, to plan, to look ahead, standing together in that store making decisions. Instead I had teeter-tottered, like a child in woman's stilettos, only a single point touching the earth, because more contact would mean being present.

Pulling the sides of my body away from the sides of the tent to prevent leaks, a memory leaked instead.

"It's all right, kids, here..." my father leans into the space above my head, "I'll just hang some of your underwear in the holes where the rain's coming in and then, see, just roll over, go to sleep but don't touch the sides of the tent. It's canvas," my father warmed to his subject, his intelligence racing in front of our faces all turned to his, all of us listening, "and it leaks if you touch it."

"If you touch it even with just your finger," I ask.

"Yeah, so STAY AWAY from it!" This is Dad's ragged voice, the one that demands I pay attention to his words, even when this means ignoring what my body is experiencing. I grow more and more able to believe his words, words about our family being normal and happy, words about how much Mom loves us and how she is a good woman and now, words about the rain, the tent, words that make me lie against my body.

Soon every window of the leaking, flimsy structure held dirty underwear in its strings, the small strings that if you pulled, opened the flap so the air came in. Except the air and the rain had come in with no pull on the strings and water was dripping down, water sieved from the torrential, non-stop storm that had thundered its way over us for the past two days. The dirty, now sodden underwear hung limply at each of the several small windows, flags of defeat.

My mother's face was a flag too, but pink and white mottled with rage until my father's look, dark as the clouds outside, his index finger in the air, emphasized his frighteningly even tone of voice, "Don't. Say. A. Word." Each syllable was clearly punctuated by a period, full stop.

Yeah, again, images of My Tragic Childhood, the thought yanked me back, a cynicism that had begun working to keep me present some of the time.

I carefully put on a few layers of clothes, loath to leave the small warmth of the ones I had worn in the sleeping bag. The bag had been borrowed and had an odd smell like gasoline and new plastic rising from its ground side, the rubberized side meant to protect from wet. It meant to protect but mostly resulted in a loud crinkling sound every time I moved since the rubber was very cheap.

I stood up outside, breathing in the damp July air. Around the field our group pattered and chatted, small bonfires beckoning with the scent of tea brewing. It appeared like I imagined a medieval battlefield would, small tents ringing the large tent where the best Warrior, the leader sat. Suddenly as though of one mind people streamed in from all sides lining up in front of that large tent in the center of the field.

I crawled back into the pup tent's tiny space, leaving my booted feet outside as I reached for my mala.

It doesn't do any good, the thought rang inside my head, but habit took over and I opened the circle of beads, slung it round my neck, stood up again and strode with purpose toward the morning's class.

I sat at the back. I sat at the back of that space because I was among the last to reach the door. I was among the last to reach the door because I felt determined to stay present, awake, to stay clear of his hypnotism. What he did felt like a mind lock that he purposely put on everyone. I was determined to laugh if I felt like it, smile when something pleased me, and ride my own derisive anger, my constant companion these days. With all this inner activity going on, I felt the need to be as far away from Dawson as possible.

I do not recall the specifics of this class until he said, "...a bridge, built in silence entirely, no hammers, no nails." Silence rang through that tent louder than a steeple bell, a silence no one dared question.

I put my hand up; he nodded ever so slightly. My body filled with contempt at him for this boon, but I asked in a mild voice, "How?"

He looked confused for a split second, as though rudely woken from a pleasant dream.

"How, Sir, how did they build a bridge in complete silence?"

The stillness of moments before collapsed upon his screeching voice. My vision tunneled down to his extended arm, finger wagging at me, his face drawn together so eyes, eyebrows, mouth all held the same lines of rage, his mouth foaming words meant to excoriate my question and me.

"You..." he spluttered, "Do you know what you are? A Doubting Thomas! That's you!"

Heads swiveled to watch this newly named monstrosity, a Doubting Thomas.

"Why, I have met masters who would make this," he snapped the index finger and thumb of one hand, "of you and your questions. You, you think you have..." and he was off, showing me his thumb as a Yod, from the Tarot. He screeched this at me and asked did I have any idea what I was asking and on and on.

As the minutes snailed by, heads turned, from one side of the room then the other, as though they expected to see my face melting, my body flayed alive, as though that was what they wanted. I sat, aware I had done nothing, except not fall under his sway. I had asked a simple question and he had come undone.

He had answered my question though. He had held up his hand, the thumb extended almost horizontally and yelled and screeched about the Yod from the Kabbalah, the same that appears as flames on the tarot card, The Tower.

The bridge is internal, the building blocks aligning with meridians in the body, including the right thumb. He had indicated the answer throughout his rant. Why? Why respond with such rage?

Why not? If he was the master of consciousness, he mirrored what I was in those moments, and despite the calm clarity of my question, I was in a state of rage. Attempting to mask it with a soft voice did not put Dawson off. He responded directly. He engaged with me at any level, excluding none and thereby widened the walls of that well, that hell in which I usually dwelled totally alone. He was willing.

Was this wrathful compassion? Or just a man too insecure to let anyone else stand tall in a tent built for him?

Then it was over. He dismissed the class early and I walked away slowly, the others cutting a wide swath around me, today's untouchable, as they headed for their friends, their fires, their comfort.

One woman spoke to me, burbling on about what great teaching he had given me, what clues he had left, did I know that a Yod was from the Kabbalah, did I understand Tarot, "he has given you a shaft of the secret teachings from the Western Mysteries," she uttered breathlessly.

I have been giving Tarot readings from the first time a pack hit my hands, giving readings while the lines from Plath's great poem, Daddy, strode through my head, "/with my Tarot pack/my Tarot pack". These words blended themselves with ones from T.S. Eliot's Wasteland, "I well may be a bit of a Fool". The Fool, my burbling friend had exclaimed, was what he had given me in teachings.

Jake had a fire going, offered me a cup of tea with the water he'd boiled for his own coffee.

"I'm just so angry, all the time," I confessed, feeling dirty and shameful.

Jake's blue eyes shot up at me over the rim of his cup. "Keep that animus going, Charlene."

His words felt like an open door after prison. Animus! The Jungian word. Was that what this was? Jake's words assured me I was growing, and these were the growing pains. His certainty brought me the first peace I'd had for a long time, even while rage still ran in my blood.

One of Dawson's minions sat as head of the next class.

"The Teacher is leaving, as we speak. He is almost packed and will be gone this afternoon."

While others gathered to make plans for the next step, I felt completely confused. He had left? In the middle of a course? Because he had stomach pains? He was heading south to the warm weather, following the sun where he'd see a doctor? All of this shook my faith and beliefs about him, about enlightenment, about everything I had assumed.

Cecilie and my brother were on this Norway excursion as well. Now, others had determined on two courses of action: one group would go north, to Finland and the Laplanders; the other group would head a bit south, to a Norwegian Teacher Training facility where it was rumored electric heaters and warm water as well as proper walls and porcelain existed.

Cecilie tried to excite me about more travel.

"Think of it! North to the Laplanders! Where they herd reindeer!"

"Think of it! Porcelain! Indoor plumbing! Maybe even modern heat!"

"You may never get this chance again… Don't you want to see the Laplanders drink blood?"

"Drink blood?" I pulled this thought inside, turned it over a few times, but no resonance, no sensation responded to it. When I thought of the words, "Teacher Training Facility" before the last word was completed warmth spread from my core. I knew where I would go.

Sitting in my single room in the Teacher Training Facility now, this silver needle pushing in and out of the cotton, pulling green, gold, pink, while the clouds outside scrabbled like underwater creatures across the sky, their shadows taking the sun, then giving it back again, thoughts rose and fell.

Dawson is awakened, enlightened. Dawson had left us and Norway, abandoned a course because he had trouble with his stomach. He had illness. What did that mean?

In my naivety and bathed in the stupendous vital aura Dawson constantly gave out, Enlightenment had meant no suffering. None. A state of deathless enchantment. A fairy tale, clearly.

I recalibrated. What is Enlightenment? What is it to be Awakened, if not that joyous compendium of no suffering ever, no illness, no pain?

Beatrice Raff, aka Chorpel, a short, squat German woman now organized us into a Teacher Training experience. She had us in classes led by those who had something to teach, attended at first by anyone interested, then increasingly under Chorpel's indomitable will, regardless of interest.

After three weeks at the Teacher Training Institute, we had to leave. Cars were assigned and at the bottom of the list the lot fell to two unlucky English people to have me ride with them. One of these passengers worked for the BBC and the other, a man, was a trained pianist, someone who had studied under Olivier Messiaen. The driver, a long-haired man in his forties wore beads and blue jeans. We were instant friends.

Down through the pink, caribou spotted fields of Sweden we drove through the ripe blossoming wild blueberry patches where we plucked and ate our fill, the driver and I sitting comfortably close to each other, while the other two sat every day in the stuffy and cramped back seat. Intent on making the rendezvous with the entire group in north Denmark by the set date, we drove for hours daily.

I sang. With the driver's encouragement and into the increasing discomfort of the two in the back seat, I sang all the hippie folk songs I knew. Over and over.

My rage had not abated. This time it targeted the two English people as supercilious, stuck up and arrogant. If I had been able to sort through my feelings honestly, I would have discovered this feeling of never being good enough. Without drink or drugs to mask my inner state, I resorted to snide comments, obnoxious behavior and petulance.

The first night out of the car we struck our tents in a dark field in Denmark and someone pulled out a guitar. We circled around a small campfire and sang. It was the first feeling of happiness I had experienced on this trip.

Storming across the dark and onto our tiny circle of peaceful joy, Tony, Dawson's first in command came yelling, "What do you think you are doing? How selfish are you? It's after midnight and I have to get up and do prayers and meditation in the early morning and that is what you all should be doing too! Stop this now!"

I did not sleep that night, the anger roiling back and forth brighter than any midnight sun. What had we done? Enjoy ourselves. What was he doing, acting like he was in charge with Dawson gone? And we were experiencing happiness, which is supposed to be what all this is for, isn't it? What was Tony doing and for that matter what was Dawson doing…until finally the rage cut clean to the bone. What was I doing?

I never felt stronger than when I was walking away. Did the unconscious memory of having my legs threatened those eight years past in northern Ontario, push its way into this world, now?

In the second cabin we broke into, Al and Gary had decided they would search for a boat. We were on the lip of Lake Superior.

"It's September," I argued, "Most people will have stored their boats by now."

Al's eyes flared, his lips flapping, "Shut up! You shut up!" He put his face next to mine, saying, "We're going to find a boat. Shut your fucking negativity up. Both me and Gary are going."

He stood up and backed toward Gary. "And we're leaving you this rifle, in case bears come. Bears or…"

"Other humans…" Gary concluded.

"I won't be able to kill anyone," I protested.

Gary again, "You probably won't have to, Charlie. Just have the rifle in case."

It leaned against the front wall, at once a threat and a friend.

"The main highway is twelve miles in that direction." Al smiled, "If you run for it…"

"I know, you'll come after me and kill me…"

"No, no we won't kill you. We're not murderers. We'll shoot the legs out from under you and let the animals kill you. They'll come and eat you, slowly, one piece at a time, Charlie. Would you like that?"

The dream from my childhood suddenly filled my inner vision. The dream brought the image of me pulling myself up and away from the walls of the slimy, creepy green valley floor, up and up until I broke through at the top. There my arms clung to the top as I hoisted the rest of my body over the rim toward what I felt was safety. As I pulled my body up, I saw the bloody stumps…all that remained of my once straight, strong girl legs.

"I won't move, Al." And I sat in one place, my body perfectly still for all the unnumbered hours they were gone.

Here in Denmark I did not have this memory, but wonder now if it pushed from below, reducing me to believing I was making a decision when in fact my history was emerging. Leaving the group felt like an enormous relief. I cajoled a young woman into hitchhiking with me and together we set out.

One memory of our travels together involves a moment just outside of Brussels. We are hitchhiking and very soon a car screeches to the shoulder. We walk over and in the Belgium sunshine I count four men, two in the front seat and two in the back. They do not look like kind people.

"I'm not getting in that car," I tell my friend.

"But we have to! They have stopped for us!"

"I don't care. I'm not getting in that car." She continues to argue with me until I walk away from the car and her, saying "You may get in, although I advise against it. But no way am I getting into a car with four men. We are outnumbered!"

What I did not know was the memory from my body that had pushed up and spilled into this moment: I had once before gotten into a car with two men, been outnumbered. The result had been traumatic. This time, I just listened to myself, despite how my friend believed I was just being difficult. I let myself be, difficult or otherwise.

We did get other rides but along the way my friend decided she wanted to go to France to a commune she knew of there. When I recognized she was leaving me, I bullied her in an ugly way.

She left and I carried on to the north of Spain, where I imagined warm sunshine waited for me. The clouds remained every day, but a young Spanish man I met wanted to marry me. I was considering this when one night I dreamed of an Angel with a fiery sword who said, "If you marry him you will not write the book." I believed she meant a book Cecilie and I would write together.

In my day mind as I considered his proposition, I imagined a small, crowded apartment with pasta hanging down, and diapers and kids everywhere. I left Spain to rejoin the group in Italy.

The field was small, the tent the same as in Norway, but the late August sun here in southern climes still warmed us.

Dawson was sitting, and I was nearby at his feet when he began to talk about communication. It was as though a light switched on inside me; he saw it in my eyes and explained, "All communication comes from the heart. That's why in some ceremonies the Teacher's beads are at his heart, and the student holds the other end of those beads at his mouth. All real communication is from the heart." Then he pulled his mala out and put it to his heart as each of us in turn knelt before him taking the other end of his mala and putting it to our lips. To me, this was worth everything.

Everyone shifted cars and passengers. My brother and Cecilie decided I'd go with them through the French Alps to Amsterdam and our plane home. Somewhere from those Alps comes this memory: deep pine woods rose on steep cliffs as the road wound higher and higher. Suddenly we came upon a structure, the first for miles, a small wooden building that served as signal post, a beacon to travelers, coffee dispensary, post office. Surrounded by the tall pine trees it looked like something from a fairy tale.

I followed Cecilie inside and was stunned immediately by the presence of a young woman in her teens. Worn ragged army boots held her feet. Her bare legs stuck out beneath a brightly colored skirt that flared over a dirty white crinoline, so stiff it almost paralleled the floor. Her jet-black hair hung straight down all around her shoulders like an extra shawl on top of her dirty white blouse and from her pale face pierced black eyes, their irises holding my gaze in a vise.

Cecilie sidled up to me, put her arm around my shoulders, and turned me toward a wall saying, "Don't stare back. She is gypsy. Staring will lead to violence. We need to get out of here. In a moment look casually at the other side of the room."

Cecilie moved to collect our coffees and my eyes flitted across the small room to a large man. A knife rose to my eyes, clearly visible from one of his black boots. Dirty black jeans covered his lower half while a soiled white shirt, whose sleeves ballooned way over his wrists, sagged about his waist. Thick eyebrows hung across his face and fat lips drooped over his chin. Nothing about him suggested compromise.

We left quickly, tittering for many kilometers about our encounter with real gypsies. Within a few hours Cecilie realized she did not have her purse. The purse held notes, including mine, notes she had collected from many of us to create a book about Dawson and his teaching. Her purse and the notes were nowhere in the car. Nowhere except the last place where the gypsies haunted.

She was devastated, had to go to everyone and apologize for having lost their notes. Many people suggested to her she was learning impermanence and non-clinging, a main theme of this trip. She just rolled her blue eyes and said, "But your notes…"

We returned the cars to Paris and the factory before heading for Amsterdam where my brother had booked a hotel for the three of us. As soon as we arrived and had bundled our baggage through the red velvet décor of the tiny downstairs bar and up the impossibly narrow staircase, my brother said, "Let's go for a walk."

"We're in the Red-Light district," Cecilie's voice held tones somewhere between "of course we're in the Red-Light district" and "Jesus, did you have to book a hotel here, with me and your sister?"

We walked along one street until to my left a large picture window appeared. Inside the window an older woman, maybe as old as thirty-five, with eyes ringed heavily in black, arched her eyebrows and heaved her bosom at my brother, jiggling her flesh a little.

My eyes caught the young woman behind her, standing bare breasted, her eyes also ringed in black but not as dark as the look shooting from her orbs. I hold those eyes straight in my own and suddenly I am looking out on the street, her eyes mine, her body, like mine, a mere ghostly presence.

The inside of the room held fake gas lamps, a foot stool covered in worn red velvet, a small vanity chair that supported most of the considerable bottom of the older woman. The picture window looked out on a world that passed this young woman by, passed her by and did not care...except I was back on the street, her dark expression of hatred falling into my eyes.

How could she know? She and I shared a past of being hurt badly and from that came the ragged edges of too many drunken days and nights, missed appointments, gone opportunities, empty direction until like her I accepted with little question whatever arose. She had no idea I was her.

Chapter Twenty-Four

Upon my return from Norway, I was called in to a meeting with the out-going chairperson of the Dharma Center of Canada.

The Dharma Center of Canada had come about because Dawson had demanded a retreat center. Responding to the growing numbers of people attending his evening classes in downtown Toronto, he had requested brochures about and then resisted lands with tennis courts, or those with swimming pools and especially any places with indoor plumbing. Instead of all the pretty places tamed and complete, ready for humans to inhabit, he'd chosen this property, a former mink ranch, home to the world's most abundant black fly population. Mosquitoes thrive in the swamp land which covers much of the 400 acres. At the time of purchase, 1965, the land had one building nearly a century old and a second equally antiquated. There was not even an outhouse. By this point a dozen years later not much had changed.

As he was the first recognized Tibetan Buddhist teacher of Vajrayana Tantra in Canada and as he was the first meditation master of Caucasian descent to be recognized by the 16th Gyalwang Karmapa, so too was the Dharma Center the first meditation retreat center in Canada dedicated to both Eastern and Western teachings.

Here in this meeting the outgoing chairperson began, "We want you to run for chairperson of the Dharma Center."

I laughed, "That's not going to happen. I can't do it. I have no training. I'm not qualified." Dawson had been cajoling us to act upon our convictions, to avoid being "armchair politicos" as he liked to put it. He urged us to get involved, so I had volunteered the previous year to be secretary for the Board of Directors of the Dharma Center. In that role I had typed a few letters to a few of the other Dawson inspired centers around the world. I had done little else. From that to chairperson seemed a ridiculous leap.

"The only other person who has stepped forward to run is your brother. Now imagine your brother running the Center." The chairperson looked into my eyes.

The air in the room suddenly fell still as the impact of his words sank in. My brother in a position like that? My mind conjured vivid images of how much destruction he'd cause the Dharma Center and its functioning if he had access to power.

That was the conscious part of me. Below the surface seethed toxic rage against the boy who had raped and humiliated me.

The cells of our bodies know. They hold all the memories of each important event of our lives, guarding their precious knowledge as closely as a dragon her gold. We live in a chamber of secrets, the compilation of moments of emotional patterns woven from our experiences. The only question is whether we consciously accept and act to release the emotions that hold the patterns of behavior in place, or whether we choose to ignore our emotions, push them back into our bodies, into the unconscious, where they command our daily behavior and choices in repetitive patterns.

Those cells, when full of unreleased and unfelt negative emotion, block lymph, slow blood and oxygen, provide the stagnant conditions in which disease flourishes. That swamp of stagnation results from trauma.

I did not remember a summer afternoon with seconds of bliss with my brother. I had no recall of his stalking me ever after, no memory of his words of humiliation and degradation. Although no conscious knowledge existed, something in me leapt to the chance to keep my brother from what he desperately wanted to be: Chair of the Dharma Center of Canada.

I was elected Chair by a sweep, and spent a few weeks basking in the role, talking with people as though I understood what I was doing. Then, one night, I shot upright in bed from a sound sleep with one thought shouting in my mind, "The Karmapa is coming, and nothing is ready!"

Now a small, hardy and completed devoted band of folks emerged to make the three-hour drive from Toronto every weekend, to drywall, rake, clear ground, clean, to paint walls, hammer, goop and prime, to do whatever we could to facelift the Center enough to satisfy our dignity. My brother showed up once, maybe twice, then had lots of excuses and his finger-pointing at others whom he deemed lazy knew no end.

We installed the first indoor plumbing on the land, in Hill House, where we wanted His Holiness to stay. This feat felt supreme to us, working as we were without visible support, without an obvious supply of money, without direction except our own willingness and the combined talents of that crew of people. I believed the Tibetans to be humble men, men of flexibility and heart, aware that the struggle for and thought behind a gift or in this case, an experience, mattered as much as the outcome.

We prepared for His Holiness and his retinue of 21 Tibetan people who needed to be sheltered, fed and properly attended to for the three days of our time hosting. The rest of his three-week Canadian stay was divided between other Buddhist groups in Toronto, and the small but growing group following Beatrice Raff, aka Chorpel, who had led us the previous summer in our stay at the Norwegian Teacher Training facility.

My first recognition after that stomach slamming middle of the night insight was that I was in completely over my head. After carefully considering, then rejecting all ideas of how to wriggle out of the situation, I was left with one question: who to turn to?

Chorpel! The short German woman with her blue eyes, her

balding head visible through her sparse white hair, with her previous life experience of escaping Nazis and setting up a batik business in India successful enough to support herself and her two sons through to their adulthood, this woman would know what to do.

I entered her apartment, sat where she indicated at the small chrome table. We chatted as we ate the German sausage she had cooked and then she began.

"Zo, you haf a big thing here."

"Yes, I do."

"First, za kitchen." She explained to me that past events at the Dharma Center had suffered because the kitchen had been poorly organized or not at all.

"You must get..." she named a woman I had long looked up to, one who seemed so sophisticated and wise.

"Yah, you vil ask und she vil say no." Chorpel's blue eyes lit on mine, holding me. "You vil ask again und again she vil say no. You do zis over und over und zen," she blinked hard once more as her face lit into a large, mischievous smile so filled with sweetness I would have committed at that moment to anything she asked. "She vil agree at ze last minute. She vil! You must belief!"

This woman, who did say no, and no, and no, and then finally, when I was really anxious, yes, created a flow through the kitchen such that everyone would have access to tea, coffee, water. We expected 75 guests.

Ted drove us. Ted lived in the now storied Beach area of Toronto, on Balsam Ave. He had an apartment upstairs from Jean, who often joined the small crew of people ready to goop and tape, hammer and saw, sew mattress covers and more in preparation for the great event.

This is the spirit with which the visit was greeted by so many of us who worked tirelessly, waiting for the arrival of His Holiness the 16th Gyalwang Karmapa and his bestowal upon us of the Vajra Crown, or Black Hat, ceremony.

The Vajra Crown ceremony, also called the Black Hat ceremony, culminates when the Karmapa enters a state of deepest Samadhi, of Enlightenment. Tibetans believe witnessing this shortens your time to attaining Awakening, or Enlightenment to only seven lifetimes. This is a snap of the fingers if you believe.

The experience of preparing for His Holiness' visit remains in my mind as a series of miracles, not by the Tibetans but through the generosity and stalwart spirit of a small band of people. Ted, Jean and Jean's daughter Natasha regularly made the journey on weekends to help with preparations. The vice-chair gooped, drywalled and painted alongside the treasurer for weeks. This treasurer created minor miracles constantly by somehow finding the money for the materials we so needed, without putting the Dharma Center unduly in debt.

Another woman, the one who had left the message at the Canadian High Commission that had so mystified Charlotte Singh six years earlier, came up with a plan for recovering all the bare mattresses we could not afford to replace. She found the material, sewed the coverings and the newly decorated beds looked splendid to our eyes.

It was a kind of madness and to keep my spirits up, I bought a copy of the song "Blinded by the Light" and played it over and over as the weeks and months flew by. I didn't call it work, then or now. What the others did was work, hard physical work. What I did was ask and negotiate, communicate and advocate, and then stand about while others worked.

During one of the rides out of the city on a Friday night someone said, "The Stones are rumored to be playing at the El Mocambo tonight and tomorrow night…"

Ted glanced over at me. Every cell in my body made the next statement, "Maybe we're headed in the wrong direction?" The layers of that question hung in the air as the others took in the possible significance.

The treasurer spoke up, "We have people waiting for us. We can't just not show up."

"Tomorrow?" I insisted, lured by the sense of rebellion constantly at the ready to tear my life open, my life and the activities of others.

"I don't think we'd get in anyway," the treasurer suggested sensibly. His common sense won out.

Then it was Friday night of Easter Weekend, 1977. We stood, great white katas (scarves) across our open palms in the dark, frigid late winter air outside the Main House watching His Holiness in a large white Cadillac get jounced about in the front seat, as his driver made the best of the deeply rutted, muddy lane.

The car stopped briefly, the driver received instructions on turning to the left, his sights directed toward the little light on the porch at Hill House, our pride of place with its own indoor plumbing!

We milled about the kitchen, aware the growing number of guests arriving already outstripped our projection of 75 people. Word of His Holiness' visit had spread like butter in sunlight. We had sent invitations to the Mayor of Kinmount, to the communities in Toronto, to our relatives and friends. We wanted as many people as possible to witness this extraordinary event due to take place on Easter morning. As our loved ones witnessed, we knew they too would have only a small number of lifetimes before achieving Enlightenment. That would be good for them, good for us and good for all humanity.

A messenger arrived. His Holiness wanted to see me, immediately.

At the door of Hill House stood His Holiness' attendant.

I smiled, waiting.

"His Holiness can't stay here," the soft clipped voice said in clear English.

"What? Why not?" Thoughts of illness, unexpected death flashed somewhere inside me.

"Because this is not a suitable environment for His Holiness..." the implications, that His Holiness, far from being the humble monk I had imagined, was a Spiritual Rock Star accustomed to all that entailed, the understanding that all the efforts of these dedicated, willing people who had given everything to create the best possible space for this revered teacher, that they and their efforts were being dismissed lit a rod, straight and unyielding, a rod of clarity and anger within me.

"This is the best we have to offer."

"Well," the attendant continued, "His Holiness can't stay here. You must get him a hotel."

"We don't have any money for a hotel! There are no hotels near here, and anyway we don't have any money for a hotel!"

The Karmapa's stocky frame appeared behind the man and to my left. Instinctively I turned toward him and saw from my heart a sudden stream of golden light, warm, soft and invincible flow between us.

He stepped toward the attendant, garbling in soft Tibetan syllables. The Karmapa's eyes never left mine through this, even as the attendant said, "His Holiness says these accommodations will be fine."

I put my hands at my heart, held my eyes on His Holiness, bowed, thanked him and turned toward Main House, confusion falling everywhere inside me. Why had his attendant been so sure our offerings were not suitable? Was the Karmapa a man who demanded luxury and wealth? How did this demand co-exist with my sense of him as completely consciously mature, a developed human being? Surely, because he was enlightened, he was also aware of human feelings? He must be a man of emotional and moral integrity since he was, according to all, Enlightened. So I then believed.

Back in the Main House, the kitchen's small lights threw an orange warmth, focused like the early paintings of Van Gogh's Potato People. And like in those paintings, where the light shone a contrasting darkness also fell.

People trailed in and out as I stood in the center of the kitchen, waiting for the next thing that needed my attention. A teacher I'd never met before this evening stood off a little way, draped in his black, floor length robes like some medieval priest, complete with paunchy belly and attitude of entitlement.

I had made it known to him, via one of his students who requested sleeping space for the dozen or so of them, we had no space for them. They had arrived without invitation and without letting us know they intended to be here. A second messenger now arrived from this same teacher.

"Why doesn't he ask me himself?" I inquired of the short, slight person who stood to my left. "Why are you his messenger?"

His face broke into a soft smile, the kind reserved for children or challenged adults. "He is my teacher," he stated the obvious, "and I do this as service for him."

"The answer is no. The answer was no an hour ago when someone else from your group requested permission, and it will be no in the future. No one sleeps on the temple floor."

"Excuse me, excuse me, my teacher wants to speak to you." Another of his students!

"I'm just wondering," this teacher began, "why you are so negative towards me?"

"Not negative," I started, the last of my patience gathering against the grain of his insinuation. "You show up here without warning with about a dozen people and then make demands about the temple floor, to accommodate your group. Why didn't you let us know ahead of time?"

The sudden rosy glow under his skin signaled I had him.

"Are you a Libran?" he deflected.

"Nope."

"Are you sure? I'm an astrologer..."

"So am I. I am an Aquarian. I know my chart."

My Impossible Life

"Do you have any Libra in it?"

I felt like I was in the card game children play, Go Fish. "Regardless, I have too many people, not enough supplies and too much to do. If you'll excuse me..."

"No. Just tell me..."

I looked at his washed-out pallor, his pale blue eyes and I tallied. The fastest way through was to give what he wanted.

"I have two planets in Libra. Saturn directly on the mid-heaven, exalted at 15 degrees Libra and Neptune, 21 degrees beside it in the 10th house."

"Oh." He smiled, some real warmth seeping through his smug superiority, "That's it. I'm a Libra and your Saturn is on my Sun exactly."

No, I thought, *your stupidity is on my nerves, precisely.* What I said was, "All right then. Now I must go."

Just then someone else needed something, a decision only the Chair could make. I made it and then retreated to the dark outside for a cigarette.

A tall man emerged from the steady blackness. He wore a long trench coat, hardly enough to keep him warm in this chill; he kept his hands in the pockets of that coat the whole few minutes we spoke. His dark blue eyes behind the wire-rimmed glasses shone in the porch light's yellow stream, displaying a kind of confusion backed up by the softness of his voice.

Suspicion rose in me. I felt that softening thing inside, the one I had to dismiss because there was too much to do. Instead I told myself he looked like a traveling salesperson. He was certainly a stranger.

"Are you Charlene?"

I was beginning to regret this was so.

"Yes."

"I have to ask you if I can sleep on the temple floor tonight."

"What is it with you people? You show up here unannounced

and expect everything to just go your way." That was it. I had broken the rules and behaved badly as the Chair of the Dharma Center; I'd behaved badly as a woman and now this would be a mess.

"You must have worked very hard for this event."

I stood speechless for a moment, feeling the sincerity of his empathy.

"Are you a Libra?" I asked.

"Sagittarius."

"Oh. I have Sag rising..."

"I have four planets," he said, "in Sagittarius. We should get along fine."

His warmth bothered me. I preferred my state of outraged indignation since it covered my underlying sense of being deeply, totally in over my head.

"My name is Dale," he carried on, "and it's got to be hard for you to have put all this together."

"Well, I had lots of help..." I muttered.

"Look," Dale went on speaking softly, "all these people are here to see the Vajra Crown ceremony. We all, many of us have been traveling across North America to see as much of His Holiness while he is here, as possible. I came from California. It's been a hard trip, an exhausting trip..."

"Hey, what you do with your time is your business. Not my responsibility."

"Wait," his hands were in the air grappling against the invisible wall suddenly between us.

"I just mean, it's okay if you soften..." He kept talking. Maybe he hypnotized me, but before the conversation ended, I had given permission for him and half the over fifty extra people already streaming around to sleep on the temple floor.

The morning of the Vajra Crown ceremony broke open with the sudden warmth, clear blue sky, and still, fragrant air that makes all Canadians forget the harsh darkness of winter. I climbed from the sleeping bag in the bedroom above the kitchen in Main House, grumbling, "Again with the sleeping bag," reminded myself to be positive, regretted there was no warm shower to climb into, and offered gratitude downstairs for the cup of hot tea put before me.

If I recall that morning at all it feels like a fat warm pulse of goodness. The sun shone and everyone seemed to move lightly, as though fueled by some inner strength.

My parents who had been aware of my intense commitment to this ceremony arrived as they had promised. My brother also shuffled through the crowd, although I had had much less contact with him throughout my time as chairperson. When he had to address what I was doing, his responses came out as sarcasm.

"Oh, there's our girl," Dad's words didn't bother me, as he turned Mom toward the door of the Main House where I stood, smoking.

"Hi, honey," Mom looked as if she expected someone to question her about something for which she had no answer, but she also looked happy to see me. "How's it going?"

"Oh, you know."

I walked shoulder to shoulder with them along and down the now dry road leading away from Main House toward the back of the property, up the steep hill to where the temple sat, its Tibetan prayers flags in green, red, yellow, white and dark blue beckoning in a light gust of wind.

"Just wait here. It's out of our hands. Now we wait for Tibetan time."

I left my parents at the front of the temple, walked in and sat on the floor which appeared to have suffered no wear in its transformation from holy space to dorm and back to holy space. A place in the front row was reserved for me. Beside and one row in front of me all along the width of the building sat the monks, prepping with prayers and mantras. My white woven linen dress came to mid-thigh as I crossed into a full lotus posture, behind the little prayer table about six inches high in front of me. It was a traditional Tibetan prayer table and was covered in a traditional white cloth. I turned my awareness to my breath.

"Uh, Charlene," Tony, Dawson's main servant for over 20 years, leaned into my right ear. "Uh, the monks think it isn't proper for you to be sitting here with your bare legs showing."

"Well, I can't...I mean I don't have anything else to wear..."

"Is there some way you can sit..."

As though it had a mind of its own, I watched my hand strip the white covering cloth off the little prayer table and lay it across my legs. It covered every inch of offending flesh.

"There..." I smiled.

The throne rose to my left and in front of me. *Back to getting ready for this Vajra Crown. Will His Holiness walk up to that throne? How will he get through the crowd?* I wondered before trying again to meditate. Behind me I heard the inevitable sounds of laughter and talking, humans 350 thick.

A commanding male voice sounded from the door of the Temple. "Stop talking! Prepare in silence, meditate or pray!"

I didn't turn around. *Let someone else take the lead, I thought. My time at the front is nearly over.* This was the first real moment of rest for over three months. I welcomed that, as I welcomed the sensation of relief of just sitting.

In. Out.

The minutes trudged along. Still no Karmapa. Still no ceremonial prayers marking the start.

"Uh, Charlene," Tony, again in my right ear.

"Yes." I leaned my ear toward him, wanting to move as little of my body as possible.

"Uh, His Holiness is worried. He says not everyone can see him."

What, I thought, *another Prima Donna, needing all the attention to be focused on him and him alone?*

"Yes, and...?"

"He says there are too many people outside the temple. They won't all be able to see him when he places the Vajra Crown on his head."

"Couldn't he do the ceremony twice?"

"The Karmapa is not going to repeat the ceremony."

"What then?"

"The suggestion is we have to saw the doors of the temple off..."

"Saw the doors...? Are you all crazy? We can't saw the doors of the temple off. What happens after that? We're left with a temple with no doors..."

"No, the doors will be replaced. It's the only way we can do this..."

I paused thinking as hard as I could, but no other ideas came forward. "No, all right, saw the doors off."

"That's your answer? We have permission?"

What he was really saying was if I gave permission, I was taking responsibility for the doors coming off and going back on.

"As long as it's understood the doors have to go back on..."

Now I see the whole experience, from being elected to working with others to create this event as a kind of graduation, one in which I was successful in the outer world. At those moments, all I knew was a moment by moment growing relief that the responsibilities and being center focus would soon be over.

I stood outside on the hill with the rest of the over 350 people who had arrived. We watched in silence as the vice chair, treasurer and a couple of other men tugged and pulled the temple doors off leaving an unfinished, raw edged rectangle. Next, the same men jimmied the large wooden throne painted in brilliant reds, blues, oranges, yellows with the reverse swastika, the symbol meaning "good fortune", shoved and shimmied that throne into the roughly framed door space.

Now one Tibetan man, the ever-present monks holding his hands as he navigated the short steps to the cushioned seat of the throne, climbed up and sat himself on the throne, facing the crowd. He seemed oblivious to our hushed attention, as he wrapped his robes more comfortably around his body.

Then with supreme simplicity and utter focus, he held the crown up on his head, his right hand steady on the side of the crown. His face remained neutral as his eyes seemed to pierce into space.

What I saw as he sat in deep meditation was the same as what I had seen moments before. The same people gathered in silent respect, the same green trees, beautiful grass on the lovely hill in the April sunshine, same monks in burgundy robes, some with large head dresses with red feathery centerpieces, that made them look like horses with manes, those same monks and there in the newly enlarged temple doorway a man, leaning slightly to his right, holding with his hand the Black Crown upright on his head.

I saw all that, but I saw it as though everything, every detail, the silence except for a lone bird call, the multiple colors of everyone's Easter Sunday clothing, the feel of the warm sun, everything danced on an ocean of light, transparent and impermanent.

This Ocean of Light was conscious, humorous, loving and so incredibly intelligent. It was the source and the place to which we would, each and every one of us, return, as a beloved child. When this happens, we will know our separation as a kind of game, the necessary mask of the costume for the game.

The uniqueness of each of us comes at such a cost and our sense of loneliness and separation provides a vitalizing energy to our individual roles. Our sorrows, our loves, our losses and fulfillments all will ultimately be seen as expressions of this Light, this warm intelligent, living Light, who loves us beyond our wildest hopes and who never for a moment ever lets us go.

Chapter Twenty-Five

FOR THE NEXT FEW WEEKS I LIVED IN A FEELING of deep belonging. All emotions, thoughts and sensations rose and fell while every moment felt complete, like living in a dream or like being high. Before I had felt life as a thistle bush, tugging and snagging at me with every effort I made; for this brief precious time every minute felt smooth, flowing.

Certainly, some of this new feeling rose from the relief of having the Black Crown Ceremony preparations behind me. I had helped achieve something visible, valuable and successful. But this didn't explain all of the positive uplift, the feeling of almost floating that buoyed every day.

Neuroscience describes how when therapists work with clients, it is the therapist's neural pathways, presumably stronger in positive ways, that the client's brain tries to mimic. This is at the heart of therapy, that our brains try to copy the neural pathways of those who experience more joy, freedom and clarity. Is it possible this is what took place through the Vajra Crown ceremony?

In the decades since that morning on the hill in Kinmount, I have sat in the audience, mesmerized by Yo Yo Ma who drew me into his state of utter absorption, such that nothing else existed, if only he continued to pull the strings of his cello. I stood witness in downtown Toronto to Rudolph Nureyev surrounded by acolytes and sycophants, a small living room fairly bursting with the intensity and vitality of the physical aura Nureyev threw.

Karmapa practiced consciousness. Did his neural pathways call to the brains of those present, encouraging our brains toward a clarity and joy we might call transcendent?

As all things are impermanent so too this feeling would not last beyond a few days, maybe a week but while I was still immersed, His Holiness extended an invitation for me to visit him in Toronto. It arrived as an invitation but was a command performance in much the same way royalty everywhere issue invitations but intend compliance. The men who had guided me through lawyers and zoning petitions and who had worked so hard to bring the Karmapa to Canada offered a warning: His Holiness was going to ask me to give him the Dharma Center of Canada. I had to refuse.

I climbed the stairs from the second to the top floor of the semi-detached house in an older Toronto neighborhood, watching my feet on the steps. The idea that I alone had been invited to an interview with His Holiness the Karmapa wafted through my brain. In this moment nothing seemed quite real. I opened the door, walked in and folded myself on the floor.

The room was a long rectangle with a slanted ceiling and windows through which the sun beamed on the single piece of furniture, a couch. His Holiness, dressed in the maroon and yellow robes of a simple monk, sat there, playing with a small grey and white kitten. The kitten hid behind the considerable girth of Karmapa's body. Karmapa, clucking like a mother hen, pulled the small beast out, petting it in long, single strokes that took the kitten's hair back, leaving its eyes looking like slits before Karmapa released his hand. Its eyes sprang wide then the kitten playfully frisked to hide again. Both clearly enjoyed the game.

Achi, His Holiness' interpreter, arrived, wearing the signature cowboy hat he'd worn the first time I met him. During that meeting, he had taken my hand in his, petting and massaging it, as he looked deeply into my eyes. This unexpected and blunt attempt at seduction had irritated me and I'd yanked my hand back. Then as now I had needed to talk business.

He bowed to His Holiness.

"Hello," he said, turning his face briefly to mine before turning back to His Holiness.

After a short silence, I managed, "You invited me here today for a reason?"

"Yes. Actually, His Holiness wanted a visit with the head of the Dharma Center of Canada."

"Yes."

Silence. Both men stared at me. It took a long pause before I realized their struggle.

"I am the Chairperson, the head of the Dharma Center of Canada."

Achi gabbled in Tibetan with His Holiness.

"His Holiness asks are you sure?" Achi addressed me in English.

Still so honoured at having been invited at all, my voice kept an even tone, "I was elected Chair of the Dharma Center of Canada last November at our annual general meeting."

More talk between the men. In the years since I have come to understand what happened. His Holiness did not accept that a woman was able to lead anything except a kitchen. It would have been difficult enough for a man to refuse to give him the land, but a woman saying no would have been doubly frustrating, perhaps even shameful.

Then Achi said, "His Holiness says if you are the head of the Dharma Center, you want to do what is best for the center."

"Yes."

"His Holiness suggests you give him the land then, because that will be best for all the people."

"Ah. I would like to give the land to His Holiness, but it is not mine to give."

"You are the head you said? You are the leader of the Dharma

Center of Canada, right?"

"Right."

"Then you say what happens; you can give the land to His Holiness."

"No. I am the head, yes, but I was elected by all the members. I am their servant and can only do what they want. They don't want to give the land away."

While speaking at length with Achi His Holiness did not alter his facial expression, but several times lifted one forearm returning with some force his palm against the leather arm of the couch as he spoke. The emphasis was clear.

"But it's up to you, no? You are the leader. You can give the land to His Holiness."

"No. Here's how it works. I might put out a vote, requesting the members to vote on whether they want the land to stay as it is, or give it to His Holiness, but I can tell you right now, most would say no. That is how we determine things."

Achi pushed back the black brim of his hat, leaned toward His Holiness and again the syllables, liquid and light flipped back and forth as dust motes streamed and gathered, bumped and collided in the sun shafts pitching through the window.

"His Holiness says if they don't agree you can just give him the land anyway."

"No! This is a democracy. This must be done by the will of the most people."

The two men sat quietly observing me as though I was an alien from space.

"A leader leads his people..." Achi began. I would learn many years later this was the Tibetan take on democracy—if the leader of a board of directors wants to go in a direction different from those board members, he abolishes the board and starts fresh with people who will do his bidding. The leader is always male.

"Not in this case. Not here. Besides the transaction would have to be approved by Namgyal Rinpoche (Dawson) and he already said he doesn't want it given away to anyone."

"How do you know?"

"Tony, who was Namgyal's assistant for twenty years has said so. Perhaps you would like to talk to him?" *and get me off this uncomfortable hook.*

"Yes," Achi quickly agreed, "His Holiness will talk with this man. Make arrangements."

After a beat I ventured, "Why does His Holiness want this land? He has so much land everywhere, in the Yukon, and all around the world."

His Holiness understood my question and began answering in broken English before Achi interpreted.

"In future much suffering, many suffering…all centers…" the Karmapa chuckled and spread his arms out to show he meant all when he said all, "all the centers have much struggle coming. If under Karmapa less suffering."

He was correct about the centers. After his passing in 1982 many of the Tibetan centers and their organizations faltered and failed through greed and immoral behavior of the so-called leaders, both Tibetan and Caucasian, found guilty of sexual abuse of students as well as financial fraud. I have not heard whether being under Karmapa's protection helped any of them.

"Duj ju." That's the sound I remember from all Tibetan language, a kind of liquid note of satisfaction at the end of a long paragraph. It is a lovely sound.

It meant the meeting was over. I left and stood on the busy street corner waiting for a streetcar. It occurred to me I had just completed a complicated task and done so with some measure of grace. I felt good in a way that was almost new.

Tony went along to see His Holiness and talk with him about the land in Kinmount. Later that summer in a room full of students in a villa on the island of Crete, Dawson would speak.

"Charlene, I'm told you tried to give the land away to the Karmapa."

The formal use of my name brought my spine to soft attention, my insides to caution.

"No, Sir, I did not."

"Then why would someone tell me that?"

"Because, Sir, whoever they are, they are lying."

Dawson rolled back slightly in his chair as though I had delivered a light and unexpected slap on his shoulder.

It would take a few decades to unravel what likely happened, and to quit laying mental blame on Tony whenever this memory twigged. It was likely that His Holiness and Achi, in their desire for the land, suggested to Anthony I had been willing to give it to them.

At the time, I believed His Holiness was awakened, that he was enlightened. At the time, I believed this enlightenment meant moral integrity, including qualities such as truthfulness, honesty, strength of character, kindness, etc. all Christian virtues. It did not occur to me for several decades, enlightenment may mean strengthening what is already present, what talents, such as a talent for shrewd business, even deception, already exist.

Dawson, eager to disrupt our unconsciousness, disparaged what he knew were our childishly simple beliefs. With contempt in his voice, flinging words like knives, he declared, "You people think the enlightened state is one of gentle Jesus, meek and mild!"

Even his sneering challenge did nothing to dislodge the jejune belief that wreathed my heart and mind, coiled up, covering consciousness even as I made efforts to become conscious.

Carl Jung recognized there is a dark part of each and every one of us. He called this the Shadow and said it contains everything we suppress in our behavior and our consciousness, everything we devalue, everything we try to shut out of who we are and how we perform our daily lives.

I was unaware of the Shadow, that spring of 1977 when I had

to refuse the Karmapa our land. The Karmapa, so I reckoned, had been the source of those days and nights of feeling relaxed after the Black Crown ceremony. My faith, that enlightenment conferred conscious morality and integrity of character, would in time be upended. For now, it held in place all the pins of whatever I saw as life goals. I did not believe I might achieve enlightenment, but I held a deep conviction I might improve, heal, get better at life in some undefined way.

Yet it was not the notion of enlightenment that compelled me. It was the stories, the whispered tales about events woven as though from a golden hand, tales that recreated our world and our lives into a powerful saga of profound beauty, terror and mystery. Whether I believed all the words about seven lifetimes, or any lifetimes, awakening and enlightenment, what caught my attention were the stories, the mystical events, the rumored swirl of colors, people, happenings, larger than life, stories that implied a glorious expression of life just beyond our physical senses, stories like the one I had just recently heard about Karmapa driving to California the year before.

Achi had regaled me with this story before the Black Crown ceremony at Kinmount. He said they had been driving south from Vancouver towards California the year before, when the Karmapa began to say, "Turn here and then turn here," to the driver. Down long, twisty roads that made no sense to him, the driver now followed Karmapa's instructions because with the Karmapa that is what is done.

After a long time, Karmapa said, "Stop." The driver stopped, and the interpreter looked around. A Native American village appeared a short distance away and here, walking toward them was a stocky, barrel-chested Native American man with a red head band across his forehead. They had arrived at the Four Corners, home of the Hopi.

The Karmapa climbed out of the car and embraced this man, one of the four leaders of the Hopi Nation, as though they were old and very dear friends. Then the two men climbed up a local mountain. That's when the rain began. The Hopi had had a three-year drought and all through it they recalled what their legends said, "When the Red Hat comes, rains will end the drought."

The Karmapa heads the Kagyu Sect of Tibetan Buddhism, also known as the Red Hat sect. Although Tibetan Buddhism contains many such stories from the past, this one was here, right now in my time. As a doubting Thomas I yearned to know if the story were true, or some kind of PR management package handed out to susceptible Westerners.

As life spins itself with seemingly quixotic webs, in the early 1980's I would work with Thomas Banyaca, one of the four leaders of the Hopi, would meet and spend a few days with him and his family, some of that time spent camping in the Sawtooth Mountains of Idaho, the state I came to know as home.

And many years later, in the 1990's, back in Toronto a woman I have just met will help me find a table in my favorite downtown dive. She will tell me she is a student of the Native way, the Red path. Before all the lights dim for the music to begin, I will say, "I feel I must tell you a story." I will relate the story of the Karmapa, the interrupted drive, the Hopi leader and the rain. She will listen with deep, calm attentiveness.

"The thing is," I will confide, "I wish I had some way to know if it was true. It sounds so great, but so many stories are just stories..."

"It is true. I was on the reservation when it happened. It happened just as you said."

In the moment her words found my ears, my heart fell open. I felt as though time itself unfurled into physical space—opened and turned upon itself such that material world did not so much march in a thin straight line, but danced in graceful, endless spontaneity, layer upon layer, fractals emerging endlessly, endlessly unique and endlessly bound by the same Mandelbrot set.

So it was this story about the Karmapa even back in 1977, the intensity of his Black Crown meditation and my private meeting with him opened a thread of wonder, of possibility and of curiosity about this world and life itself. This thread along with a tiny dash of hopefulness Dawson provided that summer in Crete incited a vaguely felt sense of future—life might be more than one endless darkness.

What this and stories like it offered was hope. Later that same summer Dawson would offer more hope through a meeting he requested with Cecilie.

After morning class one day, Cecilie said excitedly, "Namgyal wants to see me. You can come too."

Our three bodies crammed the tiny kitchen of his rented villa. As ever, Dawson played the moment to its hilt. "Are you ready?" he asked coyly.

"Yes, I am," Cecilie giggled.

"Close your eyes."

She did and he held out to her offered hands a wooden pencil case with lovely reds, blues and yellows on the horizontal sliding door.

"Oh, it's beautiful," she cooed when her eyes opened.

He smiled widely.

"Look!" She included me. "The door slides across the surface and ohh!" Inside were three pencils. You'd have thought he'd given her a pencil case full of gold the way she went on.

I felt resentment and then immediately an embarrassing desire. I too wanted a gift from him and suddenly I heard a clear voice in my head stating loudly, "I want one too! Where's my present? I want a present!" My body filled with shame.

He turned and looked at me as though I had made the demand out loud.

"Oh, oh yes..." and disappeared around the kitchen corner.

He returned a few minutes later with a soft, woolen object which he placed gently into my open hands. I stared.

"It's a sheep."

"Yes, yes Sir, I see that it is a sheep."

When I continued to stare and say nothing, he continued, "It's the best New Zealand wool, 100% wool." He said this with a slight shrug of one shoulder.

"Yes, Sir, I see."

"It's a sheep."

"Yes, Sir, I see it's a sheep. But it's black. It's a black sheep."

"Oh, yes, it is," he giggled briefly, smiled sweetly and left.

That afternoon he delivered a two-hour lecture on sheep, their place as powerful because of their numbers, their reluctance to follow unless they are led by one of their own.

What I recall even now is his description of how the black sheep, which may originally have been a black goat, was part of ritual absolution. In villages a long time ago a spring ritual included tethering a black goat, or sheep in the town square. Each person from the village came to touch it, offering their sins from the previous year to the baby animal's body. Then the small thing was released far enough from the village it would surely die, taking with it the sins of all the people, leaving them cleansed. This is what they believed.

In my memory I was leaning against a wall and so at the side of the roomful of students, watching Dawson deliver this lecture. I saw the room of heads all turned in his direction. Then he threw his brown eyes toward me as he spoke about the leader, which had to be a sheep because sheep do not trust any but their own. I saw a wave in that room rising from the attention poured toward him, as though everyone was in that moment a sheep, a wave cresting and funneled through the leadership of one sheep, just as he said.

Dawson had named a central part of me, of my life's path and in that naming opened a place of belonging in the Western culture into which I'd been born. This sense of belonging softened my sense of being deformed, a mistake, something Nature herself had tried and failed to make whole from rejected ends.

Dawson gave me the symbol of my personal mythology. True to it, I had been exiled through rapes and torture to the hinterlands but unlike the black sheep of old, I had stumbled across this teaching, this teacher. Even if I never made my way fully back to the village, to my culture again, I had a way for my soul to understand what had happened to me.

Although it would take many decades of hard emotional work for me to glimpse all the layers of being a black sheep, I read fairly soon after I received his gift a notation from Carl Jung about the importance of finding a life myth. One central need of each of us is to understand our place in the world, even if, as it is for black sheep, a place of being rejected.

We left Crete to spend a few days in Epidaurus, where during one class, Dawson held up some black, ceramic worry beads of the kind Greek men often use while in conversation, or at the market, or drinking coffee.

He said, "These beads belonged to the great writer, Nikos Kazantzakis." I held my breath. "They need restringing. Who would like to…" My hand shot up and miracle! the beads, still warm from Dawson's hands, clicked as they slipped onto my palm.

Next, I sat under a tree, the truth of my ignorance pleading against stubborn determination.

I don't know how to do this…really? These beads belonged to Kazantzakis? It can't be. That's ridiculous. Probably some beads he bought at market, or… or found lying about and he just decided to make it seem like…but what if these very beads were in the hands of the man who wrote Zorba the Greek, The Last Temptation of Christ, Saviours of God? *What if…* Something of immense potential weighed on me.

I did my best, returning them next day into Dawson's proffered hand.

"Uh, yes," he hesitated, dangling the beads in the air in front of him where the eyes of everyone in class might see, "but not sensual enough. You see?"

Internally I screamed, *Let me try again, I cannot fail at this, it is too important.*

Wordlessly he plopped the insufficient beads back into my outstretched hands, his voice lilting, "It needs to be more sensual."

More sensual. This from a man I would learn was a serial rapist and sadist.

The irrefutable evidence that this was so would not reach my ears until the first decade of the next millennium. Before that in the 1990's the Dharma Center and its supporters would be rocked by the truth revealed. The Center would be rocked and then would put a tight lid covering everything.

Dawson had forced sexual acts—rapes— on his male students. Chorpel, that woman whose guidance had led me to the right woman for the kitchen during the Black Crown Ceremony, had been his accomplice in delivering pain. He had used whips, and knives. And while he delivered the physical violence, many of his men attendants, some of whom would become "teachers" approved of by him, stood around silently abetting the horror that would remain on the bodies of these victims.

It came to my ears years later that some men who were treated thus felt it was a great healing for them, perhaps in the way the woman in Mexico had experienced being beaten to a pulp by one of the facilitators and by Dawson as a healing.

I had heard for years rumours of Dawson's intense verbal and emotional abuse upon those men whom I had always seen as "privileged", as "special" because they performed service for him. While I took the rumours to be true, I surmised a greater teaching held those minions to Dawson's side. I had assumed they gained something from the experience.

By the time I learned of his sadism I was far away from him in time and life experience. This new knowledge felt like a tiny pebble of "oh, yes, that makes sense," in an ocean.

But in that time of continued ignorance of all the dark side of the teaching and of teachers, I took his second chance at stringing these beads as a second chance for me. Had I had the strength to whisper to a close, close friend, I might have admitted what called from my deepest heart: writing.

Israel was the next country. We arrived by ferry across the Mediterranean to Haifa home of the B'nai B'rith. Their headquarters were not open that day, so we pressed on to Bethlehem. I recall most vividly the steps leading up to the market, Al Souq and the swirling colours of the robes of men and women sashaying their way through the open streets and darkened alleys.

Someone rented a bus and we drove to Nazareth, to the River Jordan where we swam, to the Dead Sea where we were swum in the buoyant viscosity. One large memory is visiting the Ein Geden Oasis.

We walk single file through an arch of green shrubs and up some steps, continue a bit farther and there before us spreads the waterfall, the shallow pools perfect for bathing, beautiful rock formations and green growing vegetation. It is lush and welcoming and I know in an instant how the Song of Songs came to be written.

We stayed in Bethlehem, exploring by day the Suk and many places supposed to be holy markers of Jesus' life. At night all of the women slept in a convent in a single large dorm room. There the mosquitoes feasted upon us. All the other women used repellent oils on their bodies to stave off the insects but I had purchased coils. The smell rose and stank in the nostrils of everyone, including me but when one woman kindly requested I use oil, generously offered oil to me, I refused. My toxic rage still burned.

In Israel, we were a group of nearly 30 people gathering every day. Our letters were opened, our phone calls tapped and no doubt our classes were under surveillance. But it was when Dawson dressed in camos with his canvas hat rolled up on one side, took four of the young men in a jeep to the Golan heights where he stood with binoculars for a long time surveying the surrounds, it was then we had to leave.

Someone from our group had to phone someone back in Canada to vouch for Dawson, to keep him, and perhaps us, from jail. The course broke up early and we left the next day for Italy.

There Dawson began with an afternoon class in the living room of his rented villa. We crowded in, the 30 or so of us present in this leg of what continued to be Dawson's constant travels.

"Well, I thought," he began, "I'd ask what you might want to explore for the next few weeks." He began at the opposite side of the room from where I sat to his right. Hands rose and he nodded or made a comment as many wonderful ideas drifted about. The Fra Angelica paintings, the mystery of St. Francis, the many Christian martyrs in the area, the political history of Italy, the Abbhidhamma (a work called "The Higher Teaching" in the Tibetan canon), insight meditation—as each idea arrived, I noticed more and more clearly what was happening in me.

Each of those ideas ought to have excited, impressed or interested me, but since Crete a growing sense of the futility in life accompanied a physical feeling like a slight buzzing in my body, especially in my legs. I felt daily a desire to lie down and never get up again.

I had first noticed this negativity in Israel but had, through years of practice, pushed it away. Now I had no reserves left. I blamed myself for being inadequate to what surely was a gift: a summer of travel to three exotic countries, Crete, Israel and Italy with classes on history, religion, psychology, meditation and more. My current state offered more proof to the sharply clawed vulture in my head that I was, as always, the problem.

Finally, I was the last student with a hand raised. "What Sir is the meaning of despair?" That was it. I knew my experience as despair.

I anticipated a sneer, contempt, a verbal put down. Instead, his response was the first of many over the next several years in which he taught me as I was in the moment. He taught me when I asked a question from the truth of my being, and not some theory about how life ought to be lived, a real answer rose.

"It is not so much meaning, as a statement of life purpose…" So began a lecture for an hour and a half on despair and while I was too far in the experience to be able to take notes, and while his deeply respectful response was too far outside my realm of experience, two memories of what he said remain with me.

He said that despair marks the beginning of maturity, because it signals that depth consciousness is starting to stir. It is a time of putting aside child's toys, in favour of some deeper, more mature approach to one's life and life questions. This did not make sense to me then but would in time.

The second thing he did happened at the very end of the lecture. While talking he created with his words what I saw in the air in front of him—a yellow flower. Of course, the flower was not actually there, but I saw what he invited me to see: a yellow flower, "maybe a chrysanthemum" he suggested to which I said, "a daisy" and the flower in the air which I saw was a daisy, a yellow daisy with as many petals as a chrysanthemum.

That image offered the full bloom of hope and from that moment the buzzing of energy in my body did not bother me, but seemed a harbinger of some kind of change, possibly for the better. The buzzing would not stop for many months but continued any time I focused on my body. What I did not recognize was this was the first time since I was sixteen, since I was held hostage for three days, that I had felt the inside of my body at all.

The buzzing sensation I would come to learn is called streaming and is the opening of kundalini energy, also called life force. It was the beginning of my body healing.

Another event of healing took place that summer in Italy. We stayed at Villa Santa Tecla on a small mountain top. The building had once been used by pilgrims as a way station. Now the monks in charge offered us severely discounted prices to sleep dorm style inside or for even less to camp around the outside of the building.

A balcony spreads across the second floor at the back of Santa Tecla Villa to this very day. Under this balcony a portico leads through a set of double doors to the men's dormitory on the first floor.

It was here, inside the dormitory I took shelter. The afternoon rains had just begun, and the air hung upon my skin like heavy rags. I lay down on one of the beds and focused on the cool air circulating lightly through the cement walled room. The shutters were mostly closed so the light fell in soothing dim shafts.

Soon a young man from the group walked in and saw me. He came to my side and gently said, "Would you like a massage?"

Inwardly, I groaned. "I don't…"

"No, I mean a massage…"

I took a chance. He firmly and with tenderness began to massage my arm, then my leg, then as he walked to the other side of me, four other men, guys I knew by site and name, arrived. They too began massaging my body and soon I had five pairs of male hands showering my legs and arms, head and feet with tender, protective masculine energy.

If my neural pathways had shut down almost completely, as they certainly had, through the horror and physical pain of Al's rape and torture, my brother's humiliation, my mother's beatings, here was the opposite: many hands, human hands, touching and massaging gently all the appropriate parts of my body with great and tender love.

When the hands slowly finished their heart healing touch, my eyes opened ever so slightly. I saw smiles on their faces as they nodded to each other signalling it was time to leave.

Chapter Twenty-Six

WHO CAN RESIST ITALY'S SUMMER CHARMS? This was the last country I would visit, the last summer I would travel with Dawson because I fell in love.

I recall sitting side by side with my love on that small mountain rise, with Villa Santa Tecla behind us and the panoramic vista of the towns Perugia a little to our left, and Palazzo to our right down among the lush green vegetation. The sun was setting, and I felt something wondrous: serenity.

I believed with utter conviction that because we both followed Dawson our marriage, which took place later the next year, would last. It did not occur to me my reasoning was deeply, regrettably flawed. I believed and that belief stood, a tiny matchstick within the forests of life itself.

Two years later I sat in the front seat, my husband driving, our little boy on my lap. My husband, a US citizen, wanted to live among Dawson's followers. Our destination was Boise, Idaho, where some of the group had established the first Tibetan Buddhist center in Boise.

Far from that idyllic scene on the Italian mountain top, I soon found I was not up to the very real demands of both marriage and motherhood. I separated from, then divorced my husband. School had always been an ace in my back pocket, a thought of what I might do if…now was the time.

I found a farmhouse with an unlikely landlady. I first saw her beneath the very large pine tree that dominated her front yard, hair dyed blue, large turquoise rings flashing on her 70 plus year old hands as she drove her maroon MG convertible along the short driveway and out to the road. A farm girl from Colorado, she would become one of the mainstays in my life for the next decade. Her earthy wisdom and continual generous support made life possible for me and my son.

Our home, right next door to my landlady's, had 6 by 8 ft. windows, two facing the street and one opening to the north where a large empty lot spread its lush green grass under tall poplars and a mature yellow walnut tree. The farmhouse had three large basement rooms, where windows offered enough sun light to prevent the dark depressive states of many basements. The house more than made up for the antiquated fridge, old stove and leaky windows through its generous light and all the green that surrounded it. I loved living there. I felt comforted knowing my landlady lived next door and was available. Most of all I was proud to offer this nurturing combination of city and country to my son.

My first semester began. Now I interviewed people to be roommates to help defray living expenses and because I have always believed it's good to live with others. Eventually we had a full house, which I organized and mostly ran; I had all the joys and responsibilities of being a mom and all the arduous work needed for school.

Looking back, I see how a deep intelligence within knew how to access the energy I needed for my new and rigorous daily life. From the overwhelmingly terrifying events of almost a dozen years ago the real memories and their life defying truth had been shut out of my mind. In an act of inexpressible compassion, through an instinct as old as our species, unimaginably ugly events had been shut away, into a pit in the unconscious. The instinct to survive had kept the lid on ever since.

Now this deep intelligence knew I needed the energy expended on that lid, needed it for my daily life and the life of my little boy.

But to take the energy away from the lid meant releasing unimaginably horrifying memories. I had, in effect, to recall and heal all the memories that had traumatized my body, soul and mind.

Some of what I remember remains as a fragment, a scene that may not have a joining thread to what comes next, or what came before. It is the truth of my experience, and that truth forced itself fully into my mind one night.

Lying on my bed I could not sleep. Suddenly I felt a vaguely familiar chill, damp and cool as though death itself hung in the air. My senses startled to attention while my mind hurled up a list I had not known I had: my son asleep and safe in the next room, roommates accounted for downstairs. Was this a precognition, like my mother's and grandmother's ability to foresee who was going to die? I found no pulse of emphasis on the name of anyone I knew.

I waited, my breath coming in shorter and shorter spurts. Then my body jackknifed into fetal position and I felt, as though it was physical, the metal ridge of his knife against my back, the ache of my neck being pulled to one side by a hand grabbing my long hair.

It is the third day I am hostage. It is now a ritual. Al and Gary make me stand back while they take a long look around, craning their necks at the bushes, suspicious of the trees. Then Gary bends over and picks the lock clean, bursts through the door, followed by me, then Al with the shotgun.

This cabin holds a rising tension. I feel it smothering us. Al shoves a broom into my hands, slapping me about the head, yelling, "Get to work. You're going to start doing things a woman does. You're going to start doing your share and acting like a woman. Now...clean this up and get us food."

I take the broom and I'm gone. Gone is an experience of no senses, no memory. My senses instinctively know to curl, small as an atom and leave instantly, come back when necessary. Now I am back.

I say, "I have to use the bathroom."

Al looks at Gary, who looks back at Al.

"You can't go out there by yourself. Gary here, he'll go with you and have the rifle on you the whole time. Don't think you can run because he'll shoot you, won't you Gar?"

Gary's head nods halfway.

"But I'll need to close the door."

"No, you can't close the door..." Al's leer slimes all of me.

Gary picks up the shotgun. We walk outside in the sunshine along the small dirt pathway toward the outhouse.

"You can at least let me close the door," I say softly.

"I'm not sure..."

"Look." I point our eyes slightly ahead to the outhouse. "The outhouse has four walls. If I break out of one of them, you'll see me and there's no place for me to run. You'll see me and be able to shoot. You think I want you to shoot me?"

"I don't want to shoot you."

"I know that." I bat my eyes at him. My lashes feel like tree trunks, heavy and matted.

"All right then. Close the door. But if you run, I have to shoot you."

I enter the small grey outhouse, close the door, sit down. I see posters on the inside walls, posters of Alice in Wonderland, posters like the pictures in the book I have at home, a 1946 edition, exactly like that.

I whisper, "How likely is it that the inside walls of an outhouse in Northern Ontario have these exact posters of Alice in Wonderland?"

I gaze at the posters, expecting them to disappear. Then I raise my fingertips up and along the edges where paper ought to meet wood. Surely if I can feel the textural change...but my numbed senses, already trained in refusing this world prevent my fingertips from knowing whether the posters are there or are from my mind. Somewhere far away this understanding is very frightening.

"Hurry up. Al's waiting."

"Not finished yet."

I think, *Either I have cracked, am schizophrenic—and under the circumstances that is not unlikely—or my unconscious is sending me a message that now is the time.* I choose.

Back in the sunshine I walk toward Gary with a real smile on my face.

This vigil over, he looks more relaxed.

"I need to talk to Al," I tell him.

I wait in the bedroom assigned to me, a cottage bedroom with a double bed, a chair and a full-length mirror.

I hear Gary, "Charlie wants to talk to you."

"Yeah? Well, I'm fed up with what Charlie wants. Everything around here is about what that bitch wants. She can goddam well wait. I got some thinking to do."

"What about?"

"Look we can't keep her with us. Not all the way into Manitoba. She..she's...it isn't working out like I thought. She doesn't do anything or give anything the way...like I thought."

Silence.

Gary's voice. "We can't just leave her here."

"No, no we can't. She might run, go to the police."

"She wants to go home."

"Shut up with what she wants! I have to think. I have a decision to make. Either we give her what she wants, or...well, it won't much matter."

They whisper.

Al sits on the chair in this bedroom. "What is it, Charlie?"

"Well, Al, you know how I have not said anything to you or Gary about where I come from, or my life?"

I see something like mild interest, possible confusion in his pale fish eyes.

"Yeah."

"Well, I have been in a mental institution my whole life..."

His eyes widen, his mouth flaps open, a fish on a wharf, "Oh for Christ's sake, of all the goddam...of all the goddam people on the highway we had to pick..." he shakes his head, starts to rise. He sits back down as I continue.

"Now, I don't mean this to frighten or alarm you, it's just that I can't take care of myself. I can't. I mean if I have a shotgun and you have a shotgun you will have to kill me because I have no instinct for self-preservation. That's what it means. That's why I'm in the hospital..."

"Oh, Jesus Christ," Al says softly. "Of all the...Christ!"

"Now, I'm all right now, but soon I may go up..." I point my finger in the air, "and when I do, I need you to take care of me, because I can't, I mean...I...I...Twas brillig and the slithey toves/Did gyre and gimble in the wabe..."

I bounce up and down on the bed, reciting Jabberwocky, giving way to some very real hysteria. "You like poems, Al? You know any poems? Maybe you'll recite one, yes, come on, it's your turn..."

"Now, Charlie, I read a few in prison, but..."

"Come on, you can tell me a poem, or story, yes, tell me a story..." like a simpleton. Then, suddenly, with facial gestures, ""How like a fawning publican he looks..."" I deliver the whole speech.

"Oh, Jesus Christ....Jesus Fucking Christ! Gary...I... Charlie," Al raises his voice and slows his language down, "I....have...to...go... talk....with...Gary? You...understand?" His face is right in front of me.

"Yes, Al."

From the other room I hear Al tell Gary, "You might as well go in there and get what you want. Go on."

Gary resists.

"Look Gar, she's says she's from a mental house, she's batty as hell. You can take what you want because no one will ever believe her..."

"What if she's lyin'?"

"She ain't lyin'. Go on in there and look at her, listen to her..."

"Nah, I just...."

"Well, then I'm going in."

I lie on the bed.

"Charlie this is gonna feel real good. You ever done this before?" His face close to mine, his body leaning in, his arm, hand curved around the knife, pushing against my back.

"No."

"Well, it's gonna feel real good..." His tongue in my mouth, I go empty, soft as a raw egg.

"What's the matter? You have to do this too! I can't do this all by myself."

"I'm sorry Al, I don't know what to do. I've never done this..."

"Come on! You've had boyfriends before...do with me what you did with them!"

"I really...I," how much will he believe, "I had one boyfriend, but we didn't do this."

"Never? I don't believe that! Any man...now put your arms around my neck..."

My limp arms land on his neck.

"No, not like that..." He grabs my hair, wraps it around his hand, uses it to stabilize his pounding while he tries to enter me. His penis is soft.

"Oh, help me!" he whines into my face. "Do what you do with your boyfriend. Pretend I'm him."

I wince from the pain of my hair being pulled hard.

"Stop whining. Make it happen," his wretched breath fogs near.

I think about yelling, about Gary somewhere close by, how he will come running if Al...

"And if you call out—" Does Al show me the knife, turning it so the light shines from its blade? "I'll cut right through your spine."

I lie still as he attempts again and finally pushes some of his partially limp flesh inside me.

"Al!" Gary's voice a soft yell, from just outside the window.

"Fuck! Not now!"

Gary makes noise rustling through bushes.

"What the fuck is he…" Al snarls, tightening his grip on my hair, flattening his chest against my breasts as he leans up.

"Al, I think I hear someone coming…" Gary's voice insists.

"Oh shit," Al is pulling his pants on. He leans down again close to my face and sneers, "You're ruined now. No one, no man will ever want you. Not ever." He smirks down at me and streams out the door.

Gary comes into the room and lies about three inches from me.

"I didn't want to come in here, but Al made me…" he says.

"Oh," I say, looking up into his eyes.

"I…really like you," He leans in and kisses my hair, my cheek. His mouth is soft.

It is easy to lie. "I like you, Gary."

His hands roam the length of my body, impressing gently on the curves and crevices. I feel nothing.

He lies on his side, his eyes intently on mine and asks, "Did he… did Al break his promise?"

I must be sure. "What promise?"

"His promise not to rape you. I thought I heard him…breaking his promise. I thought I heard him…breaking his promise so I made up that story about someone coming…" he whispers, softly.

"Oh." I wait.

"Tell me if he did, because," Gary leans up on one elbow, looking down at me, "if he did, if he broke his promise and hurt you, I'll take that shotgun and blow his fucking head off."

I look at the ceiling. It fills with blood, blood all down the walls, a wave of blood everywhere. Al shot, lying on the floor, Gary shot and me, on the bed, blood everywhere. I know none of us will get out alive.

"No, Gary, he didn't break his promise...he...he did about the same as you. He didn't hurt me." To make this real, I must believe it.

I lied to protect my rapist from certain death. His death would mean my death. I lie to keep us all alive, despite not knowing whether Al will kill me or let me go.

In my farmhouse in Boise, the initial breakthrough to Al's rape spewed a landscape of rage across my psyche. For three months whenever the thought or the word "man" crossed my path my mouth volcanoed hot lava of hate. Soon but not soon enough, I recognized the pain in my small son's eyes whenever this happened, how he withdrew his little body to a farther part of the room. Once I allowed myself to see, I knew I had to change.

I see now in this brief but impactful time for my sweet son, the unremitting laws of consciousness. I had been scarred deeply during my fourth year as a child. My son, too, bore scars from my language, as clearly as if I had hit him. His body language elicited in me the love I felt for him and that drove my determination to change, to be better.

I decided to speak with more kindness and did, but still knew I needed to release more emotional excess, possibly more ugly memories. I had to have someplace, some time to vent the overwhelmingly powerful emotions surging still through my mind and body.

I remembered how in meditation retreat everything had been scheduled so I made a plan. Every Friday evening when my son was soundly asleep, I took my journal, a pillow and my memories to my room. There, for one hour I tempted the demons. I dredged any moment from the week before, any lingering memory of words from men at school or in my home, any news items about malicious male behavior, of actions I witnessed or heard about that triggered a negative emotional response. When the week had been relatively smooth in this regard, I chased one of my memories, starting with the memory of rape.

For an hour any emotion needing release, terror, pain, vulnerability, rage, sadness, poured into the pillow I held to my face. Then I wrote. I wrote the immediate experience and I wrote old memories. Whatever presented itself, cynicism, sarcasm, idiot half phrases, or long expositions, I wrote. Gradually, along with this writing I discovered a thin stream of curiosity: what else was inside?

Every week after I dredged and wrote I took a bath. Although the bathroom was a humble one, I made sure it and the towels and everything ready to touch my body was clean. Then I stood at the bathroom door, repeating, "I am safe here. All I have just experienced is behind me. Now I enter to cleanse away the present moment." That was the tenor of my thoughts. Sometimes it was a feeling I held onto as I sank into the warm water. Then I pushed my mind to positive moments from the week at school, or with my son. My love for him has been always the foundation inspiration and strength for my healing.

While drying off, I reminded myself that any thoughts or emotions about past pains now had to wait until the next Friday. I was done for this session. My job during the week was to keep as positive as possible.

In this way, the internal pressure released, slowly and safely and eventually led to a second breakthrough. This primal erupted with all the physicality I had grown to recognize—sweat pouring out of my body, breath in spasms, sobs, muscles in my face, neck, legs, arms, belly contorted in anguish as the truth rose from its fleshy tomb.

After the rape I am in my panties and bra, Gary somewhere else. Al stands in front of me, the rope in his hands. He uses it to bind my ankles, too tightly so they fight each other. He binds my wrists behind my back for that infinity of time which eats everything. He ties the gag in my mouth, so the cloth digs at the corners of my lips. He bites my breasts, sucks dark flowers to their surface, slaps my face. He loosens the gag, demands I tell him I love him, and I do.

I am able to because this is the love of my mother.

Al takes the tip of his cigarette and brings it toward my cheek.

At the last minute I say sadly, "It will leave scars."

He stops. "Nah, I'll leave the burning tip on your skin just long enough it starts to smell. Then pull it away. That way there's no scar left. It's a little trick you learn in prison."

"Someone might know."

He hesitates. He brings the burning point to my arm, my back, my chest, my calf. He burns me and the smell just starts to register then nothing.

Gary stops in front of me.

"Oh, Jesus, Al, what are you doing? Leave her alone. Jesus Christ, Al! Not this! You all right, Charlie?"

"Hi Gary. I'm all right. It's just..." my eyes plead with him.

"Watch this, Gar...tell me you love me, Charlie. No, watch Gar, watch this..."

Al excited dances, a skinny, brittle marionette, brings the burning tip of his cigarette toward my young flesh.

"Al, for Chrissake, stop..."

"No, look, it doesn't hurt her, does it Charlie? Tell him. Tell Gary it doesn't hurt. It's a little game we been playing..."

I look steadily at Gary, "It doesn't hurt, it's all right, I love you Al..."

It goes on.

With the horror of the memory flooding into consciousness came a release of decades old tensions held in my jaw. My mouth and jaw had been pushed out of line for whatever period of time I was tied to that chair. After the release from the tight gag in my mouth came several minutes of excruciating pain in my jaw on both sides.

I learned that it is not necessary to repeat every minute of whatever the trauma may be, only enough to allow the original flow of blood, oxygen and lymph to fully route again through those areas. We know that trauma, whether physical or emotional, shuts down regenerative oxygen, blood and lymph to the area affected, setting the stage for disease and degeneration. When memory releases the unconscious emotions that kept the area depleted, rushes of fresh blood, oxygen and lymph pour back into the area, as they once had in the pre-traumatized body.

My body still holds small, round white spots, especially visible whenever I have been in the sun, but easily seen by the naked eye even in winter. On my arm, a few on my legs, these are too regular in shape to be the natural changes of skin over time. Besides I have had them since I was sixteen, my cells offering tiny white flags in the shape of the burning cigarette tip he held to my skin repeatedly in that room of the third cabin.

They are my victory medals in an unacknowledged war. Like so many before me, burned or scarred in other ways, those whose skin displayed their victory and fearlessness, so too, these scars show me for who I am: a triumphant warrior.

It was in that cabin I called upon my earlier training with my mother, whose illness grew in proportion as my body did. She would slam the leather whip against me, her words an acid poured on those open wounds, then she'd beg my father to help her.

He did. He made me stand in front of her and apologize. For her rage.

Thus, I was schooled and prepared for what lay ahead of me.

Offering Al the pain I was in may have triggered in Al a need to shut me down, to stop my expression of pain from bringing to consciousness what he was doing: hurting me. Since I had been taught by my mother, "stop crying or I'll give you something to cry about" I learned from her not to show my pain. Not ever to show my pain.

Now we know about mirror neurons, those nerves at the front of our brains, neurons that help us learn to mirror others. Did my apparent lack of pain allow Al to mirror me, my insistence I was okay? Did his belief he was not hurting me, that he was not a bad person, allow him to experience torturing me as a game, a word he and I used to describe what he was doing? If I had shown more suffering, would my anguish have escalated his knowledge about what he was doing and in the only way he knew how, would he have escalated the torture, even to death, to stop his own pain?

All I knew at the time was what I had learned in grade 10 physics—everything vibrates. I believed this as it registered with the teachings of Diogenes I'd read about when I was 12. This idea colluded with my early religious training about Jesus as an example of the power of love. In the first few desperate hours, before I learned to go away inside myself, the belief that if I could love these men, if I could raise their vibrational energy even a little they would not be able to hurt me, offered hope.

I believed so deeply that when I returned home that refrain, "they did not hurt me" only capsized after fifteen years. Whether this belief, that my job was to love them, to make them my friends, had any effect on those men or the outcome, I know it held a tiny shred of possibility open while the rest of the universe had caved in upon me.

I continued diligently while living in the Boise to engage these weekly sessions, sometimes on Fridays, sometimes on Sundays when my son was with his father. I came to think of these times as "visiting my little shop of horrors." Then a third and even more cleansing memory rang through every one of my senses. It was the moment Gary, under Al's command, shot a man.

The memory floods, totally unexpected, flushing through me with a force of heat, sweat, tears and muscular spasms that verify the truth. Vomit rises to my throat and bits stream out, as in the original moments. This memory is the one wound so tightly, so deeply inside, it had split my mind in two. Now it unfolds.

September 1968

I SLIDE INTO THE NEW POWDER BLUE PONTIAC, leaving bright autumn leaves, late summer air behind. Nothing can go wrong. I left in the dark the night before, hitchhiked out of my old life onto the black highway of this unknown. No longer compelled by dictates of parents, teachers, even friends, I am free to decide, free to do as I please. I am sixteen, everyone everywhere from commercials to pop songs to poems, promotes freedom and personal choice; it's my life and I am free.

Miles spin beneath as I stare at the blurred bushes and trees that line the TransCanada Highway, north of Sudbury. I lean my cheek against the cool window behind the driver.

'How far you planning to go?" the driver's watery blue eyes stare at me from the rear-view mirror, a slightly twisted grin on his soft, large lips.

"Edmonton." Into the small silence I add, "And you?"

"Oh, me and Gary, he's…" the driver nods in the direction of the handsome, swarthy young man whose brown eyes had hypnotized me into the car, in the front seat, "…he's Gary."

"He's Al," Gary responds as though this is rehearsed.

"We're just free, you know? We go wherever we want, don't we Gary?" Al chuckles without mirth.

I nod, "I know what you mean."

"Do you?" Al shoots back at me, but glances at Gary. "What's your name?"

"Charlie."

"Charlie. Charlie," he repeats as though trying to remember something.

"What do you guys do for work?"

"What?" The word slices towards me. I see a taut snag at the corner of his mouth.

Gary absorbs Al's tension. "We just do whatever we feel like, don't we Al? We're free."

"That's right, Gar, just free to do what we want."

"That's us, free and easy."

"We just hang around, go wherever we want, right Gary?" Al repeats.

"That's right, Al." Gary looks out the window.

"We don't believe in being tied down, kept on other people's time, wasting our lives working for the man, that right Gary?"

"That's right, Al."

"What about money, what do you do for money?"

A short pause.

"You see that canvas bag back there?" Al, his watery eyes claiming mine, asks. "Well, that canvas bag contains two shot-guns. Gary here has sawed one off, right Gar?"

"Yes, I did, Al," Gary nods shyly.

"Those shot guns are the ones we used to shoot the legs out from under a gas station attendant in Welland, after we broke out of prison. You know where Welland is, Charlie?"

"Southwest of Toronto." Inside, all my pieces separate, fall away.

Now we have broken into the first cabin and are walking away. We walk back toward the highway away from that first cabin and keep walking, in the drizzling rain, in the dark, Al talking nonstop, "…up the TransCanada. Ditch the car. Gotta ditch the car because the cops will be looking for us and it…"

"I don't think the cops are looking for you yet," I offer.

"Yeah," Al rips the air, "well, I don't think you know everything. You may be a Miss Smart Mouth, but you don't know nothing."

We walk on.

Slowly I begin to notice I am having trouble breathing. The image of a hospital fills my head, those warming yellow lights and nurses in white uniforms.

"I, I think..." I stop and pant, leaning over.

"What now?" Al snarls.

"I think I have pneumonia...I've had it before many times, and this is what it feels like...I have to get help..."

"Oh, Christ!" Al mutters. "We're not going to a hospital, not going to happen so get that out of your mind."

"Okay, but I can't walk anymore..." I pant and lean and lean and pant and try to sit, stand up and try to take a step, wobble.

The two men confer.

"Jesus Christ. We can't let her get sick."

"She's no good to us sick. We're not taking care of her."

"Can't we take her to the hospital, drop her off, let her walk in by herself..." Gary's voice.

"And then what? Lose her as bait if the cops come after us? No way. She stays with us..."

"We can't do nothing. Pneumonia is serious. She could die."

"Think I don't know that?"

"Let me go back and get the car, Al, let me go get the car, then she'll be inside it..."

"Gary's gone back for the car," Al announces to me as though I had been gone.

Al stands next to me on the shoulder of the highway as we wait for Gary. The wait takes infinity.

"You sure it's pneumonia?" he asks.

"Pretty sure. I've had it..." pant, pant, "before." I know these men are of little brain, but I am not sure where the boundaries are, how much I can make them believe.

"That Gary, he likes you," Al starts as though we three are at a junior high school dance. "I like you, too."

I do not gag, but lean over, panting as though I can't talk. Then I say, "I like you both."

"That Gary, he's a good man, he likes you, he's gone back to get the car, now I probably wouldn't have done that, but Gary now, he goes right ahead and gets you what you need. You need the car, me and Gary will get the car…That's how it is Charlie, we be good to you and you be good to us…"

I ignore his sickening implication and try not to go away, to the place I have discovered where there are no dreams, no sensory input, no dissociation, just nothing. I come and go from this place throughout these three days and nights.

Large yellow headlights seek us out, pass us by.

Finally, Gary pulls up, Al gets behind the wheel, I climb in the back seat and am gone.

When I come back, it is cold in the car. The engine is off.

Outside the window we are surrounded by trees in early autumn, a dirt road underneath us, no one around. It may be early morning.

Al announces to me, "We are almost out of gas. No more running the car for heat. Gary here," he nods his head toward Gary, "will go and find us some gas, won't you Gar?"

"Yes, Al." Gary gets out.

I have the same silent reaction, Don't leave me, don't leave me with this man, but the reaction slides instantly into that place where there is nothing.

"Where you from, Charlie?"

"Oh, somewhere," I mumble.

I never tell never tell them oh never tell them. An urgent sense of immense importance warns me: I must not tell them anything about myself.

"I remember when I left home…" he regales himself with his

life story.

Gary returns. Al tells him to go, and Gary leaves again. When Gary comes back, Al and I get out of the car and follow him.

We stand outside the trailer, an older one sitting up on cinder blocks. Gary leans down toward the gas, a thin rubber hose in his mouth, splashes liquid fuel into our red can.

A grey-haired man in red plaid flannel jacket and blue jeans suddenly stands in the doorway of the trailer.

"What're you young punks doing?"

"We're taking your gas," Al answers, that twisted sneer on his face.

"Oh, yeah? Well, I'm calling the police, we'll see how smart you are then..."

Gary raises his head toward Al.

Inside I yell mutely to the man, Stop, they are dangerous let them take your gas but Al nods and says softly, "Do it."

Gary cocks the rifle, one soft snap of air before a loud crack splits the universe. What emerges from the wounded universe is a man dangling, one eye falling out of its socket, the other gone, his grey and red brains spewing across his forehead, his body, full of mouths spilling blood, dangles for a moment with the impact of Gary's sawed-off shotgun. Blood splays in every direction and the smell of sweet burning human flesh violates my nostrils, hangs inside my nose like stuffing.

A scream crowds my ears. *That person better stop screaming because Al won't like that,* I think.

Gary fills my vision. "Stop!" He is urgent, something important is happening.

I begin to smile.

"Oh Christ," he almost yells to Al, "she's in shock."

Al snarls something I cannot make out.

"Move," Gary commands, "walk now, come on Charlie, walk" but my legs do not respond.

Gary, his dark brown eyes targeting mine, whispers in my face, "If you don't move, Al will do to you what he did to that man."

Half pulled, half dragged, behind Gary, I make it to the side of the trailer, let go of his hand, turn back and spew vomit.

"Yeah, don't feel bad, I did that too the first time I saw something like this..." Gary's tones of comfort.

"Like what?" I ask.

Gary's eyes flicker, something I don't understand, then he turns to Al watching us from a few feet ahead, "She's all right, aren't you Charlie? She can move now."

I nod.

I come to in the parked car. Al is asleep behind the wheel, and Gary's snoring body slumps against the passenger window. I am locked in between them. A moment of anguish, then I recall the small paring knife I have in the bottom of my satchel. I might slit Al's throat. I know Gary is soft on me and I see us running together, escaping, under the law. I see us in cheap hotels, one after the other the vision continues but it seems I cannot smile again. Dirt everywhere, covered in dirt always, I can't get clean and I no longer smile.

That vision clears and I stare straight ahead where a flood of blood flows vertically behind Christ on the cross, his head lolling to one side. He took the pain. I accept the message and do not think again of the knife, or of hurting anyone.

Remembering the shooting was my third major breakthrough. This, the most powerful trauma had been laid down on my neural networks before the rape, before the torture.

When I first recalled the rape, I believed that was the primary layer.

By the time of the second breakthrough I began to feel a small slice of curiosity about what else might be inside.

And when the memory of the man's body spilled out, it birthed with it a return to the sensory world, the world I had lived in before the first apocalypse of my life when I was 3 and 1/2 years old.

In my bedroom in Boise after my body responses and the memory itself subsided, my senses rushed to life. More potent than any drug, more intense than any encounter with any meditation or teacher, my brain and body filled with a rapture that warned me to move very, very slowly.

It is a sunny Sunday afternoon. I am alone in the house. I walk slowly, palms to the wall of the hallway into the living room. I recognize my eyes feel raw, as though suddenly stripped of layers they had grown used to, as though the way I had been living was through visual impairment, a semi-blindness I had not known I had.

My tactile sense also begins to register. As though I had lived wrapped in a thin layer of plastic, and now had been cleansed of this, I feel my clothing against my skin. The world seems to pour itself into me, through me, my ears, skin, eyes, nose all receiving as though for the first time.

Light coming through the trees outside falls in filigree details upon the carpet where colors reach up to be caressed by the sun, the sun's light caressing and being caressed by my eyes. My eyes almost hurt. Almost but not really. The smell of damp spring air opens inside me like a presence, as though my organs breathed back to the sweet air flowing in.

I push the radio button, and Mozart's music dances upon air waves, enters my ears evoking immediate and large body sensations of happiness. My body responses tell me I am in the terrifying world of beauty, of sensuality, of having my senses working as they had been meant to all along.

I recognize I am close to sensory overwhelm. I lie down on the patterned carpet and breathe slowly, knowing my brain needs time in this new exquisite world, the world from which I had been exiled so long ago, the world I had despaired of ever re-entering.

In those few hours my senses reorganized themselves in the new spaciousness, the emptiness created by conscious remembrance of the bloody remains of the man's body. I had crowded myself against myself, expending much energy to keep the sound of the trigger, the smell of the blood, the sight of what remained of his body locked in my unconscious.

I say "I" did, but the truth is a force of health and sanity much stronger than any I might conjure had buried the horrifying moments and their aftermath safely in my cells where the only damage was a dampening of my senses, and a loss of some present moments. The dampening was to protect me, but in protecting me had muted the world and in that muting had altered the very center of me. Deep within me, a knowledge and love greater than any I might invoke knew the exact order the traumas needed to be re-experienced to return me to my senses: rape, torture and then witnessing the murder.

I also recognized this last trauma, witnessing the man's violent death, had blown a chasm in my psyche into which some major life events had fallen. This experience was the source of my dissociation. I had dissociated over being forced to visit the Reclining Buddha; I had dissociated over being forced to camp on Vancouver Island. In both cases, the men had believed in their ability to make decisions on my behalf; on my side I unconsciously believed if I did not follow them, they might kill me.

This is how trauma works: the psyche will split itself against its own will, in order to increase chances of physical survival.

Dissociation is nature's way of keeping us alive in what is believed to be a life-threatening situation. Dissociation is a survival skill based in our instincts. I have never recovered memory of the Reclining Buddha, nor do I recall what venom pouring out of my mouth at high decibels in that Vancouver Island campground, decibels and language harsh enough to cause all other campers to stop and stare. I will never have those memories; I do not need them.

The underlying terror, kicked off by survival instincts, led to my tempest on Vancouver Island. I went, as all who are threatened do, into big anger rather than display how helpless and vulnerable I felt.

Lying on my living room carpet that Sunday afternoon in Boise, I knew I had returned from the partial death which had wrapped me since the moment Gary's shotgun had exploded. This was the farthest dungeon of my own hell. I had reached that dungeon and had the power to return, more fully restored, to life on the surface. I would return to the surface and then go back, many, many times to empty all the rooms of their corpses.

From this beginning through a series of such primal breakthroughs I put together the whole story of those three days. From the time of the third breakthrough I felt whole. I felt sensations inside my body rather than as though I lived only above my eyebrows. With every day I recognized more the value of being in my senses, the joy of simply walking and being aware of walking, the contentment of making a meal for my son and myself.

Where before I had known intellectually that I was doing things that were supposed to be satisfying, I now felt the fulfillment. I felt other things as well: sorrow, sadness, anger, excitement, the full gamut of human emotion opened up gradually along with my senses. In the experiencing of all of these emotional responses to daily life I knew I was living my life, for the first time since I was sixteen.

Not all of my breakthroughs were internal. My confidence and strength found new outlets in the risks I was willing to take in the outer world.

My friend and roommate George sat across from me at a restaurant booth. We may have been having a quiet beer together, or a coffee. He was concerned, "Look, I hear you, sometimes the others in the house hear you, in your room crying. I don't think all that crying is doing you any good. It's weird. I hear sounds like a baby crying in there."

I tried as best I might to explain to him what I was doing and why it was for me a positive thing, a good release. Then I said, "And I have learned through this that I was raped."

I sketched in a few details he had not heard before about having been held hostage, how I had believed nothing bad had happened but now, through the work I was doing, the memory of being raped had returned. I may have said with fervor, he raped me, I was raped, something like that.

George's blue-green eyes fixed directly on mine, and he said with his top lip curling, "You were so angry a minute ago. When you talked about being raped, you were so angry!" He made it sound like I was wrong.

I remember going still in my chest, like in a jungle when all the animals and birds suddenly go silent. In the silence I heard this thought, Notice this: you cannot expect many men to offer sympathy or support.

Dawson came to give teachings in Boise and of course I attended. After one class I asked for an interview and he suggested we walk together a short way. As we did, I explained to him that I had remembered I had been raped.

"What do you expect me to do about it?" he snarled.

Instead of warmth and support, he had snarled. Inside I saw a bridge and said, "Nothing sir. I just wanted a sort of confession, like to a priest…"

"Oh" he relaxed, "yes, of course, well then…very well." I had erected a bridge entirely in silence. Thus it was I learned to be cautious, to consider the man before I spoke my truth.

It was different with women. I learned from the very first woman friend I told that women had matching stories. Almost every woman I have told over the thirty or so years since I remembered what happened, has had a story of being raped, molested, beaten, confined against her will or a combination of all of the above. It was staggering to listen to their pain and incredibly comforting to hear their words to me, "I am so sorry you had to go through this. I wish you had not had to endure anything like this." I learned from these courageous women I was not alone, either in how men had hurt me, nor in my instincts to keep quiet about my experiences.

One afternoon I was in the Writing Center where I worked as a teaching assistant. No one was currently booked for help, so four of the young men who worked there crammed into the small office with me. The men began complaining about how they often hated working with women students.

"Yeah, their stories are so..."

"Like, you know, I was raped by a garden hose when I was a child..."

I saw their smiling faces. I felt myself rise from within my body, almost as though a different person made the decision to speak, as I said, evenly, "I was raped. I can tell you it was no joke." I looked at each face and left.

At home I found on my kitchen table a single flower in a small vase. The card beneath the vase contained these few simple words, "I am so sorry. I will never laugh at rape again." It was signed by one of the young men. I wept and still weep remembering.

Another evening I was working with two of those same guys, again in the Writing Center. One of them started talking about Cannery Row, having seen it on television. The other man began talking with him comparing the book to the program, when the first looked at me, to include me in the conversation.

"You know, *Cannery Row*?"

I recognized I was falling into a flashback. Two men, in a small space, one looking directly at me and talking in a way I knew I was supposed to understand. But I hadn't read *Cannery Row*. A sense of threat rose all around me.

"Uh, yes...uhm, I have to go now." My conscious mind had just enough power, just enough energy garnered through those explosive breakthroughs, I remained conscious. I walked across campus and drove home, talking to myself all the way, *You are safe. You are home and you are safe. You are not back there; that's over.*

'Back there' meant the recently released memories and their

truth but something else too. What had emerged from that chasm of terror was a fully developed figure, harsh and unremitting, who would help me survive.

Al calls me out. "Well, Charlie, I've made a decision. We're gonna let you go."

Small muscular relief, and "Thank you Al, thank you so much."

"Now Gary found a small boat, it's just a ten horse but it'll get us along the shore. We'll drop you off somewhere near civilization. We don't want you to be left in the woods where the bears might come. We'll drop you off, but you have to promise, you must promise us you will not go to the police. Do you understand what I'm saying?"

"Yes, Al, I understand. I promise I will not go to the police."

"At least, not until Gary and me have a chance to get across the border into Manitoba."

"No, Al, I won't go to the police, not ever."

Back in the bedroom, I am looking into the free-standing mirror. Does the mirror exist? I can't be sure, but there stands the burned, bruised and ugly body that is what remains of me.

I see me swim as though to a surface, but I cannot break through. Instead, a third energy, another personality leaps forward, stares back at me, defiant, enraged. A knife in her hand, she says into my eyes, "If this is what it means to be a woman, I won't be one." She will be the numb creature, the me who returns to Toronto, who takes on drinking and drugging and partying as the only response to her world. In short, she will carry all the behaviour of what will decades afterward be known as PTSD.

The small boat contains us within the endless grey waters of Lake Superior, Al behind me guiding the ten-horse engine, Gary in front but turned to look at me.

Al speaks to Gary about sightings on the shoreline, possible places to let me go.

"We could just let her go, anywhere," Al's decision to rid himself of me grows more demanding.

"Ahh, but then she might...I mean, there're bears around. Animals."

"Yeah, you're right, Gar."

Gary flashes a look at Al, once, twice, then says to me, "I wish I had met you under different circumstances."

I offer a small smile say nothing, but a wave of laughter builds. I must not.

Wind scuttles across the water. Waves lap against our purpose.

Gary repeats, leaning closer, "I wish we had met under different circumstances."

I say, the edge within dangerously close, "Yes." I nod with what feels like vigor but might be a tiny head motion. "Yes. Under any different circumstances." I smile inside laughing, try not to show this.

They spot a golf course. I want to argue with them, maybe I do, not likely a golf course up here, at this time of year.

They step onto the shore and help me, hold my hands so I will not fall. The men walk as before, one in front of me, one behind, this time for protection. Al says, It's bear season up here.

When we stop in a small clearing, Al standing between me and the golf course, says, "Don't go to the police. We're giving you your life and the only thing we ask is don't go."

Gary to my right, says, "If you do go, give us some time. We need to make it to the border."

I nod, all agreeable. We shake hands, each one in turn saying good-bye, all the best.

I sit, alone. I sit, knowing I have given my word to not shout, not wave my hands, jump up and down, go to the police.

I turn and walk westward, out of the small forest toward the lush rolling green hills of the golf course.

Of course, a golf course, language now spills inside me, or out, an idiot's babble. Of course, why not? I smile to myself constantly, life is so strange.

Inside the dark, empty building I see a coke machine.

I pace quickly up and down wondering where anybody might be. I can't tell how much time passes.

A woman appears—or was she there all along— a woman who looks at me and starts back.

I register this but I might be talking, talking, talking so many words. "They want me, they said not to go…I should go…I probably need to go but they asked me not to, they didn't hurt me or well, they let me go finally, they were my friends, now I'm not sure…I should go to the police."

I sit on the wooden stool, then rise and walk pacing up and down between the coke machine and the woman, who shrinks visibly away from me, behind the counter.

More words, "A coke, yes! That's it! I haven't eaten in three days," I say this jubilant, satisfied I have solved a life-sized riddle. I reach into my blue jeans, find a bit of change and say, "I don't have any money. We bought cookies, you see because we were hungry and it seemed the only thing…I mean they bought cookies, I just ate them…"

"It's all right…here, have this." She offers me the dime I need. As her hand reaches out then drops the small coin, I see in her eyes the dirt on my skin, the oil in my hair. She's staring.

"Oh, thank you, you are so kind, that's really nice of you, I mean I'm just a stranger and this is your livelihood, this is how you make your living and here are you…"

"Really, it's all right," she insists.

We share the space, my fractured psyche falling to pieces; gradually her desire to run from me gives way to advice.

"You better call the police."

"I told them I wouldn't go to the police for a few days, maybe three days or at least two hours or sometime for them to get over the border."

"Really, you should call the police right now," she insists with increasing authority as she realizes I am messed up, but no threat.

We discuss this, rolling the sentences and their meaning back and forth a few times before I agree.

She dials and holds out the receiver to me. I say into it, "You don't know me but I'm coming to see you." Hang up.

I ask the woman's relieved face, "Where is the police station?"

"Across the highway, around the back of the mall. It's clearly marked."

"Thank you so much, thank you, you have been so kind, thank you."

I stride across the highway noticing the emptiness of the mall, no people. It's Wednesday, I can calculate that much, it's Wednesday, the sun shines, early September and no one in at the mall, all the stores closed has the apocalypse occurred while I have been away all the people gone wouldn't surprise me at all, life so strange…

The uniformed officer sits behind his desk but looks up as I place myself in the chair in front of him.

"Hello. I'm a runaway from Toronto and I want to go home."

He laces his fingers behind his head, leans back in his chair and puts his feet up on the desk.

"In my experience with runaways..." he begins.

I slam my fist on his desk.

Epilogue

THAT MOMENT, WHEN MY FIST HIT THE DESK in the police station in Marathon Ontario, marked the moment my path was chosen: whatever twists and trials life might take, I would follow my inner guidance, the forces that had brought me, scarred and deeply traumatized but alive through those days. No matter how bizarre, how upside down or how much a black sheep I would appear to be, from that moment until this I have lived by that guidance.

Sometimes this has been, as it was in those first years long ago, the guidance of Angels. They have continued to visit, rarely manifesting visibly. More often they speak to me in their tones like bell chimes, offering guidance and direction because my daily mind does not function, to this day, very well within this culture. I believe firmly Angels are with all of us, ready to enter our hearts whenever we turn towards them.

I stumble around in poetry and want to turn everything, from doing my taxes to sitting on my terrace into poetry. Whole stories rise up as I wash the dishes. I am besieged by tantalizing ideas just by walking across the room. Language! Where had I learned to use language also as a weapon?

I learned from my brother to use the one weapon I had: language. I learned to create sentences he could not understand and fling them at him whenever we were in front of Dad who always glowed at me with pride for this. Then Dad would laugh at my brother saying, "Well, she got you there…do you even understand what she's saying?" Dad implied that he understood and, in this way, kept both my brother and I salivating for his approval.

Through language a tiny portion of hope—hope I might prevail one day— stayed alive in my heart. And eventually it was through words I stopped my brother's carnage on my psyche. After Dad explained his version of the facts of life, I arranged for his words to fall into my brother's ears until my brother knew his dominion over me was ended.

My brother remained married to Cecilie for seven years. During the time I lived in the US, he abandoned Cecilie in a most ignorant way, parading his new paramour throughout the group of those still hankering after Dawson. His humiliation of Cec reminded me of how he had had to humiliate me as well.

The Christmas of the year he left Cec and brought his new girlfriend and her children to my parents' home for the celebration, I sent a card to him marked Do Not Open Until Christmas. In it I described how I would never receive his new partner as part of the family and how my loyalties remained with Cecilie whom he had treated so poorly. My last sentence stated he was no longer my brother.

When the phone rang on Christmas day, it was my father. "I hope you know you have spoiled Christmas for all of us…how could you send such a card and make sure…it was even up on the tree…" He said *tree* as though it was a symbol of something pure, something almost holy that I had violated. "Your brother spent most of the day crying in the other room, your mother was in tears…"

I replied I had meant to hurt my brother. I said I had done what I had done deliberately. All the while I was talking, I felt a kind of warmth across my chest. I had crushed him, finally, as he had me all those years ago.

It was language which drew my heart to Cecilie, and in heart kept me close to her for many years before she passed away from injuries sustained in a car accident. Her friendship helped me heal, helped me describe a path from my innermost being to the world through the power of poetry. The deepest parts of our friendship wove us together through the power of language.

At sixteen, faced with two criminals who had shot a man in front of me, I used language to create webs: webs of comfort, webs of lies, whatever was needed to keep me alive. It was all through language.

Jabberwocky spoke to me of how language creates without saying anything directly. I had been compelled by unnamed forces inside me to memorize it from the first time I read it. I used the poem as a way to introduce to Al a plan I had not known I had: a plan that appeared to me consciously only in that outhouse, on those walls, a plan that ultimately helped save my life.

For most of my life I believed my language had saved me. I believed I had so befuddled Al his final decision was to let me go. I believed I had done this on my own. Only recently have I seen differently. It was Gary's language, soft and persistent against Al's desire to kill me, that kept me alive. It was Gary's insistence, gentle but honest into Al's ears that made Al decide in favour of letting me live. Gary's language, coming from the heart of love he had for me, saved me. And so, a murderer, he who had pulled the trigger on the shot gun and rent my psyche in two pieces, was the same man who saved my life. He did it through his language soft and relentless all through that one night.

I have no way to know whether those posters of Alice in Wonderland, the ones I saw on the inside of that outhouse, ever existed in this realm. What I know is what I knew: I had a choice to make about what I perceived, and I chose the path that gave me the most advantage, stopping short of hurting anyone else, or myself. I chose to believe my own experience. I have been choosing this way ever since.

Dawson repeated like a mantra, "You have no choice until you choose. Then once you choose, you have choiceless awareness." I did not pretend to understand. It made no sense for many years but gradually I began to see how my choices had been dictated by the thrust of something deep within, something unconscious. The only choices I would have made had I stayed in Toronto would have been to drugs, drinking and partying.

The choice to travel with Dawson was propelled by that inner, unconscious knowledge. Traveling shook everything up. The neurons clinging to pathways of repetitive negative behaviours, my habitual actions, had no place in India, or in retreat in New Zealand or any of the places my feet set me down upon the earth. "Neurons that fire together wire together" meant that traveling interrupted the neuronal flow and made new wiring possible.

Travel and Dawson's outrageous behaviour and claims, his visionary articulation of a world both dying through its ignorance and aflame with the hope and experience of renewal, lit my imagination. Life was possible! Through his passion for articulating his vision of a better world, I began to believe healing existed for us all.

The birth of my son birthed in me a new and positive direction. I had not been able to establish a persona, an identity to enable me to fulfill a role within this culture until I became a mother. Through this new identity my life stabilized and I veered away from Dawson. My own life was more important than traveling with him.

Thus when I heard the rumours in 1993 of a student coming forward with strong evidence that Dawson and Chorpel had raped and savagely tortured this person, while a group of Dawson's chosen men, many of whom would go on to be "teachers" in his lineage, stood around watching, it all seemed a long way away from what mattered in my life.

Dawson fell into dementia. That his great brain shredded was kept hushed up by his closest circle and he passed away in 2003. Then in May 2015 the evidence, this time irrefutable, re-surfaced and I had to accept what is still impossible: the man who had been most instrumental in healing my devastation from rape and sadism was himself a serial rapist and sadist.

Many students rushed to claim his actions were pure through something called "extraordinary intervention". They make the claim his sadistic behaviour caused healing. Many other students abandoned Dawson, stripped of their belief in him and sickened by everything he ever said or did, in light of this information.

My encounters with Marion Woodman, Jungian dream analyst, helped me through this conflict. Our Shadow must be integrated. With Dawson, his two sides: serial rapist, sadist and powerful healer both attained conscious expression, but he lacked the strength to hold his violence and hatred of others in his own consciousness.

Tibetan teachings indicate that everything at its base is pure. It is, but regarding human beings everything at our base is pure when we have struggled to control our own evil energies, our dark shadows, to recognize and keep them away from harming others or ourselves. Dawson's narcissistic arrogance allowed him to run his ugliness rampant over others. Perhaps buoyed by the worst in Tibetan culture—its misogyny, hierarchical structure, medieval power grabs— or perhaps out of his own sense of entitlement his Shadow remained unintegrated. He hurt others as though they deserved it. In this he was the worst kind of psychopath.

The power of his consciousness in the positive side remains. From a meditative perspective, he entered a state of profound union with his words. In this, he encouraged our brains, practiced at self-concern and petty anxieties, to let go, to get caught up in and absorbed by, his visions of and enthusiasm for life, culture, history, sexuality, gender, physics, astronomy, Tarot, astrology, mysticism, spirituality, Tibetan Vajrayana Tantra, the list goes on. He spoke with equal ease and depth on all these and more.

I, the "I" who had fainted right away as he had so succinctly observed in our first meeting, that I slowly found healthy interest in the rest of the world. For what is health? It is the same as spiritual well-being: a growing sense of balance between the well-being of self and the well-being of the rest of experience. From this perspective, his travels, classes, encouragement, humour and insight helped me heal. My sluggish neurons, corrupted and rusted with trauma, found new life as he provoked my fascination for life, by virtue of his own.

In one of our encounters, Marion Woodman spoke about the three P's, how therapists must offer Presence, Patience and Paradox to their clients. What Dawson did, serial rape and cuttings, burnings and more to his students and how that stole what had been a precious vision from others of his students has no place in a world of real human beings. His charisma cloaked the truth of his stunted and regressive emotional illness. His extraordinary intelligence, his gifts of demonstrating the path to healing even if, like Moses he was unable to enter the healing land, the holy land, covered his evil shadow for much of his life. His continual traveling kept many from catching on or catching up to the evil he was doing.

At Dawson's memorial service in Kinmount one of his oldest students told me a story. He said Dawson had confided a dream. The dream was of a snake, a giant snake wrapped around the globe, chasing Dawson wherever he went.

Dawson could not sit still. He projected himself as the prime example of enlightenment: financially free, emotionally unattached, verbally superior. And the many miracles I did witness in his presence spoke directly to something.

But everyone around him was a sycophant, wanting more for their own glory than to help him remember his humanity. No one stood up to him and he would never have allowed anyone such equality. He encouraged students to see him as other than human, as a being who had no need of relationships based in the warmth and acceptance of human flaws and failings. He failed in all areas of moral decency and ethical integration for even while he sometimes alluded to these things, he did not embody them.

No humanity but a real ability to create miracles. He communicated telepathically while I was in many of the rooms in which he taught. The vision of him that had propelled my initial journey to India seared into my awareness an inkling that human consciousness contains latent powers of immense proportion. That awareness fed unconsciously into my belief healing was possible.

And he helped me heal by emphasizing the healing powers when they arose. The power of his mind to recreate the dream he discussed in Mexico, about descending some stairs, opened in my mind the same image and he knew this. His easy acceptance of my dream of healing tiles, and my interpretation of it, encouraged me.

My study of my night dreams has offered wisdom, healing and hope. While the world sent me bitter herbs instead of mead, and thorns as pillows, my night dreams expressed a different world, one of unrivalled love and intelligence. As a child the three recurring nightmares described my future and a way through it. When I remembered those childhood dreams, they helped save my life. Dreams brought me news of the tragic end of my beloved friend, Tim and although I was unable to prevent how his life energies resolved, we shared an intimacy that marked me, and I hope him, with deep caring. The thread of our love streaming across the globe demonstrated the profound power of dreams.

Continuing study of my night dreams has brought me the reasons for life's bitterness in the expression of salt. Salt is the daily pinch, whatever little or large moments twist a bit of skin or tug at a tag of emotion in an uncomfortable or even very painful way, salt is the bitterness. We all need a little salt. That is Life's offering. With a little salt the sweetness of life rises to our mouths and we grow grateful and content.

Dawson's optimism, for example when he'd break out smiling and look at us and say, "Well, kiddies, come now or come later. You will all come to enlightenment at some point. It is evolution," activated within me my father's vision of our world. My father's blindness to what was going on in his own home, the brutality of my mother, the humiliation of me by my brother, lay counterpoint to his vision of his world as sunny and our family as normal, healthy, the best. While my father's optimistic vision did nothing to protect me, his message of health and a happy life lay within me, another stream of wholesomeness that fed my belief I might heal and in healing live such a life.

My mother's curse grew on me into a blessing. "Where there's a will there's away Charlene and you are the most willful person god ever put on this earth." So it was I had the power to stay the course through all the storms, physical as well as emotional. I was able through my willpower to eventually release the demonized layers of energy holding me hostage to an experience long since gone.

My mother's fury also gave me permission to express mine. None of my energy turned inward toward depression and if I have had to struggle toward being calm when vulnerable, if tenderness has been a learned experience, my rage sustained and held me through so many decades when I needed to be strong in a world that does not like women or children or vulnerability.

A personal quality, that of discipline, emerged with that rage. And discipline through willpower enabled me, when I was an impoverished single mother, a university student and the main cog in a communal house to take an hour a week for myself to deliberately remember and process the traumas I began to let myself remember. The containment of my "little shop of horrors"—as I came to think of those memories—and the wisdom to turn to the positive thoughts for most of the week came from meditation as I learned it under Dawson.

Eventually I developed a daily meditation practice, but always kept up the deep emotional release work of bio-energetics and deep release breathing that leads to primal expression. I learned to focus on and encourage good feelings through two activities I've always loved: singing and dancing. The joy I have found in music elevated me to believing I might hang on, even if sometimes that meant just for one more song.

Underlying everything the love for my son wrought the filigree of enough power that I knew I would succeed. I would because I had to. I had to because I had him.

Later, I began to see how much wounding so many of us have experienced at the hands of others and my search for healing morphed into something much larger than my search.

It must be that others have had the same experiences of rape and brutality because now so much health and healing information and guidance are available.

Today I live contentedly in a cottage by a lake. My family have grown, and everyone is healthy. My partner of many years, a man who bears his own scars from war in a foreign place, continues to offer stability and consistency.

I am so grateful for all that has happened. Although this is not the life I thought I was headed for, it was not a detour, not a mistake. This life, this path was chosen long ago, through the endless eons of suffering we have inflicted upon each other. My life emerged from that swamp of pain and suffering, joy and release and as a tiny drop at the crest of a huge wave, whatever healing I have been able to achieve flows back toward the greater archives of our species. For this, for being allowed to participate at all, I am immensely grateful for My Impossible Life.

Last Words

THE STORIES WE EACH HAVE OF OUR INDIVIDUAL LIVES matter now more than ever. As we see cultural institutions, churches, temples, mosques, synagogues, universities, political office tumble through immoral and indecent behavior we need more than ever to learn the heroic stories of how each of us has coped with, come to terms with and healed from the struggles of our lives. In reading the stories of others we come to understand more fully how our own lives make sense, how our own struggles are not unique and how we ourselves with our pain and our sorrows simply in the end belong to the human situation.

I hope you enjoyed reading **My Impossible Life**. If you have a few seconds to spare, even the shortest of reviews help authors gain attention. Something as small as "I enjoyed reading this book…" or "A good read" helps support us.

I'd enjoy hearing from you. Please feel free to email me at

charlenej@rogers.com

If you are interested to listen in to my 15 min podcasts of other authors, please go to www.soulsciences.net click on podcasts on the left side and scroll to your heart's content.

May you learn to live with all the faces of love as your guide.

Manufactured by Amazon.ca
Bolton, ON